SHARING ARCHITECTURE

SHARING ARCHITECTURE

Robert L. Vickery, Jr.

University Press of Virginia,

Charlottesville

THE UNIVERSITY PRESS OF VIRGINIA
Copyright © 1983 by the Rector and Visitors
of the University of Virginia

First paperback printing 1989

Library of Congress Cataloging in Publication Data

Vickery, Robert L.
Sharing Architecture

Includes bibliographical references.
1. Architecture I. Title.

NA2500.V5 1983 720 82-13614
ISBN 0-8139-0973-2 (cloth); 0-8139-1234-2 (paper)

Printed in the United States of America

For those students who have shared

Sharing Architecture

PREFACE

When reprinting a book there is always the temptation to rewrite and make more current the subject matter. Certainly, if I were to start over, and write a new and longer book, I would add a substantial chapter on the delicate balance between what is built by our society and what exists in nature.

I am afraid that unless we change our attitudes away from mindless material, and ever more construction, we shall awake one day (soon) to discover an environment with no differences in quality between urban, suburban, and farm life, and no wilderness left at all.

But such a book lies beyond the more simple scope of this book: to begin to appreciate and understand architecture, we must first learn what it means to build — to make a mark upon the land — to modify and change the world within which we live. We must first study what architecture is, why it comes to be, and how it is designed and built. Once these lessons are mastered we can then begin to appreciate the role of architecture within our larger environment.

Once we begin to grasp these basic principles, we also begin to love architecture, to care for it, and to share it. This book remains as first intended, to serve as a beginning.

Feb. 1, 1989

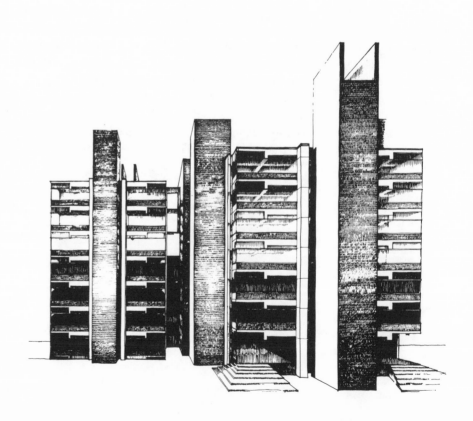

INTRODUCTION: ON SHARING ARCHITECTURE

This book is intended for the serious reader who is interested in understanding architecture — what it is, who it is for, and why it is built.(1)

The issue of understanding architecture is an important one, for as we are ever more rapidly reshaping the world into a man-made environment, we need to pause and ask, Why? Are our architectural intentions honest? Proper? And how can we formulate appropriate value systems for judgment so that we may build a symbolic and inspiring architecture rather than a commonplace environment.

Unfortunately, understanding architecture is a long, complex task, filled with years of difficult questioning. But this is to be expected, for even in the best of times, the practice of architecture is difficult. The final aesthetical result of the the man-made environment has always been beset with problems of fluctuating economy, changing technology, shifts in social need, vagaries of building laws, the whims of clients, and the fancies of architects.

In our present age, however, there is a fundamental philosophic issue that makes understanding, designing, and reshaping our environment especially difficult. For at this point in our cultural history it is hard to find a base of common agreement among professional critics and architects themselves as to what our basic values for aesthetical judgment should be. The choice then of an architectural value system is difficult even for the seasoned architect, the most advanced of students.(2)

Nevertheless every serious professional wrestles with his aesthetics, continually questioning the merit of his work, re-examining his attitudes and values. How then to begin? This book will argue that the

(1) Serious reader *may be interpreted as meaning anyone who questions, and wants to learn why the man-made environment has a particular form.*

(2) The point that there exists a striking lack of reasoned agreement as to the proper direction of future aesthetics is well shown by any of the works of Louis Kahn.

In his design for the Richards Medical Center laboratories at the University of Pennsylvania (see sketch), Kahn carefully created large, open, flexible laboratory rooms, with the many mechanical services separated out and then carried in attached, but powerfully formed, towers. Kahn thus differentiated between the "spaces being served" and the "service spaces."

Kahn's work has been called obfuscatory, contradictory, and willful. And it has been pointed out that the laboratory areas are not, in reality, open and flexible, but rather are broken up into many small rooms, used for research projects.

Yet many architectural students looking beyond the pragmatic questions of use, continue to be influenced by Kahn's work. For what they see is a possible new direction for architectural form — a difficult existentialist blend of simple geometric forms shaped through a return to basic structural ordering systems.

Kahn's key role in modern architecture will be more fully discussed in chapter 10.

logical starting point for understanding architecture is first to provide a limited framework of agreed-upon terminology — a basic architectural language, which may then be used to explore the meanings of selected conceptual ideas. By studying how these conceptual ideas are reflected in architectural form, the reader may then begin to formulate his own questions and answers, his own values for judgment, his own aesthetic, and his own understanding (no matter how tentative) or what architecture is.

What I am suggesting is that any study of the meaning of architecture must proceed from the asking of questions, and that the study of architecture cannot be separated from the study of architectural theory.

(3)   No book that I am aware of specifically addresses this issue. There are, however, a number of worthwhile books with which the beginning student might well become acquainted. Among these are: S.E. Rasmussen, Experiencing Architecture *(Boston: MIT Press, 1962) — basic observations about architectural perception; Gordon Cullen,* Townscape *(New York: Reinhold Press, 1962) — a straightforward approach to sketching the richness of sequential spaces; Kevin Lynch,* The Image of the City *(Cambridge, Mass.: Harvard University Press, 1960) — a book that at the time helped refute the idea that city planning consisted of coloring zoning maps; N. Luning-Prak,* The Language of Architecture *(The Hague: Mouton & Co., 1968) — a more difficult book, but one that shows the importance of relating cultural history and aesthetics; Siegfried Giedion,* Space, Time, and Architecture *(Cambridge, Mass.: Harvard University Press, 1967) — a difficult book for the beginner, but still the classic treatise on how baroque spatial concerns led to the modern movement.*

For many years there has been an acceptance by many architects of their role as being simply a member of the building profession. All around us are the tasteless results of this abdication of moral, philosophical, and aesthetical leadership — grossly scaled shopping centers, inhuman housing developments, frightening highways that blight our cities and scar our human consciousness — ugly constructions devoid of the rich meanings and symbolic contents of architecture.

In the spring of 1970, when I first began teaching an introductory, first-year college course in "Concepts of Architecture," I was forced to address head-on this lack of a reasoned architectural aesthetic. In preparing the lecture notes for the course, I soon discovered that it is difficult to teach philosophy to students who, for the most part, do not know what philosophy is, and who have never examined (or been asked to examine) the structure of knowledge. Furthermore, how can one who is beginning a study of architecture progress beyond the asking of general questions to an examination of a specific field of philosophy (aesthetics) that examines a specific field of art (architecture)? How can one examine concepts of architecture if he does not understand what constitutes conceptual thought?(3)

As suggested earlier, the answer to this dilemma is, in theory, deceptively simple - provide a framework for the intelligent questioner, and he can philosophize for himself.(4) As the mathematician and philosopher Bertrand Russell says, "The only way to find out what philosophy is, is to do philosophy."(5)

The difficulty, of course, is in asking the right questions.(6) And to ask these questions, one first needs a base of knowledge that identifies and differentiates the areas of agreement from those of nonagreement. (This book will also argue that despite the disagreements as to direction mentioned earlier, the actual areas of agreement as to starting values are, surprisingly, much larger than commonly believed).

The subject matter for this book, then, lies first in discovering a basic framework for questioning what architecture is, and second in using this framework to examine certain selected concepts that affect architectural form. That these two aspects of intellectual inquiry — that is, asking the question and discovering the answer — are inseparably linked, will be shown later.(7)

Above all, however, the reader must first clear his mind of preconceptions. He must ask, Why? For whom? How? What for? And yet again, Why? For in the beginning, the answers are not as important as the questions. The first purpose of this book is to make a beginning toward understanding the questions.

(4) One may substitute method *for* framework *if desired. The analytical method of questioning with which we are most familiar is, of course, the dialecticism of Socrates as expanded by Aristotle (discussed in chapter 4).*

(5) Bertrand Russell, Wisdom of the West *(New York: Crescent Books, 1959), p. 7.*

(6) The critic in this field [architecture], where everything is transient and temporal, hopes that something may testify to his efforts. He expects no miracles, but he is an optimist with some fairly tough beliefs. In architecture and urbanism those beliefs must be based on history, art and humanism. They must have strong ties to modern sociology and technology. And they must be grounded in a knowledge of the past for the shifting present and the uncertain future. . . . But only mock philosophers pretend to provide answers for the questions they raise; the purpose is to provoke thought and the possibility of solutions.—*Ada Louise Huxtable,* Will They Ever Finish Bruckner Boulevard? *(New York: Collier Books, 1972); p. 2-3; my emphasis.*

(7) As thoughtful students have long known, the answer to any question can only be stated within the framework or nature of the question itself. (See chapter 4 for a further discussion of this issue, in particular, note 21.)

During the Senate Watergate hearings of 1973, a former attorney general of the United States stated that the committee was impugning the integrity and ability of the FBI by suggesting they were not finding the right answers. A committee member retorted that he was not impugning the FBI's integrity, only wondering why they had been directed to ask the wrong questions.

(8) This presumes that intelligent disagreement should be encouraged, and quibbling ignored.

(9) Intuitive thought is always involved when we ask such questions as: "What does the form mean?" "What does the building want to be?" "What is the conceptual idea of shelter / habitat?" The reader's participation (and tolerance) in this section of the book will be critical, for there are no easy answers to intuitive questions concerning form.

(10) A sampling of other issues: (1) What are the conceptual issues in evolving city form? (2) How is architectural form affected by changing technology? (3) How does evolving national social policy affect architectural form? (4) What is the purpose, or meaning, in erecting landmarks?

The format of the book has been carefully constructed, and the first chapter begins by introducing a terminology so that discussion itself can proceed.(8) Chapter 2 continues in the same vein, with an analysis of the determinants of architectural form. Chapters 3 and 4 deal with questions of philosophy, specifically the difficulty of practicing architecture today, a difficulty caused by both our inherited past philosophy and our most commonly practiced present philosophy, pragmatism. In this initial section, careful attention is given to understanding the differences between pragmatic questions and the historically earlier analytical questions of Aristotelian logic.

At that point in the book, the framework having been laid, the emphasis shifts away from classification and analysis, and the reader is asked to participate directly in a discussion of broader issues of intellectual concern. The first such discussion, on selected concepts affecting architecture, investigates in chapters 5, 6, and 7 two specific conceptual ideas: first, the Gathering Place and, second, the Shelter / Habitat — examining how they are expressed in architectural form. This section on conceptual ideas will also make the point that intuitive thought is a valid addition to our earlier framework of objective analysis. That is, that our final framework will have to be an intuitive as well as an objective architectural language.(9)

The second broad intellectual area, the impact of the individual artist, investigates how the competent architect may make a unique contribution to his profession. While other architects are mentioned throughout the book, it is the work of Frank Lloyd Wright (chapter 8) and Le Corbusier (chapter 9) that is most closely examined in this section.

In this middle portion of the book, no attempt has been made to mold these areas into a simple theoretical method. The issues of architecture are too complex — what is intended is to sample a few diverse but critical issues, so that the participant-reader may go much further and question additional issues.(10)

Chapter 10 shifts the emphasis to discuss the modern movement and its origins, intentions, and potential future directions. An attempt is made within the text to discover those paths of architectural form along which we are currently being led by our society, and its architects, and theorists. The formal argument ends as it begins with the question, Why?(11)

A few final comments should be made concerning the eleventh and last chapter of the book, Education and an Afterword. This chapter is a personal reflection on learning and the state of our architectural profession. If any single bias exists in my mind, it is in the old contention of the famous historian Jacob Burckhardt that the acquisition of knowledge consists of humanely studying the great interconnected conceptual ideas of man's cultural history.(12) This is a humanist view, but it is a broad interpretation, which not only stresses man's right and need to reason, but also acknowledges his susceptibility to error and failure. This acknowledgment converts knowledge into a more profound humane wisdom, a wisdom that happily shares its cultural achievements.

This last chapter will attempt to reaffirm that in this day of relativity and multi-leveled value systems, we need more than ever to experience again the simple human joys of building together and of sharing architecture.

(11) In chapter 10, the emphasis will not be so much on historical classification as on historical perspective — i.e., if we can begin to identify at this point in time the shift in social cultural values, we can also begin to postulate which emergent theories of architecture are likely to affect future physical form.

(12) Burckhardt's contribution to humanist teaching and learning is more fully discussed in chapter 11. Another distinguished scholar, Jacques Barzun, House of Intellect (New York: Harper and Brothers, 1959) distinguishes between our basic "intelligence" and our inherited "intellect" — inherited intellect being the vast store of cultural history passed down to us by the preceding civilization. Barzun argues that we should use our intelligence to preserve and to add to our inherited intellect (p. 1-4).

An opposing view is held by the writer-philosopher Claude Lévi-Strauss, who in all of his works has claimed that humanism has failed man. A major purpose of the discussion that follows in this book will be to refute that particular contention, despite Lévi-Strauss's personal brilliance in argument. It is not humanism that has failed us, but we who have failed humanism.

I DEFINING THE TERMS

As Aristotle understood well, and as recent linguists and symbolic logicians have rediscovered, no serious discussion can occur without there first existing a base of common agreement. Thus, one cannot really ask what architecture is without first having some general agreement for the meaning of words such as *art, beauty, aesthetics, form, style, creativity,* and *architecture* itself.(1)

That this is a basic problem may be shown by a simple experiment. Start by thinking of four spatial environments of widely different character. These should be environments with which one is intimately familiar — for example: 1. a walk along a countryside stream, 2. a drive through a small town's main street, 3. a visit to a national landmark (such as the 630 feet high St. Louis Arch), and 4. a trip to a strip-development hamburger drive-in.(2)

(1) In the beginning, it is necessary to agree upon a few terms so that discussion itself can proceed. But as one progresses in any field of knowledge, basic definitions are modified, rearranged, and built again by learning and experience.

(2) This sketch of a typical drive-in illustrates that one's visual and aesthetical perceptions change if the drive-in is considered a part of the strip development (the drive-in is hidden within the outlined area.) The experiment, as stated, did not differentiate which perceptions were to be used.

(3) One way of performing this experiment is to look at photographic slides of the different environments, and then construct graphs that record individual responses, later tabulating these into group statistics. (One such individual response is shown here.) While such experiments are interesting, they are statistical tabulations only, and prove nothing as to the quality of architecture. They only become meaningful when every participant agrees on what part is being evaluated, and to what degree an environment may or may not be architecture. That is, only after we basically agree on how to determine art, architecture, *and* beauty, *will statistical data become useful.*

Environment	Art?	Arch?	Beauty?	Comment
① stream/walk	yes	no	yes	God's Art is always beauty
② main street drive	no	yes	no	didn't like all the signs
③ landmark – (St. Louis Arch)	yes	yes	no	"too big" to be beautiful
④ Hamburger drive-in	no	no	no	couldn't stand it !!!

TYPICAL INDIVIDUAL RESPONSE

(4)The written and spoken language we use is already an abstraction of the real subject matter. That is, the word architecture *is already an abstraction of an event, an object (or thing).*

(5) Webster's New World Dictionary *(New York: World Publishing Co., 1960). The other definitions are not entirely irrelevant, however.*

After listing them, one should then reconstruct his remembrances of these spatial experiences, recording all of his pleasurable (or unpleasurable) sensations and feelings. After this is done, he should ask himself three questions about each listed environment: Was it art? Was it architecture? Was it beautiful?

The results will be surprising. One group that has participated in this experiment was evenly divided on the question of whether the St. Louis Arch was, or was not, beautiful. The same group could not agree on whether a specific hamburger drive-in, with which they were all familiar, was architecture. Each individual response reflected highly personal reactions.(3) This suggests that one proper start towards understanding architecture is to define and agree upon a limited basic vocabulary.(4)

Even agreeing on this basic vocabulary is difficult, however. Webster's dictionary lists no fewer than ten definitions for art: one being "cunning," and another "trick or wile." The principal definition for our purposes, however, is the first one: "creative work generally, or its principles; the making or doing of things that have form and beauty."(5)

Webster's of course is not the only authority for defining art. But virtually every artist who has written of his profession agrees that the performance of art requires creativity, as well as an interpretation of events through form that reveals symbolically an inner or new meaning for man.

Frequently, however, *art* itself is never defined by the critic or historian — rather its aim or purpose is discussed; or its subject matter and style are evaluated. In the first instance, consider Aristotle's classic statement: "The aim of art is to represent not the outward appearance of things, but their internal significance." Or again, Marcel Proust's statement: "True art rediscovers, grasps and reveals to us that reality far from which we live, from which we get farther and farther as the conventional knowledge we substitute for it becomes thicker and thicker."(6)

An evaluation of *style* is even more difficult. Consider one of President Harry Truman's better known quips in 1951, on seeing an exhibition of the paintings of Yasuo Kuniyoshi: "If that's art, I'm a Hottentot!"

These difficulties must initially be swept away by simply agreeing on certain postulates as starting points, with disagreement over minor terminology tabled for later analysis. The rest of this chapter will put forth a series of postulates concerning the terms *art* and *architecture*.

A postulate for art: *Art is a creative statement about the human predicament.*(7) If this definition is accepted, art will deal with life, discovering (sometimes hidden) reality while exploring meanings to be found in the relationships between humans, their environment, and their ideas.(8)

This postulate needs a number of subpostulates, which will flesh out and give substance to the definition. The first of these subpostulates will be: 1. Art is a human endeavor. It is created by humans for human understanding and enjoyment, and while this definition allows for diverse subject matter, it does imply that art's meaning is found in human concerns.(9)

(6) Two other well-known definitions can further obscure the issue: Gauguin's statement, "Art is either a plagiarist or a revolutionist," and Picasso's "Art is not truth; art is the lie that makes us realize truth."

(7) If the word predicament *is disturbing, it may be replaced by the word* condition.

Two former students have written provocative definitions that on first reading appear to have different emphases: "Art is a statement resulting from creative inquiry into reality, needing three elements for completion — source, medium, and receiver (Gordon Smith) and, "Art is the outward expression of an intense personal perception of reality," (Steven Semes), This last definition continues: "The artist's perception is rendered in an outward expression called form. *Great art always captures reality in a highly structured form."*

(8) If this definition is generally correct, then art is related to education — for understanding great art is always a rich educational experience.

(9) The idea that art has subject matter is more fully explored in the third subpostulate.

(10) The fact that the universe apparently has an inherent and magnificently ordered form was Albert Einstein's argument for the existence of God. (God exists because no human artist is capable of ordering, or fully understanding, the form of the universe.) The Spanish writer and philosopher Miguel de Unamuno argued a similar point, but from an existentialist position — all men desire order (and meaning); thus: God exists, because if He did not exist, man would have had to invent him.

(11) Jerome S. Bruner, On Knowing *(New York: Atheneum, 1965) p. 18. This book is quoted from frequently in the text, because no modern psychologist has done more than Bruner to destroy the notion that science and art are natural enemies.*

(12) Ibid. p. 3.

(13) Ibid., p. 18. An example of effective surprise is the brilliant eleventh chess move by Bobby Fisher against Boris Spassky in their third championship game of 1972. Diagram (a) shows the board just after the move. (Fisher is playing with the black pieces.) Placing the knight (or horse) on the edge of the board is considered a poor move by chess experts. One does not need to understand the game to see why this is theoretically so.

The knight (or horse) advances by moving

This definition does rule out often beautiful works of God or Nature, since these cannot be created by man, nor may their inherent beauty be manipulated. God's Art may be enjoyed by man, but only God controls the form.(10) If one reconsiders the four earlier environmental spatial experiences in this light, the walk along a stream may be beautiful, but it will not be art.

The second subpostulate will be: 2. Art is always creative, creativity being the placing of things in a new perspective, or the discovery of new meanings by rearranging known relationships into new forms. J. S. Bruner, in his excellent small book *On Knowing*, suggests that the clue to whether an act is creative or not occurs when the rearranging produces an "effective surprise."(11)

Bruner claims that effective surprise produces "metaphoric effectiveness": I.e., it produces a surprise within our mind that lies beyond and outside the expected practical result. "It is not simply a taking of known elements and running them together, . . . to create consists precisely in not making useless combinations."(12)

This does not mean that the combinations must be complex in themselves. "The content of the surprise can be as various as the enterprises in which men are engaged. It may express itself in one's dealing with children, in making love, in carrying on business, . . . or in painting a picture. What is curious about effective surprise is that it need not be rare or infrequent or bizarre and is often none of these things. Effective surprises have the quality of obviousness about them when they occur, producing a shock of recognition, following which there is no longer astonishment," and, ". . . the triumph of effective surprise is that it takes one beyond common ways of experiencing the world."(13)

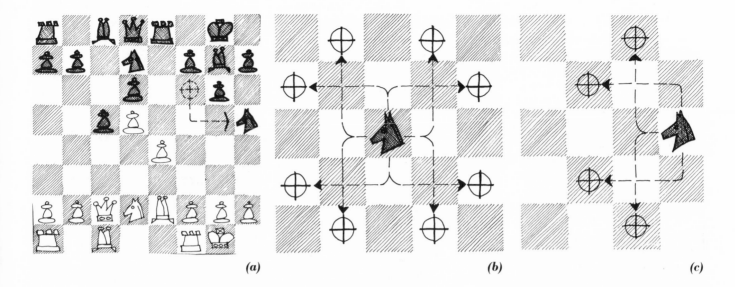

(a)	*(b)*	*(c)*

In her book *Problems of Art*,(14) Susan Langer, another serious student of art, carries Bruner's thought a step further. She discusses the placing together of pigment, canvas, lighting, etc., to form a picture that is an illusion of space. Likewise, an architect creates a building by arranging together stone, mortar, wood, grass, etc., to mold our spatial perception. Langer suggests that effective surprise occurs when our feelings produce a symbolic transformation within our mind.

one square in one direction and two squares in another direction. In diagram (b), we see that if the knight is located in the center of the board, the piece can theoretically move to eight positions on the board. As Fisher placed his pieces, however, there are only four options on future moves — diagram (c).

Nevertheless, what actually occurred was that this creativity was the beginning of a brilliant attack that won the game for Fisher. The move caused consternation, "effective surprise," astonishment, but it led to a useful combination that produced victory. This game is simply explained in Fisher / Spassky, New York Times Report on the Chess Match of the Century *(New York: Bantam Books, 1972).*

(14) Suzanne K. Langer, Problems of Art *(New York: Charles Scribner's Sons, paperback ed., 1957), chap. 3.*

(15) The importance of symbolic transformation will be discussed more fully in chapter 4.

(16) Diagrams can help explain this difference. Langer's process (a) leads to a new thing — in this case a house — which is then perceived in the eye of the beholder as being a work (or nonwork) of art.

Bruner's process (b) stresses human relationships, which are rearranged creatively to produce an altered combination. If this rearrangement has sufficient "effective surprise," we can metaphorically interpret the rearrangement as art.

(17) Many artists have philosophically dealt with creativity. Among those who have written with perception, and who may be profitably read by beginning students, are Ben Shahn, Louis Sullivan, and László Moholy-Nagy. In each case their discussions of creativity should be read with care, for as Le Corbusier has said in his book of the same title, "creation is a patient search" -- and, as one student pithily observed, "it is also a lot of work."

(18) Certain schools offer courses in creative writing, creative arts, creative salesmanship, etc. Is there any such thing as noncreative salesmanship?

(19) Jacob Bronowski, Science and Human Values *(New York: Harper and Row, Torch Books, 1972).*

Langer is using *symbolic transformation*(15) in much the same way that Bruner uses *metaphoric effectiveness*. The principal difference is that she stresses creating something new (i.e., that did not exist before) out of material things, while Bruner stresses creating a new relationship of activities or human enterprises (i.e., showing a relationship not realized earlier).(16)

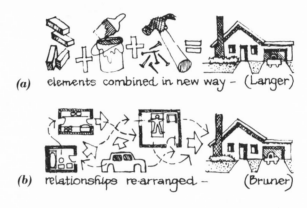

(a)   elements combined in new way - (Langer)

(b)   relationships re-arranged -   (Bruner)

I have discussed the thoughts on creativity of these two respected scholars, not because other definitions do not exist, but rather because both their definitions stress an underlying issue of great importance to one who is beginning an understanding of architecture — that creativity is at the core of art (and architecture), and that it is a serious business.(17)

One final point about creativity needs to be mentioned — it is not an act reserved for the artist. Businessmen, even scientists, can (and need to be) creative.(18) As Jacob Bronowski says in his book *Science and Human Values:*

> You can not have a man handle paints or language, or symbolic concepts of Physics, without instantly waking in him a pleasure in the very language, a sense of exploring his own activity. This sense lies at the heart of creation, ... I have had, of all people, a historian tell me that science is a collection of facts, and his voice had not even the irony of one filing cabinet reproving another.(19)

The third subpostulate for a full definition of *art* will be: 3. The beauty (or the aesthetics) of art comes through the shaping of its content.(20) We could say, "Art has form," and that form is the way the whole thing is put together.(21) Or, that the content of art must be ordered or shaped into some form for us to understand it.

It is important for us to realize that in our age the subject matter (or content) does not have to be of world or national (or monumental) scale to be of value. It is rather the manner in which the content is shaped that helps us better understand or experience the world.

This unconcern with the monumentality or the greatness of content is of comparatively recent history. Consider the ancient Greeks, whose tragedies are always of kings, queens, and the gods at war and peace. Yet in the twentieth century, Arthur Miller can write a major tragedy, *Death of a Salesman*, about an unheroic, inconsequential man, Willie Loman.(22)

Picasso has stated this position even more strongly: "What a sad thing for a painter who loves blondes but denies himself the pleasure of putting them in his picture because they don't go well with the basket of fruit! What misery for a painter who detests apples to have to use them all the time because they harmonize with the tablecloth! I put in my picture everything I like. So much the worse for the things — they have to get along with each other."(23) Contrast Picasso's position with the work of a classical painter such as Velasquez, whose portraits of kings and queens are in regal attire and in god-like poses (even Velasquez's masterpiece *Los Borrachos* which depicts drunken peasants, has them arranged around the god of drink, Bacchus, who dominates the composition).

In architecture, this change in concern over subject matter and content can be seen in recently published books on architecture history. Before 1900, one is hard pressed to find a book that covers indigeneous (or people's) architecture in a serious analytical vein.(24) Today we have books that cover the historical development of a single village (often without any acknowledged great buildings). For example, the

(20) This phrase is borrowed from Ben Shahn, The Shape of Content *(New York: Random House, Vintage Books, 1960).*

(21) This is paraphrased from Langer's Problems of Art. *One difficulty with all philosophic definitions is that they finally must be reduced to terms that themselves are not completely definable — such as the phrase "the whole thing."*

(22) While it is true that Shakespeare wrote "there's a special providence in the fall of a sparrow" (Hamlet, 5.1.230), it is also true that Shakespeare's principal characters are kings, queens, princes, lords of state — characters whose actions result in the gain or loss of kingdoms.

(23) Picasso quoted in Bruner, On Knowing, *p. 21 — Of course, Picasso's unique genius was in making pertinent and unusual combinations that significantly changed our understanding of painting.*

(24) This excludes guidebooks of picturesque villages, as well as coffee-table pictorial essays.

(25) The sketches of government housing (1960s) in Spanish Morocco show the effort made to provide through air-circulation, as well as the traditional courtyard design. The plan of a single unit (a) provides two private courtyards. The "group-form" plan (b) shows that by interlocking the units, a public street of alternating narrow and wide spaces is formed. These sketches were adopted from "Plan de Construccion de Viviendas en Ifni y El Sahara," published by the Spanish government in 1966.

(26) The sketch of Kahn's design shows his concern for ceremonial (or ritual) entry and progression, even in a small building. There is a strong philosophical relationship between this simple building and Kahn's later, more complex work.

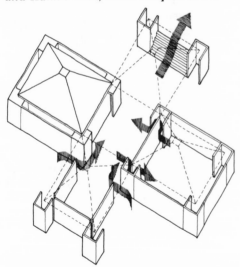

(27) The concern for social content may well have peaked around 1970. Later American architectural work shows a retreat (or a new direction) away from social concerns toward individualistic personal positions.

government of Spain has published a series of booklets describing new villages for workers in its African colonies, in which stress has been laid upon efforts to give the houses a traditional courtyard form.(25)

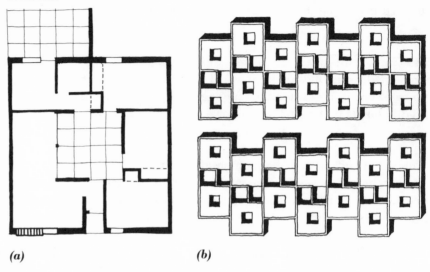

(a)   *(b)*

Another example of this new concern for nongreat subject matter is Louis Kahn's bathhouse for Trenton, New Jersey.(26) In this 1950s building a simple function — a place to change clothes at a public beach — has been given the most careful shaping, so that the form is a careful manipulation of: 1. separated functions (entry, changing rooms, locker storage, and access to the beach), all defined and articulated; 2. structure (the U-shaped columns used as baffles into the dressing areas); 3. construction (the open spaces in opposition to the closed spaces, which are roofed over); and 4. sequential movement, so that human progression through the building produces a constantly changing environment, culminating in arrival at the beach. The resultant form is a building charged with high symbolism.(27)

Particular attention has been paid here to the nature, or "content," of art, because this is an area of extreme confusion between the lay public's view and the present artist's view. The public view is quite clear: It expects architects to deal with the large (usually civic), "important" structures such as the city hall and the post office —

monumental buildings that should have "culture" (i.e., art). The idea that artists might also be concerned with linked transportation systems, or with subdivision layouts, is anathema to the larger public.

Meanwhile, artists and architects blithely continue in directions of social consciousness (design for society) on the one hand and individual artistic theories (or form for its own sake and art for artists) on the other. The fact that society as a whole only accepts Picasso's artwork uneasily and does not accept public housing as an aesthetical problem of any concern (in both cases on the grounds of inappropriate content) appears not to concern many architects.

There is no answer to this general dilemma — each artist, through a painful and slow personal experience, must decide for himself how close to the functional truth his content must be. The subject matter for art has never been agreed upon.(28)

This brings us to some discussion of *how* content may be shaped, or what constitutes form? Form certainly has a structure — although in a larger context we should probably use instead the word *order*, to differentiate from the architectural use of the word *structure*, which denotes the actual steel and concrete systems that hold buildings together.

Order implies an organization by which the form presents content to us in a way that is symbolically powerful. Every field of art has numerous organizing systems of form by which this is done.(29) Let us take a haiku poem by the Japanese poet Issa (1762-1826) as an example:

Tsu-yu no yo wa
Tsu-yu no yo na-ga-ra
Sar-i na-ga-ra(30)

(28) In the bathhouse example shown with note 26, the metaphoric effectiveness is brilliantly handled, yet it is doubtful if many laymen think a bathhouse is important enough to worry about(?) — certainly, not for an artist!

The English filmmaker John Grierson, a leader in discovering beauty in the simple aspects of Canadian life, thought all things were beautiful as long as they were in the right order.

(29) As an art form, music obviously has a special language. Skilled musicians can enjoy reading the score of a Bach concerto while playing it. Within this special language, music also has special forms — such as melody, ode, fugue, concerto, symphony, etc.

The recent addition of perfectly pitched electronic equipment allows two types of sound progressions (or scales, the basic note forms of the language) — one based on harmonic progressions, the other based on pure mathematical progressions. As musicians move further into disharmonic music, they face the same problems of audience acceptance and appreciation that troubled Picasso, Jackson Pollack, and other recent abstract painters.

(30) As a special poetic form, haiku strives for an intense intuition in which the image is so clear that it has its own

meaning. Kenneth Yasuda, The Japanese Haiku *(Tokyo: Tuttle Co., paperback ed., 1973), says: "such an image is a kind of poetry the West yet seems timidly to accept as valid, ... it [Haiku] is poetry without ideas, though there may be ideas in it. ... A successful haiku renders then a speaking, vibrant image." (p. 19)*

Haiku is poetry without a stated concept of meaning. It is rather an image, not of meaning, but of being. Yasuda carefully makes this point by quoting from numerous haiku; specifically, the famous haiku by the Japanese poet Basho,

> *On a withered bough*
> *A crow alone is perching;*
> *Autumn evening now.*

Yasuda explains, "he [the haiku poet] reads, in a few epithets what he experiences, so that imagination will fill those spaces with all the details in which the experimental value of the images reside. He does not give us meaning; he gives us the concrete objects *which have meaning; because he has so experienced them," (p. 7). Haiku poetry has obvious connections with the Zen philosophy of Japan, but it has striking parallels in Western thought and art as well. Consider Wordsworth's famous line that "poetry is emotion recollected in tranquility"; see also the imagist and symbolist poetry movements, and, of course, existentialist philosophy.*

Taken as is (particularly for those of us who have no knowledge of the Japanese language), this poem has little impact. If, however, we know that the haiku is a special form of Japanese poetry in which there are generally only three lines — the first line of five syllables, the second of seven syllables, and the third of five syllables again, we begin to perceive an order in the poem, and if we add to this an English translation, the content begins to take a shaped form that communicates to us:

```
1 2 3 4 5
Tsu-yu no yo wa          The world of dew

1 2 3 4 5 6 7
Tsu-yu no yo na-ga-ra     Is a world of dew, and yet

1  2 3 4 5
Sar-i na-ga-ra            And yet.
```

If we further understand that in haiku one precise phrase from each line is usually repeated in the following line, we begin to see the skill with which Issa shaped his content:

```
1  2  3 4 5
Tsu-yu no yo/ wa

1  2  3  4  5 6 7
Tsu-yu no yo/ na-ga-ra

1  2  3  4  5
Sar-i/ na-ga-ra
```

If we return to the English translation and consider Issa's intent, the poem becomes a complete entity of content in a shaped form:

Thought A	The world of dew
	Is a world of dew, and yet
Thought B	And yet.

Thought A tells us that the world of our everyday life is only a temporal existence — a "world of dew" when contrasted to Buddha's everlasting world. Thought B expresses Issa's lingering doubt — that we never know for sure that this is *only* a "world of dew."

This poem was written after Issa's last child had died. We can imagine his friends comforting him on the transiency of this life. Issa sits down and, not consciously thinking of structure, pens his lines.

Years of training have perfected his style, and within the few lines of haiku, he makes a powerful statement. The third line, which repeats "and yet," is not a cry against Buddha (or God) — rather it is a deeply felt, quiet plea — Why do I not understand? Finally, it is not unfair to say that because this poem relates to a common human experience, and because it may be read on several levels of meaning, it is a better work of art than the trite phrases so often found on sympathy cards.(31)

Architecture, of course, also has form, and the pyramids of Egypt are a good example of its importance. In this case the form itself is symmetrically perfect and pure, responding for all time as a mark upon the land. Their scale, dominance, and mass let us know that only a powerful god-king could leave such sculptures behind.

The most common way to shape form in architecture is to manipulate the physical structure -- such as laying down a structural grid and then infilling this grid for functional use. Among the more interesting examples of such a structurally determined form is a proposal made during the 1960s by the architect James Stirling for the *barriada* (squatter) districts of Lima, Peru.(32)

(31) Haiku imagery is not always sad or wistful. Issa also wrote this delightful poem:

> *Living in the town*
> *One must have money even*
> *To melt the snow down!*

(32) Sketch (a) shows the structure; sketch (b), the mechanical chases and possible connecting points. Sketch (c) shows several building possibilities. Note that each house which is infilled is different (depending on the need of the family). This systems approach to architecture was intended to encourage poorer squatters to build their own houses. (This is sometimes called participatory architecture.)

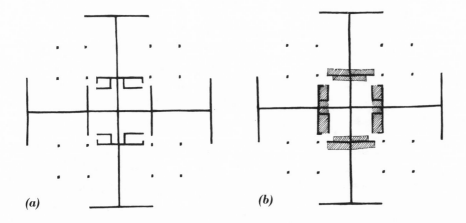

(a)   *(b)*

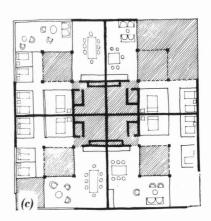

(c)

One should be careful, though, in giving physical structure — such as post and beam wood construction, or brick bearing-walls, or skeletal steel systems — too prominent a role in shaping the content. Architectural content may also be shaped through circulation systems, land formations, use patterns, sociological beliefs, cultural mores, etc. This subject — the determinants of architectural form — will require the entire second chapter for discussion; at this point, however, it is important to remember that the symbolic content will determine the artistic value. It is how we understand the meaning of the architecture (or what it stands for) that determines if we shall value it or discard it. It is Langer's point about symbolic transformation that we must keep in mind. The form of the content allows us to see beyond the obvious and commonplace meaning. In this context, the bathhouse by Kahn is more than a bathhouse; it is a statement about our culture.(33)

(33) Likewise, the example (note 25) of a Spanish courtyard house built for the people by the government, is a world apart philosophically from Stirling's courtyard house to be infilled by the people. Actually, Stirling's scheme did not allow for as many free options as a first glance would suggest. A mechanical systems approach would allow for much greater individual expression — diagram (a), assuming of course, that individual expression is a real goal. Perspective (b) shows how a simple mechanical framework might become highly individualistic.

All of these examples of courtyard housing have been chosen to illustrate that even in a housing concept that is at least 7,000 years old, the way in which the concept is shaped and given form can express greatly varied cultural and philosophic positions. Placed in an American context, subdivisions are not homogeneous, but vary greatly among social classes, cultural areas, and climatic regions.

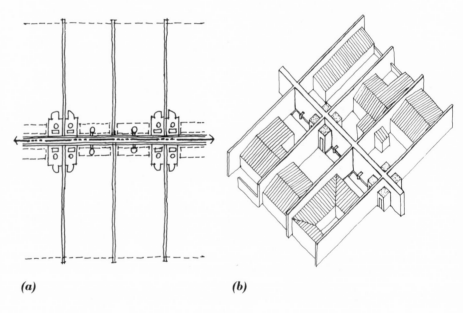

(a)   *(b)*

A sophisticated example of an integrated concept concerning suburbia, housing, circulation systems, and social order may be seen in Clarence Stein and Henry Wright's 1929 development plan for Radburn, New Jersey.(34) In this case, there is a hierarchal relationship of public car space to private house space to semiprivate neighborhood walking space. These spaces are linked not only by circulation but also by the landscape form itself (using *landscape* in the sense that includes buildings). There is a powerful and persuasive idea about how people ought to live together that comes through clearly in the total form.

(a)

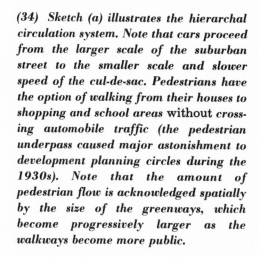

(34) Sketch (a) illustrates the hierarchal circulation system. Note that cars proceed from the larger scale of the suburban street to the smaller scale and slower speed of the cul-de-sac. Pedestrians have the option of walking from their houses to shopping and school areas without crossing automobile traffic (the pedestrian underpass caused major astonishment to development planning circles during the 1930s). Note that the amount of pedestrian flow is acknowledged spatially by the size of the greenways, which become progressively larger as the walkways become more public.

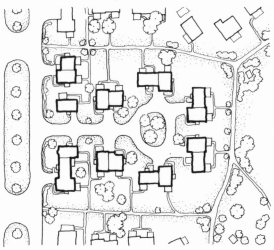

(b)

Sketch (b) illustrates one of the cul-de-sacs at Radburn. While Stein and Wright intended for the greenway to be the social gathering place, recent studies have shown that the cul-de-sac itself is the major organizer of social contact (husbands meet as they get in the car for commuting to New York City; the children play on the paved area; housewives drive to stores, etc.) Social scientists who argue that Radburn doesn't work, because it is not used as it was planned to be used, miss the point — at Radburn one has the opportunity and the choice to walk in safety. And some 47 percent apparently do walk, rather than drive to shopping centers (compared to 5 or 6 percent nationally). While children may play in a cul-de-sac in any case, it is one thing to play in a place where traffic must stop and quite another thing to play in the normal through-traffic street of the American city.

The theoretical background of the Radburn plan is well discussed by Clarence Stein in Toward New Towns for America *(Boston: MIT Press, paperback ed., 1944). For a more recent look, see "Radburn Revisited" by Henry Wright, Jr., in* Architectural Forum, *July / August 1971, p. 52. We will return to the importance of Radburn as a complex conceptual housing idea in chapter 7.*

(35) An interesting (and contentious) debate can always be guranteed by raising the question, "Is an outhouse architecture?" The answer cannot be framed without first deciding if the question is pertinent.

One is reminded that the Byzantine philosophers raised questions of how many angels can stand on the head of a pin and how much purple (the royal color) a minister of state can wear in comparison to what a priest can wear. The mysticism of the Greek Orthodox Church, the opaque and luminous mosaics of Hagia Sophia, the filtered light and dark shadows of Istanbul's sixth-century churches — all are related to the philosophic attitude of a society that questions angels on pins.

(36) This relates to the idea that collective or group form is relevant, even though individual form may not be. (See chapter 5 and its discussion of gestalt psychology.)

So far in this opening chapter, difficult words have occasionally been used without being given precise definitions: For example, *shape* and *structure*, have been treated as roughly synonymous. Semanticists may disagree with this approach but in the preceding discussion an attempt has been made to use the terms with their commonly accepted meanings.

In this light, the reader beginning to question his understanding of form is capable of seeing that content has to be shaped in some manner if it is to impart a meaning. It follows from this that art (and architecture) will make a symbolic statement that is significant, not mundane and trite.(35) Thus, if we return to the experiment proposed at the beginning of this chapter, we find that a hamburger drive-in may (or may not) be art. In any case, the design of the individual hamburger drive-in within the context of the one hundred hamburger drive-ins, window banks, and gasoline stations adjacent will not be as critical or as significant an issue as the overall pattern of highway strip development(36) that is emerging and the discussion of whether architects, as artists, can (or should) do anything about it. The question, then, "Is this drive-in beautiful?" cannot be answered unless a larger framework is considered. Is there a highway aesthetic? Should there be? And if so, what role should the architect play?

This begins to suggest that we may need different sets of aesthetical values when judging the highway scene and when judging a monumental building, such as the Boston City Hall. While this question will be more carefully explored later, at this time mention must be made of two difficult terms that appear in any theory of art: *style* and *beauty* itself. Style is the flavor of the form.(37) It improves or makes more enjoyable the content of art. Appreciation of style is taste, and although the term is not germane to development of an architectural theory, a slight digression (quoting from Russell Lynes) is warranted, if for no reason other than its excellent warning:

A great many people enjoy having taste, but too few of them really enjoy the things they have taste about. Or to put it another way, they are like a man who takes pleasure in his excellent taste in women, but takes no pleasure at all in a woman. ... the real reason for having taste is to increase one's faculties for enjoyment. Taste in itself is nothing. It is only what taste leads to that makes any difference in our lives.(38)

As a "word," *beauty* is simple to define — it is that which pleases, satisfies, and delights us in form. How to create beauty is a more difficult problem. A book may be beautiful; so may a tree; and as mentioned earlier, so may a walk along any countryside stream. Beauty, however, is elusive; those who most seek beauty (and prate about taste correspondingly) often never find the exhilarating moment of discovery. Those who work honestly within their art, struggling with their craft in an effort to express some new dimension of man and his cultural world, are more apt to awaken one morning to discover, not only that their work is beautiful, but that their doing the work has been worthwhile and satisfying in itself.(39)

(37) The individual styles of two architects, Frank Lloyd Wright and Le Corbusier, will be explored in chapters 8 and 9. Style is also alluded to in the discussion on determinants of form (chapter 2). While style itself is not a major concern of this book on how to initiate or begin a theory, it naturally is a concern of importance to any architect. This book tries to suggest that if one seriously approaches learning why he wants to build, he will, in the process of inquiry, acquire, through experience, his own style.

Style, of course, may be both individual (such as the personal style of Palladio) and societal (such as the cultural style of baroque) at the same time. An interesting but difficult treatise on this subject is Wylie Sypher's book The Four Stages of Renaissance Style *(Garden City, N.Y.: Doubleday, 1955).*

(38) Russell Lynes, The Tastemakers, *(New York: Grosset and Dunlop, 1954), p. 341.*

(39) Boris Pasternak expresses well the dedicated artist's approach when he says ". . . art always serves beauty; and beauty is delight in form, and form is the key to organic life, since no living thing can exist without it, so that every work of art, including tragedy, expresses the joy of existence." — Boris Pasternak, Doctor Zhivago *(New York: Pantheon Books, Ballantine Books [paperback] Ed., 1981) p. 456.*

(40) *A few selected other definitions: Architecture is . . .*

". . . a response to life" (Marcel Breuer).

". . . the Mother of the Arts" (anonymous; a definition fondly clung to by all architects).

". . . the play of masses in light" (Le Corbusier).

". . . the marriage of place and occasion" (Aldo van Eyck).

". . . frozen music (another anonymous quote fondly cherished by architects).

". . . composed of firmness, commodity, and delight" (a famous Renaissance statement by Henry Wotten in 1624).

(41) *The Grand Canal in Venice generally follows the channel of the original river. The smaller canals branch off of the main artery to create man-made community enclaves. Today it is no longer apparent which part of the canal system is natural and which part was formed by man.*

Let us now turn to a postulate for architecture: *Architecture is that field of art that deals with shaping the environment.*(40) This definition is purposely a broad one and, like the postulate for art, needs subpostulates to give substance to the basic meaning.

The first of these subpostulates is: 1. Architecture is concerned with the total physical environment; the creative statement will occur through the shaping of physical form. Thus, architecture is concerned not only with buildings but with all relationships of shaped places — the relation of rooms one to another as well as to the halls and to the outside; house to house, and to street; the arrangement of buildings and trees in the landscape; neighborhood to the city, and to the region. Architecture will attempt to order (and to create beauty) within this total environment by controlling and manipulating it. Only when one molds or shapes the total physical environment will he be working as both an "architect" and an "artist."

The second subpostulate follows naturally: 2. Architecture is a human endeavor and exists as a field of art for man's enrichment. The architect as an artist will need a value system by which to judge his choices. And all great architects have a highly developed aesthetical theory even if they do not consciously (and verbally) state it.

This definition, together with its subpostulates, is much wider in scope than the older statement that architecture is the "profession of building." Returning one final time to the experiment at the beginning of the chapter, we see that a walk along a countryside stream will not be architecture (although the shaped canals of Venice may be).(41)

Likewise, a drive through a town's main street will be architecture if it is a molding *by the society* of its shopping environment. (If this molding occurred over a long period of time as an unconscious expression of societal culture, it may fall into a special category, "vernacular architecture." The St. Louis Arch will be architecture (although whether it is good architecture must await further study); while the hamburger drive-in along the highway, as has already been discussed, may not be a relevant "art" and "architecture" issue unless considered in the context of the total strip development.(42)

The first note to this chapter was a caution, and it seems appropriate to end the chapter with this same thought within the text: In the beginning, it is necessary to have a few terms of agreement so that discussion itself can proceed. But as one progresses in any field of knowledge, his basic definitions are modified, rearranged, and rebuilt by his own learning and his own experience. There is nothing sacred about these definitions; they are intended for use in the beginning.

(42) The revised chart (see note 3) illustrates a possible final evaluation based on the tentative definitions of the four environmental experiences suggested at the beginning of this chapter.

Environment	Art?	Arch.?	Beauty?	Comment
① stream / walk	(no)	no	yes	God's Art is not Man's creation
② main street / drive	(yes)	yes	no	may be "vernacular"
③ landmark — (St. Louis Arch)	yes	yes	no	a personal reaction
④ Hamburger drive-in	(yes / no)	(yes / no)	no	depends on cultural context

REVISED INDIVIDUAL RESPONSE

This particular student has discovered that four of his answers (those which are circled in the chart) have changed since his first evaluations (see note 3).

II DETERMINANTS OF ARCHITECTURAL FORM

Having outlined a basic vocabulary for architecture, we should now proceed to ask what forces act upon this architecture to shape and give meaning to its form?(1) After identifying these shaping forces, a framework for discussion will be completed, and one may then proceed with simple investigations into aesthetical value.

As one outlines these forces, or determinants, he soon discovers that their number is infinite if each determinant is given a precise value difference. But the number is not as important as the idea: By using determinants, we are categorizing and separating out for study various influences on form — making value judgments based on simple analytical method possible.(2) For this discussion, four determinants of architectural form will suffice as a beginning:

1. *Functional* (need) determinant:
    The necessity of shaping environments for both public and private human wants

2. *Technological* (ability) determinant:
    The state of architectural crafts and the economic means of a society

3. *Cultural* (society's symbolic need) determinant:
    The desire of a people for symbolic art expression

4. *Artistic* (style) determinant:
    The architect's personal intellectual contribution

The order of ranking is also not relevant, since (by definition) any architectural form will be a reflection of all four determinants. It may, however, be possible to say that in a specific circumstance one determinant may be more important than another — for example, a hamburger drive-in will have to work functionally for visibility, car access, parking, etc., and the functional determinant is generally thought of as being more important than the technological determinant in this instance.(3)

(1) This can be alternatively stated: The meaning of architecture is an expression of certain forces acting upon its form.

(2) The advantages of this method from Aristotelian philosophy are obvious. The disadvantages will be explored in chapters 4 and 5.

(3) Even here one must be careful. Witness the McDonald's Hamburger stand and its change in cultural symbolic expression. In the 1950s this hamburger chain was characterized by bright lights and large golden arches (sketch a). By 1970, the McDonald's image had been greatly altered to become that of a family place (sketch b).

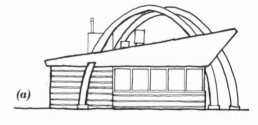

(a)

(b)

The image change was hastened by a skillful television advertising campaign. (This raises a larger question, of the relationship between television and architectural form.)

(4) This does not deny that some architectural examples may stress cultural and artistic determinants over functional ones. For example, the Campidoglio in Rome by Michelangelo uses building form, paving patterns, and visual perspective to draw attention to the central statute of Marcus Aurelius. But a careful inspection shows that while this plan was not designed for functional needs (walking, gathering, sheltering, etc.) per se, it nonetheless is highly successful as a walking, gathering, and sheltering place!

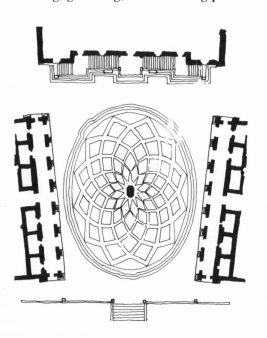

(5) For example, which is more beautiful: a hand-written letter or a typed one? Or, a hand-turned vase, or a machine-made one? The answer is relative, not inherent; it depends on the situation: who and what the letter is for; how the vase is to be used.

Each of these determinants should next be examined. One sees that the *functional determinant* may range in scale from something as simple as the need for a kitchen or cooking place to something as complex as a large seaport facility for handling ocean freighters.

The kitchen must be sized and formed to allow for one or two persons to cook and move about in it, with countertops and storage units properly located. The seaport facility must be designed to allow for the interaction of giant cranes, warehouses, railways, and trucks. In both cases, if the basic functional needs are not spatially provided for, the resultant buildings will not be thought of as good architecture.

This is a good point at which to lay to rest the belief held by many that there is some mystical power that separates function and beauty. If anything, the reverse is generally true. To be an aesthetical entity (that is, to have the potential for being beautiful), any work of architecture, must be designed with function considered.(4) Many laymen and students, and unfortunately many architects as well, feel: "It doesn't work well, but I like it, so in my terms it is beautiful."

This feeling, separating functional usefulness and "artistic" beauty, is a relatively recent occurrence, and a direct reaction to the Industrial Revolution and the implied functionalism of the machine. There is nothing inherently either beautiful or ugly about machine-made products, however. (There is also nothing inherently either more or less functional about machine-made products.)(5)

This popular misconception of beauty versus function leads to "art for art's sake," and to an equally perverse attitude concerning supposedly useful or utilitarian structures, such as a large bridge. There are no such purely functional structures; a bridge always reflects technological, cultural, and artistic determinants as well as functional ones. And the most competent structural engineer is an artist concerned with the expression of form and with the beauty of his creation.

Although the number of functional determinants is endless, we may conveniently divide them into private needs, such as shelter from the cold while sleeping, and public needs, such as a place for shopping, bartering, and exchanging. An example of private need is the rock-cut cave house of Cappadocia, Turkey.(6) That this ancient shelter form, begun before the 1600s, continues to function well is attested to by the fact that it is still being cut out of the soft stone today.(7)

An excellent example of public need would be the shopping arcade -- such as Asakusa in Tokyo(8). In this case the covered arcade begins at the first torii, or gate, leading to Asakusa temple, and ends at the entry to the formal temple courtyard. Thus in walking from the main traffic street to the temple, and in returning, the pedestrian passes by a variety of shops that satisfy his marketing needs. A more recent example of capitalizing on this simple functional-path idea is the modern supermarket, which carefully places everyday purchases such as milk, bread, and Coca-Cola in widely dispersed areas throughout the store — thus increasing visual contact for impulse buying.

(6) Sketch of rock-cut cave houses, Cappadocia, Turkey (1975).

(7) This also is a testament to the continuing cultural symbolism of this shelter form in Turkish society.

(8) A sketch of Asakusa arcade, Tokyo.

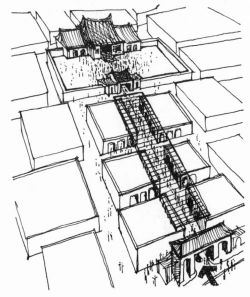

Another good example of functional public need is the castle. As an architectural form, the castle began when it was functionally necessary to protect the village from attackers. The form itself evolved from high towers to low concentric rings and star earthenworks when the introduction of gunpowder changed the military requirements for defense.(9) By the time of the Second World War, the castle as a fixed defensive position had lost most of its military value, and it soon disappeared as an architectural entity.

Architectural form frequently reflects more than one functional determinant, as may be seen in an African village layout.(10) In this case, the form of the huts themselves satisfies the need for individual (private) sleeping and storage areas, while the layout of the total village satisfies the need for a defined meeting place. Like the Cappadocia rock-cut houses, these African villages have been found satisfactory to the extent that their form has been repeated down to our present age, a fact that reinforces the idea introduced earlier — function as a determinant of form is still very much with us when we aesthetically evaluate architecture.

(10) *An African village of this type is also easy to build and easy to move. The simplicity of form in much African housing has powerful symbolic import — as has been analyzed both by Amos Rapoport and by the Dutch architect Aldo van Eyck.*

The *technological determinant* has historically been more important for what it prevents us from doing than for what it allows us to do. Each society has certain abilities for construction that strongly affect architecture. For example, the Mogul empire in India had vast numbers of workmen available (but no factory-made precast screens, or grills). The result is a series of brilliant tomb constructions, each with carefully hand-carved screens, culminating in the Taj Mahal.

A society's technology affects the detailing of wood joints in ancient pagodas, as well as in modern windows. There are even art movements that capitalize on a technological breakthrough for much of their aesthetic (such as art nouveau's fascination with cast iron, futurism's concern for the car and for speed and movement, and archigram's 1960 desire to express systems).(11) But the best way to examine technology as a determinant probably is to trace the historical evolution of *one* building-form idea, such as the covering of a large space with a dome, and then to observe how technology has affected the change in architectural form. Four examples will demonstrate this evolution.

The first of these, the Pantheon (A.D. 110), was designed and built by the Roman Emperor Hadrian,(12) but the form already had a long historical background. Preceded first by the arch then by the barrel vault, the design of the Pantheon is based on a perfect circular dome or sphere. The dome is held together by the sheer mass of the cylindrical wall that contains the outward thrust, thus keeping the dome from exploding and falling.

(11) The sketch is of "Plug-in City," designed by Peter Cook of the archigram movement. Archigram was fascinated by all types of twentieth century technologies; mechanical layouts, structural capsules, moving parts, computers, wiring diagrams — all became the basis for "systems" that would resolve complex architectural issues.

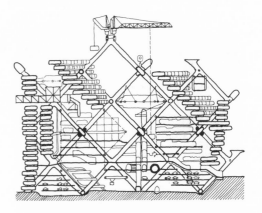

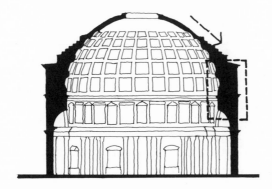

(12) The sketch is a structural perspective view of the Pantheon. Note how much material mass is above the natural breaking point of the dome. Hadrian was not only a great emperor, but one of history's distinguished architects. Unfortunately, a definitive architectural examination of his work has not yet been written. (As discussed later, the Pantheon was used as a starting point by Jefferson for his design of the Rotunda at the University of Virginia.)

(13) The sketch shows the pendentive of Hagia Sofia in perspective.

(14) This perspective sketch of the Duomo shows how Gothic vaulting resolved the problem of outward thrust by making a pointed (higher) dome out of structural ribs. The material between the ribs becomes of lighter construction than previous domes. The Duomo has often been called the last Gothic church, as well as the first Renaissance church. In this context, the Duomo, Brunelleschi's masterpiece, is a turning point in history and worthy of further study.

(15) The sketch is of Bucky Fuller's dome. Mathematically derived, the structure's great lightness makes it possible to span great distances, and to enclose vast areas. The triangulation of its parts distributes all forces evenly in every direction — which reduces the weight of the parts. One can see that this type of structure lends itself to a computerized program for design of the structure (even though Fuller's initial ideas were intuitive).

Hagia Sofia (A.D. 532-37) designed by Anthemius and Isodorus for the Emperor Justinian, takes the principle of the dome a step farther by placing a dome over a square base rather than a cylinder. This makes necessary a special brick construction called a *pendentive*.(13)

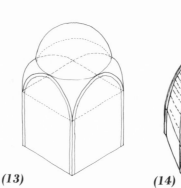 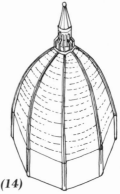

(13)   (14)

In general, technological knowledge has continually increased. The heavy domes of Rome and Constantinople give way to the lighter construction of the Renaissance — with their pointed and ribbed domes as at the Duomo,(14) the great cathedral at Florence designed in 1400 by Brunelleschi. The ribbed vaulting of the Renaissance gives way in turn to the eggshell domes of the twentieth century, and finally to the immense triangulated-hexagonal domes of Buckminster Fuller, as in the twenty-one story high American Pavilion for the Montreal World's Fair, Expo 67.(15)

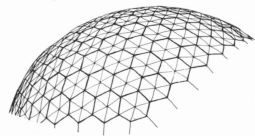

Indeed, one of the great problems of today's architecture is the very freedom from constraint that modern building technology allows. (Uncharitable critics call this a lack of restraint.) For, although we can imitate the Parthenon (to perfection with cast beams and spray plastic), this does not mean we should do so, unless by chance our cultural goals are similar to those of Ancient Greece.

This leads us into the difficult philosophical question of the *cultural determinant.* Few would debate that each society has cultural ambitions that it expresses symbolically in art form. Discovering what these cultural ambitions are is not easy, however. In earlier societies, where there were large areas of common philosophical agreement, a dominant cultural concern would prevail. There is an obvious difference in sociocultural values implied between the symbolism of the French Gothic cathedral of 1300 with its high and long directional nave leading to the altar and the Italian Renaissance cathedral of 1600 with its powerful dome and central altar plan.(16)

(16) Sketches (a) and (b) are of the plan and section of Rheims cathedral in France. (Note also that the outward thrust of the vault is contained by the flying buttresses.)

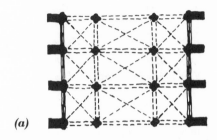

(a)

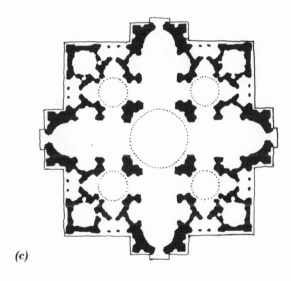

(c)

(b)

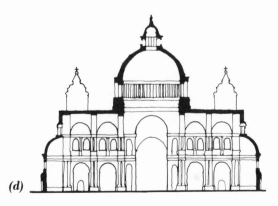

(d)

Sketches (c) and (d) are of Bramante's plan and section for St. Peter's in Rome. Bramante's plan greatly influenced all later Renaissance architectural thought — including the final plan, which was actually designed by Michelangelo.

(17)   In the two examples given, there are other equally obvious cultural determinants; for example, the great cathedrals of France are intimately connected with the emergence of the city-state and the reappearance of major trade between these small cities. A strong case can be made that the cathedrals were built higher and higher so that citizens could say with pride: "My cathedral is higher than yours."

(18)   The Sydney Opera House, originally designed by Carl Utzon, was finally completed in 1973, after more than fifteen years of debate and at more than fifteen times its original estimated cost. It is the perfect example of consciously building a national landmark.

(19)   Which is why in this book, which concentrates on theory, this particular discussion on high style is not longer. Many excellent books on high-style architecture already exist; the acknowledged classic is Sir Bannister Fletcher, A History of Architecture on the Comparative Method *(1896; rev. ed., New York: Charles Scribner's Sons, 1961, 1963).*

The tall and slender columns of the Gothic church (pointing upwards toward God?) rhythmically progress in plan toward the altar, which is *beyond* the crossing of the nave. (God lies hidden in the apse?) In the long nave, the hierarchal medieval society listens to chanting, smells the incense, and feels the mysterious power of God. The Renaissance church, on the other hand, places the altar in the middle of an often perfectly balanced form — the Greek cross with its equal arms. (God becomes more accessible and humanistic.) A man-made geometric order prevails.

While it is dangerous to be too simplistic about culturally determined symbolic content in architecture,(17) there can be little argument that significant cultural epochs create powerful symbolic art forms. For convenience, we might call these examples high style. They will normally be important civic structures that are carefully planned (usually by an architect who is remembered) and are sponsored by a powerful social group such as the church, the government, or a wealthy family. Examples include the Pyramids, the Greek temples, the churches of western Europe, the pagodas of China and Japan, the high-rise corporate business towers of Manhattan, and the cultural civic centers now being built everywhere.(18)

History of architecture courses normally concentrate on high-style architecture.(19) But pinpointing what specific cultural mores are relevant in any example will probably always remain a difficult question.(20) In his book *The Language of Architecture*, the critic Niels Luning-Prak suggests that there are two areas of high-style aesthetic criticism. The first area, formal aesthetics, he defines as being the composition of form elements, and it deals with such issues as proportion, size, mass, rhythm, and consistency. He suggests that throughout history, there has been common agreement on how to judge formal aesthetics. The second area of aesthetics he defines as being symbolic, and his contention is that it deals with the meaning of forms and not their composition. "It [symbolism] is rooted in the meaning which particular forms have acquired for a certain society at a particular time."(21)

If, for purposes of discussion, one accepts Luning-Prak's definition, he soon sees that there is a particular problem with social historical criticism in the twentieth century, for our societies are so fragmented and are changing so rapidly in their own structure that finding any large area of cultural agreement will prove difficult.

Another, more profound difficulty with analysis of the cultural determinant is in deciding whether the symbolic meaning is a conscious act or an unconscious act of the society. The historical, well-known examples we have listed are all obvious high-style, conscious acts of the society. But what of vernacular, indigenous architecture — the farmhouses, the small villages, the native markets — those places obviously not designed by a conscious act of patron, planner, architect, but that still possess architectural character?

(20) Students yearly rebel against architectural history courses that are full of facts — dates, names, identification — but never tackle what the architecture means. History must, of course, be taught as a real and continuously alive process — that this is so is the final argument in this book; in academic history's defense, however, identifying a building is often the first step in discovering what it means.

(21) Niels Luning-Prak, The Language of Architecture *(The Hague: Mouton Press, 1968), p. 6. This book is excellent for the advanced graduate student, but difficult for beginners. Luning-Prak says that architecture is made up of function, construction, and aesthetics (this is an indirect reference to Vitruvius's famous definition), but that symbolism is the most important aspect. He then proceeds in a complex process to define three levels of symbolic content — (1) an activity level (which, one may argue, is in fact function); (2) a "manifest symbolism," or a culture's style, and (3) a "latent symbolism," which is the unconscious (nonobvious) cultural philosophy of a social historical period (pp. 1-7). The third level is extremely difficult to analyze, for, as he says, "social conditions are of course not objectively given" (p. 41). While all of this may be confusing to a beginner, Luning-Prak's major point is, in fact, rather simple — the cultural history of a society is crucial to understanding what architectural form means.*

What is important is that he builds a methodology for symbolic evaluation (or a language of architecture) and applies it directly to nine case studies.

This method has serious flaws, the most important being that it slights function and construction (the first two components of Vitruvius's definition), and the analyses often makes social history seem to be only ideas rather than human drama — still, Luning-Prak's book shows the seriousness of reasoned criticism. His most telling point is that many theoreticians attempt to prove the truth of their symbolic aesthetic by taking out of context a formal aesthetic (p. 7). Thus, Le Corbusier can argue that his interpretation of the meaning of architecture is proven by the form of the Parthenon. As Luning-Prak demonstrates, however, it is possible to agree that the Parthenon is beautiful without agreeing that it proves Le Corbusier's theories.

(22) Bernard Rudofsky, Architecture Without Architects *(Garden City, N.Y.: Doubleday and Company, 1964). What appeals to all architects in this book is Rudofsky's emphasis on group forms, which are strikingly presented in photographs. Even if one accepts his differentiation between vernacular and elitist architecture, however, the question still remains: Are the examples shown architecture?*

(23) Amos Rapoport, House Form and Culture *(Englewood Cliffs, N.J.: Prentice-Hall, 1969), p. 8.*

(24) This flamboyant example is just outside the city of Srinigar, Kashmir.

In *Architecture Without Architects*, Bernard Rudofsky suggests that vernacular architecture is the unconscious will of the people over a long period of time,(22) representing a cultural attitude of the mass, as differentiated from the elite who hire architects. Amos Rapoport in *House Form and Culture*(23) supports this view when he carefully lists three categories of architecture: 1. primitive — built with few modifications by all the people on a common model; 2. vernacular — divided into preindustrial, which is built by tradesmen on a model that comes from the people (folk art), and postindustrial, built by specialists, from a model for the people (mass-culture art); and 3. high-style — built by specialists and designed by specialists (architects) for an elite cultural group.

There are examples of preindustrial vernacular architecture in almost every society, such as the thousands of Kashmir houses with their Moslem harems,(24) built high above the public spaces below, or the countless Victorian farmhouses of Ohio and Illinois, all similar but individually distinct.

The difficulty is in defining a modern vernacular. Rapoport suggests that there may not even be a modern vernacular(25) — but then his definition excludes it. If we carry his thoughts further and define *modern vernacular* as architecture built by specialists (in some cases, architects) on a model that is believed to be for the people, we can find innumerable examples. In the typical subdivision layout, each house is a variation of a standard plan sited on a land plot of given common yard size, having a common setback; and facing an identical street pattern.(26) Other examples are highway strip development, the country store, and the plans of primary schools during the 1950s.

(25) "We have seen that some of the dominant characteristics of primitive and vernacular building lost force with the greater institutionalization and specialization of modern life. . . . The clear hierarchy of primitive and vernacular settlements is lost" (Rapoport, House Form and Culture, p. 126).

The most interesting section of this book, its ending, is also the most controversial. Rapoport's discussion of the dream house suggests that the idea of unconscious will is very much with us, even if we do not define why we have dream houses (ibid., pp. 130-35).

(a)

(26) Johnson Village, Charlottesville, Virginia (1968). This layout (a), thoroughly typical of those in the United States during the period of 1950-70, shows the strong influence of Wright and Stein's Radburn, N.J., plan (discussed in chapter one). In this case, the influence was not direct, but rather indirect, through planning and zoning laws. That is, the Planning Code of Charlottesville (written by those influenced by Radburn) shaped the layout through restrictions on street setbacks, widths of lots, etc. Note that the subdivision has only one entry

and exit point. This has become important in maintaining a contained social neighborhood environment. It also eliminates all through traffic.

The house plans shown (b-c) are both variations of an identical building technology.

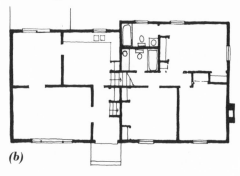

(b)

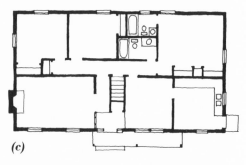

(c)

(27) Wylie Sypher, Four Stages of Renaissance Style (Garden City, N.Y.: Doubleday and Company, 1956).

(28) It is not important whether one includes society's style within the general framework of the third determinant or whether it is given a listing as a separate determinant in itself. What should be remembered is that every architect operates within a larger cultural aesthetic framework (see chapter ten).

Whether these modern examples are or are not vernacular architecture is not as important as the fact that they are being built, and they do say something about our society's culture. As suggested in the first chapter's discussion on the highway strip development environment, the appropriate question is What role should architects play? And, does this built form represent any real unconscious desire of the people, or is it merely all that the people have to choose from?

The importance to design of the cultural determinant is the most difficult of the four determinants to discover in analyzing any work, high style or vernacular, of architecture, but understanding this importance is critical to our future well-being. For an architecture that places 40,000 people in twin office towers, such as the New York World Trade Center, and then ignores how this collective mass will culturally relate to their cubicle, to their work, to their place in the air; an architecture that denies every person his sense of identity — is an architecture that indicts the clients, the financiers, the social planners, the engineers, and the architects.

The fourth and final determinant of architectural form, the *artistic determinant*, will be the architect's personal intellectual contribution. All architects are, of course, influenced by their society (or at least by that fragment of society with whom they associate), so that it is possible to claim that there is both a societal style and a personal style evident in every architectural form. One can find numerous books both on a period of style, such as Wylie Sypher's superb *The Four Stages of Renaissance Style*,(27) and on an individual within that period, such as any of the many books about Michelangelo.(28)

Although we should remember that no artist operates in a vacuum, nonetheless there are still architects who excite our imagination by the enormity of their intellectual contribution — such as Fillipo Brunelleschi, who in 1400 "rediscovered" the dome, combined it with medieval vaulting technology, and created the Duomo (shown earlier), or Antonio Gaudí, who in 1880 tilted inward the outside row of columns at his Hall of 100 Columns, to express their internal stresses.(29) In his intensely personal use of cut stone, colored-tile mosaics, naturalistic iron decoration, and bent structural configurations, Gaudí helped to create the art nouveau style, which is still little understood.

(29) The section (a) shows how the outer row of columns in Gaudí's Hall of the 100 Columns at Parque Güell leans slightly inward. This structural configuration may be tested in a laboratory and shown to be correct. The sketch perspective (b), shows how the roof of the hall was used as a children's playing field, with benches surrounding. The bench configuration allowed nannies to talk together in a semicircular seating arrangement, while still watching the playground.

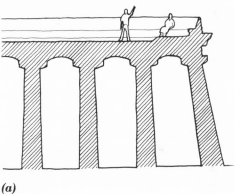

(a)

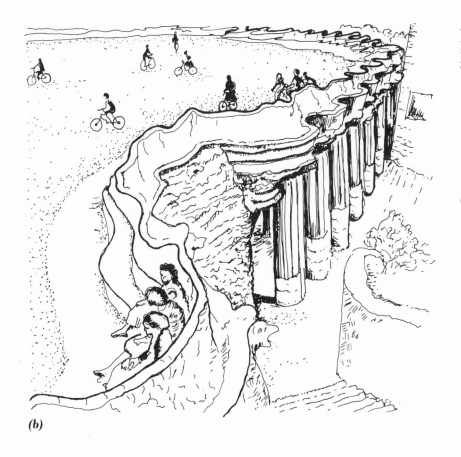

(b)

(30)   The sketches show how Alberti's new marble facade changed the original character of the entrance (a), making it appear to be a totally new composition (b). The church's actual construction is of brick.

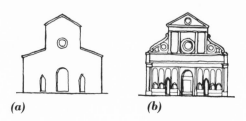

(a)   *(b)*

(31)   See the Introduction.

(32)   Our present American society places a great premium on individuality. Building a "house" onto wheels is not that uncommon an occurrence. Sketch (a) is of a house on wheels seen in California. Sketch (b) is of a house for the dead seen in Kyoto, Japan.

Personally, I would exclude both of these examples from being architecture on grounds of insignificance, but this does not deny that they exist and are being built. And they certainly have societal importance. Many students have argued that

A fine example of a unique and individual artistic contribution is Leon Battista Alberti's use of the volute in remodeling the church of Santa Maria Novella in 1450. One can imagine the church fathers asking Alberti to redesign their Florentine church in the new Renaissance style. How to make the front facade appear to be one unified whole instead of being a high nave with two lower side aisles (which of course it remained in the interior) must have bothered Alberti until he came up with the idea of using a geometrically curved form, the volute, to make a graceful transition from high to low.(30) This solution was so original and so perfectly in harmony with Renaissance thought that it was copied endlessly — long past the Renaissance and into the present day, where it now appears in strange dado designs for railings and porches.

More-modern examples of individual architectural style include F. L. Wright's flowing horizontal planes growing out of the land (his "organic architecture") and Rudolph Steiner's fluid concrete plasticity used in his Goetheanum building near Basel, Switzerland — a project little known by architects, but not overlooked by Le Corbusier, whose equally astonishing concrete masterpiece, Ronchamp, is barely one hundred miles distant. Or refer to Louis Kahn's Richard's Medical Center shown in the Introduction,(31) which separates the open laboratory spaces from the mechanical service spaces.

In any evaluation of the artistic determinant in architectural form, one must always raise the question: At what point does the personal artistic expression cease to be relevant within the context of a larger society? Is an architecture created for only one person —- the form-maker himself — in fact architecture? Is a jerry-built home on wheels ridiculous or sublime?(32) The answers to these questions are difficult, but they will be bound up with the issue of significance: Is the example significant enough to merit architectural study?

(a)

(b)

The reader must also understand that the preceding discussion of the four determinants is not all-inclusive — one may add other determinants: "climate," for example.(33) Nor has there been any attempt here to draw sharply defined boundaries around each determinant.

Any architectural example is a complex intermingling of all the determinants. A good case in point is the Parthenon — for centuries it has been known and appreciated that the end columns are spaced closer together than the central columns. The commonly accepted reason for this is that different optical illusions occur when one sees sky behind the end columns (see plan).(34) The sky makes the columns visually appear farther apart, and the Greeks thus moved the columns closer together so that when one stands in front of the Parthenon, the columns appear to be evenly spaced. The spacing is therefore the result of either a personal stylistic concern (determinant four) or a long-ingrained cultural symbolism (determinant three).

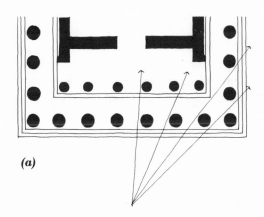

(a)

these examples and others like them constitute a new type of architecture that should be called personalized vernacular. This raises the interesting question of the architect's role. Should he provide the spatial mode, which then can be individualized by the owner? If so, a complete rethinking of current standard aesthetic responsibility will be necessary.

(33) Climate might also be considered a subcategory of the functional determinant.

(34) A plan (a) and a perspective elevation (b) of the Parthenon. Very few visitors realize that the columns are not evenly spaced or that the floor is slightly bowed (higher in the middle). The latter is another optical illusion and a highly effective one, since visually the floor appears level.

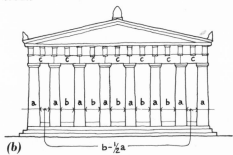

(b)

The great modern Italian engineer Luigi Nervi claimed that the above hypothesis is nonsense, and that the real reason for the column spacing is technological(35) — the Greeks having been limited by the maximum size of the solid-stone spans of the lintels that they could cut and then move. On studying the Parthenon, one does find that all the lintels are cut to the same length. The end columns were then moved slightly inward, so that the column capital is totally covered by the lintel.

(35) Pier Luigi Nervi, Aesthetics and Technology in Building, trans. Robert Einaudi (Cambridge, Mass.: Harvard University Press, 1965), p. 11, illus. fig. 1. Since the lintels are the longest individual stones cut for the Parthenon, Nervi's hypothesis is more than reasonable.

(36) Performing this experiment with a class of 120 students and using as examples (shown via slides) Hagia Sofia, the Parthenon, and a hot dog stand (one shaped like a hot dog), produced the composite results shown in chart (36).

	FUNCTION	TECHNOLOGY	SOCIAL	ARTISTIC	TOTAL
HAGIA SOFIA	2	2	2	1	7
PARTHENON	1	2	2	1	6
HOT DOG STAND	1	3	2	4	10

In this student ranking, a number 1 rating was considered as the highest and number 10 as the lowest; thus, the Parthenon is seen as being the best architecture. Remember that this form of polling is a game, and a tool that gauges popularity. Polling is not architecture itself.

(37) Chart (37) represents the actual reranking in the experiment with the three examples from chart 36.

	FUNCTION	TECHNOLOGY	SOCIAL	ARTISTIC	TOTAL
HAGIA SOFIA	1	1	1	1	4
PARTHENON	1	1	2	1	5
HOT DOG STAND	1	2	2	3	8

With due deference, it seems reasonable to assume that both theories are correct. The Greeks certainly understood optical illusions, while at the same time they were working within the technological limitations of their time. In all great architecture ("significant art," to use a phrase from chapter 1), as in the Parthenon, the four determinants will be powerfully fused and expressed within the form. Other examples, all mentioned earlier under individual determinants, spring to mind — the Pyramids, the Pantheon, Hagia Sofia, the Duomo, St. Peter's, Rheims, the Parque Güell, the Sydney Opera House, etc.: All may be discussed as integrated and complete works of art.

Up to this point, we have outlined definitions for art, beauty, and architecture, and we have discussed a limited number of determinants of architectural form — in short, we have created an abbreviated analytical vocabulary or framework for discussion, which we can now use to examine and evaluate architecture itself.

An interesting experiment is to have a lecturer or photographer take a number of architectural environments with which the viewer or student is not familiar; have the viewer then look at slides or pictures of each environment, and then rank them as to their value or worth under each determinant.(36)

An in-depth study of each example should then be undertaken – a study that examines when the architecture was shaped, for whom, and why; that examines the technology of the period, its cultural aspirations, the architectural style prevalent, and the contribution of the architect. One then reviews the slides and reranks the examples. The shift in one's value judgment is usually considerable, and the change in rating is almost always to a higher ranking (demonstrating that a little knowledge is better than none at all.(37)

This experiment might be called the ranking game because there is always a natural curiosity to see which environment ranks highest.(38) It is also related to the experiment in the first chapter — and it suffers from the same handicaps in that an actual visit to the site is needed after the determinants have been discussed and studied.

Perhaps a better way to use this determinants methodology would be to apply it to an analysis in depth of only one superior architectural complex, recognized as being significant. To demonstrate this, let us make a more careful analysis of Thomas Jefferson's design for "the Lawn" at the University of Virginia.

Built from 1819 to 1825, the Lawn constitutes the center of the present university. The original functional determinant is simple enough – there existed a need for a new university to help in educating the young men of a rapidly expanding state. This new university would need to have academic buildings, athletic facilities, lodging hotels, professor's houses, and service buildings. And Charlottesville was the logical place to locate the new institution, since the town was close to the center of the state's population, and already possessed a small college that could serve as the nucleus for expansion.(39)

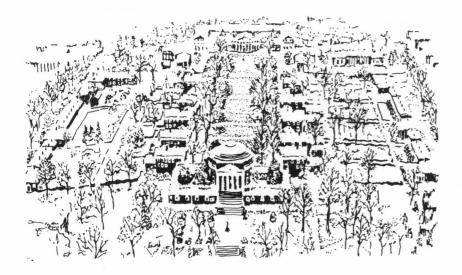

The first student ranking was obviously affected by the fact that many students had heard of the Parthenon, so it rated highest in their esteem.

The second ranking is affected not only by the knowledge gained through the lecture (although knowledge does help) but also by the fact that in this case the lecturer happens to admire Hagia Sofia. An interesting point is that the shift in opinion is generally uniform — that is, that within any relatively uniform social group such as college students, the change in ranking occurs similarly and uniformly throughout the group.

(38) One would expect Hagia Sofia to rank higher than the hot dog stand on the grounds of significance, but a cogent argument can be made that the hot dog stand cannot be viewed out of context — i.e., it is only one of a long grouping of similar structures on the beach; therefore, its importance as a cultural symbol is relative to the situation.

(39) An aerial view of the Lawn during the winter makes it clear which buildings and outdoor spaces Jefferson designed. One would be foolish not to recognize also that as chairman of the state site-selection committee, Jefferson had more than a little to say about locating the university within visible distance of Monticello.

A superb account of the beginning of the university may be found in Dumas Malone's The Sage of Monticello, *his sixth and last volume of* Jefferson and His Time *(Boston: Little, Brown and Company, 1981).*

Technologically, Jefferson's buildings were not dramatically new, but they did employ the most advanced techniques of the building crafts as they existed in the new republic, particularly when one realizes that Charlottesville was little more than a hamlet of forty-eight houses, far from the cultural centers of Philadelphia and Williamsburg. The buildings, colonnades, and garden walls were all of brick, and the dome of the central building, the Rotunda, represented a formidable construction task.

(40) The walls undulate in the natural arc of the reach of the bricklayer's arm — the undulation of the form gives the wall its structural strength despite the fact that it is only one brick thick.

Nor did Jefferson hesitate to order Italian marble for his column capitals when the native stone was found to be soft and susceptible to chipping. And while not a new idea, the now famous serpentine walls built in the gardens had never been greatly used in the state of Virginia. (40)

Using his books on architecture for a reference (specificially Giacomo Leoni's 1721 London edition of Palladio's *Four Books of Architecture*), Jefferson was probably the most innovative architectural technician of his time in America. Indeed, the entire creation of the Lawn is so dominated by Jefferson's great intellect that it is difficult to analyze any of the determinants as independent from his thought. This is particularly true of the cultural determinant.

One can see the concept of the final built form of the university, implanted in Jefferson's mind in 1784, some forty-one years before its final completion. In that year, Jefferson was named ambassador to France, and there he came in contact with the second generation of the French Enlightenment, the society of King Louis XVI. These intellectual aristocrats, influenced by Voltaire, Rousseau, and Diderot, all looked back to the Roman Empire for the purity of their Neoclassical ideas. As a brilliant statesman and writer in his own right, Jefferson was an intimate associate of these men.

(41) A perspective sketch of Marly-le-Roi. The Lawn's similarity to it is obvious.

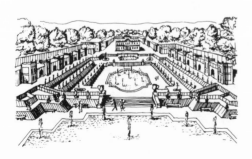

We know from letters that he visited Marly-le-Roi, Louis XIV's summer retreat.(41) In this architectural complex of residences, the king's palace was in the center of a long lawn with the dwellings of his courtiers flanking his palace along the sides. We also know that Jefferson visited Southern France (where at Nîmes he saw the Maison Carée, a Roman antiquity that he later freely translated in his design for the state capitol at Richmond, Virginia). In short, when he returned to the United States in 1789, he was thoroughly familiar with the then avante-garde movement of Neoclassicism.

As early as 1805, while still president, Jefferson wrote his thoughts on what a university should be: "A plain small house for the school and lodging for each professor is best, these connected by covered ways out of which the rooms for the students should open would be best. These may then be built only as they should be wanting. In fact, a University should not be a house but a village."(42

Already Jefferson is thinking of an academical village composed of scholars and students in close association, rather than of a large-scale single-building (and anonymous) institution. Some ten years later, in 1815, Jefferson's first Lawn plan appeared.(43) From that time forward, he and his friends actively worked to establish a great new university in Charlottesville. In this work, they were aided by the best thinkers and architects in the small nation. The new university would repudiate the Georgian style (a style named after an aristocratic king still detested by the new republicans) and would be built of simple pavilions, Neoclassic and open-ended in design, symbolizing educational growth, and of sufficient grandeur to attract young men from the west back to Virginia for their education.

In 1817, Jefferson wrote his friend Benjamin Latrobe, America's first trained architect, for advice. Latrobe's reply suggested a central and dominant building emphasizing the axis.(44) He also suggested making each of the pavilions different. Jefferson accepted both of these ideas, but as was his characteristic, he made subtle and important alterations, shortening the width of his Lawn and thus making it more directional as well as more intimate in scale. Furthermore, he decided to make each pavilion an example of the good taste of the times using his Palladian book and taking Doric, Ionic, and Corinthian classical architectural orders directly from it.

(42) Quoted from, William B. O'Neal, Pictorial History of the University of Virginia (Charlottesville, Va.; The University Press of Virginia, 1968) p. 10. O'Neal's book is an excellent source for those interested in Jefferson's original drawings. The 1815, 1817, 1819, and 1822 plans may all be found in this book.

(43) The 1815 plan — Jefferson's first recorded drawing for the University Lawn.

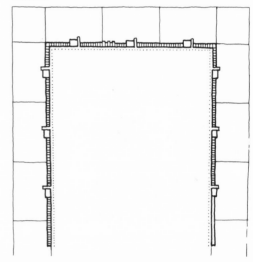

(44) A sketch of Latrobe's 1817 suggested plan. Earlier, Latrobe and Jefferson had consulted frequently about development of Washington, D.C., as a fitting capitol.

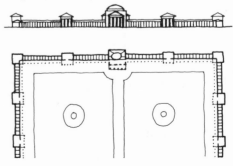

(45) O'Neal, Pictorial History of the University of Virginia, p. 15. Sketch is of Jefferson's 1819 plan. Apparently, Jefferson himself cut the drawing along the dashed line, so that he could reverse the gardens and hotels. The result is a plan that conceptually is very close to the final one shown in note 46.

By 1819, when planning the university in Charlottesville was sanctioned by the state legislature with Jefferson as its guiding father, he was far along in his design plans. One final important change still remained — his friend Joseph Cabell, a local farmer and plantation owner, suggested that the overall plan could be improved if the gardens were located between the pavilions and the student hotels. Jefferson commented, "It is a real improvement, and the greater as by throwing the hotels and additional dormitories on a back street, it forms in fact the commencement of a regular town."(45)

With the plan modified and buildings under construction, an engraving was made in 1822 and sent to prospective students so they could orient themselves before arrival.(46) This plan, known as the Maverick Engraving, is the clear final statement by Jefferson on education and the Age of Enlightenment. The points of the plan can be summarized as follows:

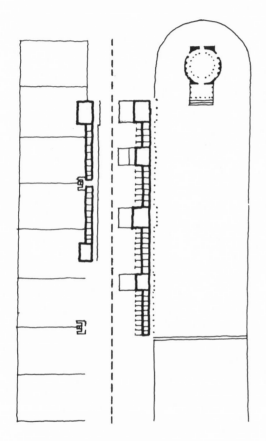

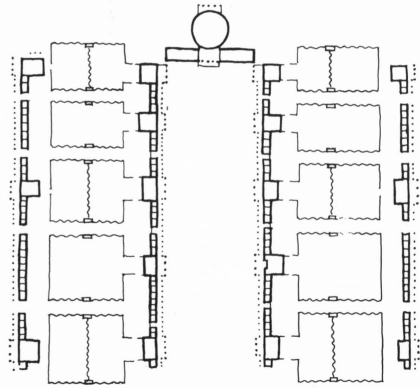

(46) A sketch of the Peter Maverick (an engraver in N.Y. City) plan of 1822. (revised in 1825) — This plan may be found in O'Neal's book, p. 47. Note that in

1. The Rotunda is the dominant element — thus, the most important building contains the most important reason for a university: the library with its books.

2. The Lawn is a common green — an outdoor gathering-socializing place exists for all.

3. The pavilions each house a professor above, with his lecture hall below — the faculty are thus living on campus.

4. The student rooms define the Lawn by linking the pavilions — the colonnade in front of the student rooms makes the entire university one continuous building form.

5. The gardens separate pavilions from dining hotels and more student rooms (linked by an arcade rather than a colonnade, as on the Lawn) — the gardens are used both as horticultural teaching outdoor rooms and as places for growing vegetables for use in the hotels. The hotels are run by staff from different countries — students thus acquire knowledge of the Spanish, French, etc., languages (and cuisine) as they move from hotel to hotel for their meals.

this, Jefferson's final plan, the Lawn ends, not with a pavilion, but with a student room. This suggests either that his intention was for the Lawn to continue toward the south with more rooms when expansion was needed or that the formal composition of the final pavilions needed to be flanked by two smaller elements (in this case, student rooms).

This plan is such a magnificent cultural idea, representing the best of young America's intellectual thought on education and architecture, that one cannot help but wonder why such a clear and distinguished idea was so soon to be abandoned in the university's expansion.(47)

In this discussion of the cultural determinant, it can be seen that Jefferson's ideas were bound up within the ideas of his society and the Neoclassic movement — that last gasp of humanism; Jefferson has in fact been called the last Renaissance man. Where Jefferson's particular personal artistic genius lay was in combining the best of so many disparate parts and putting them together in a brilliant formal conceptual statement. He drew upon only the best; the weak ideas, the poor intellectual concepts, were discarded, through forty-one long years of discriminatory thought.

(47) Or for that matter, why not return even now to the conceptual idea? Instead, new buildings at the university are placed farther and farther away from the Lawn. Each building becomes its own monument, more isolated and more disparate.

Jefferson's creativity lay in combining a wide range of elements to produce just that kind of effective surprise discussed in the first chapter. His design of the Lawn ranks as one of the finest creations in the history of architecture.

These first two chapters have established a framework for discussion, using four determinants of architectural form. If one applies this framework to a corresponding analysis of a work of modern architecture, he is apt to be disturbed. Too often we find that our physical environment is a regurgitation of uninspired thought, not worthy of being considered as architecture. Yet if our thesis that our built form should be a symbolic reflection of cultural values is correct, one sees that either we must be having difficulty in stating what our culture is or the culture itself is philosophically stymied with little left to say.

The next two chapters examine these difficult questions. What, if any, is the architectural dilemma of the twentieth century? What are the origins of our present philosophy? How does this philosophy cause us aesthetic problems? And, Is there any way out?

III THE DIFFICULTY OF PRACTICING ARCHITECTURE

The first two chapters dealt with simple definitions and analysis of what architecture is — outlining a method by which one may begin to understand how architecture is creatively formed. But we have not yet discussed how to evaluate beauty itself.(1) This is an important issue, for it is no secret that laymen, critics, architects, and students alike find a distressing lack of beauty in our most recently built architectural forms. If one considers this question seriously, he sees that agreement on the meaning of beauty can only occur if critic and public alike possess some consistent set of aesthetical values.

Of course, the problem of finding this agreed-upon philosophy has always existed, and it is a problem that must be faced anew by each cultural generation. It does seem, however, that since the end of the Second World War, this problem has increased in difficulty. This will be discussed in detail later, but if one considers almost any two modern buildings that are both thought of as being beautiful — for example, the Lake Shore Towers in Chicago, designed by Mies van der Rohe, and the Marseilles apartment block designed by Le Corbusier — he sees great differences in aesthetical values and philosophic attitudes.(2)

(1) This method does imply that architecture that reflects the four determinants will be better as a starting point than architecture that does not.

(2) Mies's housing towers (a) are pristine and elegant, encased in meticulously detailed structural steel frames. Le Corbusier's apartments (b) reflect his deep concern with the problem of mass housing — the social and physical consequences of housing a small community in one building.

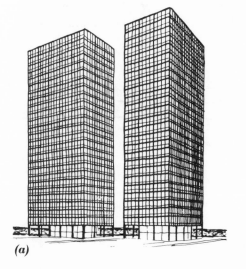

(a)

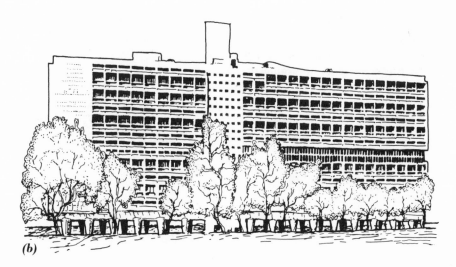

(b)

For that reason, the next two chapters will deal directly with this problem: i.e., the difficulty of practicing architecture today, due in large part to our apparent inability to find a common aesthetical value system shared by society in general and artists in particular.

This chapter will introduce the problem, suggesting that it is directly related to the philosophy of pragmatism. (This chapter will also suggest that each artist must resolve the problem through his *own* questioning.) Chapter four will then examine the roots of the problem by discussing in greater detail the Greek origins of Western philosophy, together with pragmatism and some more recent philosophic thought.

Searching for an appropriate value system is a complex endeavor, and while the discussion purposely will be kept simple, the answers cannot and will not be simple.

(3) Purists might demand the separation of a moral word (good) *from an aesthetical word* (beautiful). *These words are not separated, however, in the minds of the general public, nor were they for Socrates.*

In defining our terms earlier, we alluded to the fact that good, or beautiful, architecture presupposes that the reasoned creative statement will be a significant one.(3) It has also been suggested that in order to make the significant creative statement, the artist must have his own set of values. Let us now examine this further by asking "What conditions for creativity must be present for the architect to produce good architecture?" In this manner we can isolate precisely where the dilemma may lie in our current philosophical values. As a starting point let me suggest that there are four of these conditions for creativity.(4)

(4) Conditions *is another word chosen solely for convenience, in order to discuss the problem. A good argument can be made for there being no conditions necessary — that creativity is simply a lively process of the active mind.*

The first condition is that the architect must possess an intelligence that can be trained with the necessary technical skill to bring forth his creativity. This condition should not be difficult to satisfy in any material society of the twentieth century.

The second condition for creativity is that the architect must have the economic support of his society in order to shape the environment — more simply stated, someone must put up the money. In a general sense, this condition can be met in any society with reasonable material means. It is true that an argument can be made that when larger urban projects are funded, the architect's role has, in fact, been predetermined by quasi-legal-social funding agencies. For example, the form (or shape) of public housing may well be determined by the FHA, the Land Clearance Authority, federal funding agencies, and local building codes, all of which will specify square footages, room sizes, densities, easements, materials, even exact costs.(5)

The answer to this argument is simple — either the architect must expand his role and move into these fields, as his shaped environments increase in size, or he must acknowledge that the overall architectural form is in fact being dictated by others, and he must then accept a more specific role within the total process.

The third condition for creativity is that the architect must both be a participant in his society, so that he may understand it, and at the same time, be detached enough from that society so that he can make a dispassionate statement about it. At any instant he must be both married to his society and divorced from it! While this condition has always been present in any creative endeavor (and is thus not restricted to artists, but includes all creators), it is a condition most difficult to fulfill in our age.

The great German novelist Thomas Mann clearly understood this, and in his largely autobiographical short story "Tonio Kröger" he discusses at length his own emotional reaction to this duality.

In the story Tonio is torn between two desires. One is the desire for an everyday existence, as symbolized by the yellow-haired and blue-eyed boys and girls of his youth; the second is the desire for the clear intellectual world of the artist striving ruthlessly after meaning, as symbolized by his bohemian artist friends.(6)

(5) *The infamous Pruitt-Igoe public housing project in St. Louis has been roundly condemned as being poor architecture. In truth, however, the density of the highrises, the lack of urban amenities, and the starkness of the slab towers are all the result of a stringent Public Housing Authority program that froze the architect's possible creativity.*

(6) *I stand between two worlds. I am at home in neither, and I suffer in consequence. You artists call me a bourgeois, and the bourgeois try to arrest me . . . I don't know which makes me feel worse, . . . you ought to realize that there is a way of being an artist that goes so deep and is so much a matter of origins and destinies that no longing seems to it sweeter and more worth knowing than longing after the bliss of the commonplace . . . I am looking into a world unborn and formless, that needs to be ordered and shaped; I see into a whirl of shadows of human figures who beckon to me to weave spells to redeem them, . . . and to these I am drawn. But my deepest and secretest love belongs to the blond and blue-eyed, the fair and living, the happy, lovely, and commonplace. — "Tonio Kröger" by Thomas Mann, quoted from* Death In Venice and Seven Other Stories *(New York: Random House, paperback ed., 1963) p. 133.*

All of Mann's work embodies the idea that the artist must lead a double life — on the one hand cool, dispassionate, and objective, and on the other, involved, passionate, and subjective. Indeed, the ideas Mann introduces in "Tonio Kröger," he later develops brilliantly in his masterpiece on love, morality, beauty, and aesthetics — the long story "Death in Venice."

(7) It is not important to argue whether this dichotomy actually does exist — many artists and philosophers will agree that a balanced life is as necessary for the artist as it is for all citizens. A number of recent writers and architects seem to sense this dichotomy, however — Herman Hesse and William Faulkner in literature and Eero Saarinen in architecture, for example.

While it is certainly debatable whether the artist needs to be in anguish, torn between two worlds,(7) Mann makes the important point that each artist must stake out a position in regard to society's values. For there is always *some* interaction between the artist, his values, and those of society. This of necessity is particularly true in the field of architecture, for to be built, architecture demands considerable money and societal involvement.

Each of Saarinen's buildings expresses a great concern for functional value and at the same time for personal value — the two often in conflict: I.e., the Dulles Airport terminal has, on the one hand, a clear functional human path system from the car park to the airplane on the runway, but the form of the building itself has been likened to a bird ready for flight. In this particular case, Saarinen's poetic (emotional, personal, symbolic) vision of architectural wings hovers above man's functional work below. Many critics think this building is Saarinen's finest achievement.

If Mann is correct, involvement / noninvolvement with society is always difficult when a clear philosophy for the society is not apparent — for the artist cannot be dispassionate and removed if he cannot discover a system of societal values about which to be dispassionate. Nor can he easily form his own value system without having a larger system with which to interact.

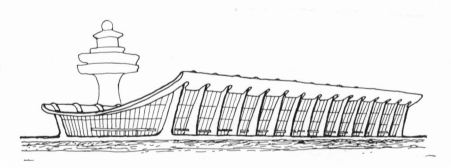

This leads us to the fourth and most important condition for creativity: The architect must have his own value system by which to judge his efforts. It is this condition that is at the heart of the architect's present dilemma. For the middle twentieth century has no common philosophy or value system — no set of agreed-upon moral criteria by which to judge the rightness or the wrongness of our actions — and no set of aesthetic criteria by which to judge our art.

This is partly due to the fact that we have many emerging societies, each at a different stage of materialistic growth. But if we concern ourselves specificially with the industrialized and generally affluent societies, we find the principal reason for our philosophic dilemma is that the dominant philosophic attitude of the twentieth century, pragmatism, does not, in fact, contain a real set of criteria.

Modern philosophers may disagree about what is current philosophy. Certainly since 1900, however, pragmatism has been the base for continuing philosophic inquiry in the United States. As espoused by John Dewey, pragmatism is the philosophy of practicality and it says the value of an idea may be measured by its utility. If it works, it is good, it has value; and we discover if it works by testing it. Pragmatism was an outgrowth of the Industrial Revolution and, as such, was a useful philosophy for America on 1900.

Useful is, in itself, a peculiarly pragmatic word — for any act that has use-value will, by definition, work, and any act that works will in most instances be found useful. In neither case is the deeper philosophic question raised: "Should the act be done?" This difficulty with pragmatism has led many to question if it is, in fact, a philosophy or whether it might better be called a method or an attitude.

This does not belittle Dewey's achievement in 1897 — for his generation saw the great potential in the machine being used to free society from materialistic worry. With true societal progressivism, Dewey pragmatically felt that the greatest good could come from that which did the most for the largest portion of society.(8)

(8) Nor does pragmatism's lack of an inner value system prevent us from using it as a method or technique to help discover for ourselves a value system. This will be more fully explored in chapter four in the discussion on operational process.

There are disturbing implications, however, in holding fast to pragmatism in our present age. In *On Knowing*, J. S. Bruner discusses some of these problems, and he stresses in particular the essential difficulty of Dewey's philosophy:

> His optimism is classically American in its rejection of the tragic view of life. He defines truth in the pragmatic spirit: truth is the fruit of inquiry into the consequences of action. He expresses a firm faith not only in the individual's capacity to grow but in society's capacity to shape man in its own best interests.
>
> Yet the very wholesomeness — the acceptance of man's harmonious continuity with society — leaves one uneasy, . . . we have lived through a revolution in our understanding of the nature of man. . . .
>
> Today we know that no person is master of the whole culture; indeed, this is almost a defining characteristic of that form of social memory that we speak of as culture. Each man lives a fragment of it. To be whole, he must create his own version of the world.(9)

(9) J. S. Bruner, On Knowing (New York: Atheneum, 1965), p. 114.

Bruner than argues that the inner failing of pragmatism is that it may help us pick the right machine to do the job, but that it does not tell us if the job is worth doing. Bruner feels this difficulty is directly related to man's need to be creative, his need to be an artist. "The reason [for creativity] is the ancient search of the humanist for the excellence of man; the next creative act may bring man to a new dignity."(10) Bruner suggests that man wants meaning in his life, meaning beyond simple action. He points up the compelling desire in the modern world for identity. We are not happy simply being useful; we want to identify with something, and thus we have courses on creative writing, creative advertising, and creative salesmanship. In short, pragmatism hinders the artist because it does not give him sufficent or proper values by which to judge his work.(11)

(10) Ibid., p. 17. A good argument can be made here that Bruner has the wrong reason: that inquiry itself may be reason enough. We do not have to be a humanist, however, to see that practicality is a justification after the fact.

(11) See chapter 1, note 18.

As an example, the United States was able to replace its troops in South Vietnam with troops from the country itself — and by obvious deduction thus to reduce American troop losses. This was a measurable act and could be shown to be useful. But the act did not answer the prior philosophic question of whether waging that war was correct.

Pragmatism can also tell the Western nations to keep increasing their stockpile of weapons so as to have more than the Russians; but it cannot tell those nations if blowing up the world is either good or bad. (Although pragmatism will tell one that once he has enough missiles to destroy everyone, his measuring system is no longer relevant — which is one reason arms limitations agreements exist.)

A final aesthetical example would be to look at highway construction from a pragmatic view. From such a view, it can be demonstrated graphically that if one wishes to travel from a suburban door to downtown, a straight highway is the most economical way to provide access. But this solution does not question whether it is morally right or wrong to tear down the houses that lie in the way, or if it is aesthetically proper to divide cities into compartmentalized sections through division by highway construction.(12)

The greatest danger in this pragmatic dilemma is that the practicing artist, unable to derive a value system from his society, will detach himself further and further from that society and, in the process, will create for an ever and ever smaller group of his peers ("he is an architect's architect!") until at last he is creating for no one but himself.

While this may be a romantic and attractive notion, it leads to the artist becoming a total outsider, with no communication with others. The third condition for creativity no longer exists, and the artist loses his ability to work — Van Gogh chops off an ear and commits suicide; Nijinsky becomes insane; Hemingway shoots himself.

In his book *The Outsider*, Colin Wilson discusses this problem of identity and reality.(13) He cites T. E. Lawrence, the British conqueror of Arabia. On being asked, "What is reality?" Lawrence replied, "unknowable, my glimpses of it cause me nothing but trouble because they ruin me for everyday triviality without telling me where to find another way of living."(14) Once Lawrence left the desert, he was never again able to adjust to life in society.

(12) A sketch of a Los Angeles traffic intersection from the air demonstrates that this city is different from the traditional city's architectural image. Although pragmatically everyone has been freed from want (via the car), the question arises: If everyone must have a car in order to live, are we then back where we started from? What is needed in Los Angeles is a different set of values for architectural judgment.

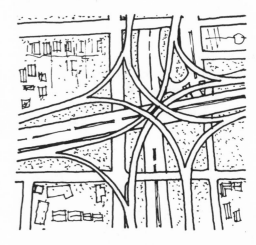

If this is true, then the older concept of a city core no longer applies, for the city is held together, not by public spaces and buildings, but by highways.

(13) Colin Wilson, The Outsider (Boston: Houghton Mifflin Co., 1956). While Wilson's call for a new religion seems highly debatable, his book is an incredible tour de force in that it brings many diverse artistic examples together in one thought-out whole.

(14) Ibid., p. 114.

(15) Ibid.

(16) I am referring here to story content and not to formal writing skill. The Old Man and the Sea does not say anything in meaning of content that is not stated in his earlier "The Short, Happy Life of Francis MacComber."

(17) The Architecture School building at Yale represents a highly personal and romantic aesthetic. With its strong stair towers and jackhammered, exposed concrete, the building has been called medieval by some critics.

Ernest Hemingway was also greatly concerned with this problem. In one of his stories, a character says that identity "is the moment when you do one thing, the one thing, the only thing, when you know that you are not merely a trivial superficial counter on the social chessboard."(15) This makes for interesting reading, and it clearly shows the dilemma of being divorced from society; but it is a philosophy that will destroy the artist's creativity. Indeed, once Hemingway developed this theme in his own work, he did not progress beyond it.(16)

One can discern this problem continually in twentieth century architecture — one good example being the continued strivings of Paul Rudolph to create new forms, such as his Architecture School building for Yale.(17)

To this point, I have argued that of the four conditions suggested for creativity, our society can satisfy the first two — *training* to develop the architect's intellect, and *economic means* by which to shape the environment. Today, however, the third and fourth conditions are not so easily satisfied, for the architect cannot both understand his society and yet be detached if he cannot discover the value system by which that society lives. Furthermore, without a personal aesthetical value system, the architect cannot even critique his own creative effort. Is there a way out of this dilemma? One can certainly see at least three avenues of escape currently being tried by young artists and architects.

The first of these is to reduce values to simplistic notions that will shortcut the difficult search for criteria. In place of philosophy, one may substitute popular communication theory; for architecture, elusive theories and treatises (rather than buildings) that introduce a steady stream of new words and new classifications whenever a difficulty arises; and for education, the lament that architects should "just learn how to draw again."

A second avenue of escape is for the architect to accept authoritarian and absolutist values. This approach suggests that since we cannot discover the values of our society, even if we try, we should choose values that will be good for us anyway. Thus, the great architect Le Corbusier could propose leveling Paris and rebuilding it as a park with huge high-rise residential towers — a city that would have destroyed and denied its past. This avenue is always a popular one for radical student movements, impatient with their slower-moving elders.

Since, as individuals, young architects can see a great deal of good in what many radicals preach (for Paris does need new housing with light and air and less squalor), there is a great temptation to let the radical speak on a wider range of issues. The result (frequently a manifesto) will stress that what is wrong is the system, and that what is needed is sweeping social reform for the good of collective humanity.

A final avenue of escape is to insist on studying process rather than content. This avenue is peculiarly attractive to educational institutions, and it suggests that if the process is analyzed for a sufficiently long period, the good value will sneak out, and the product will somehow evolve. Process is stressed *as* process, and the relativity of all things is championed. Using this avenue, nothing is right or wrong so long as a process question is asked. This is a method by which some once-fine schools have programmed and committeed themselves to death.(18)

All of these avenues of escape must be approached with care, for they bypass the essential issue that every artist must eventually face — to construct a value system, he must question the meaning of his *own* life in relation to his *own* culture.

(18)   *The study of process for its own sake is as disturbing as the old study of content for its sake — it is only what process leads to, an understanding of the nature of the problem, that makes process worthwhile.*

(19) Bruner, On Knowing, *p. 120.*

(20) While this argument will be carried further at the end of chapter 10, mention should be made here that I am not *suggesting a system of relative values (all within an embracing system), but rather a system that allows for different values given different situations.*

This means that the argument is for a con-sistent attitude that finds the proper value in the instance. In fact, if we understand the conditions that created the architecture, we can then begin to understand the architecture itself, and in the experiential process, we may comprehend its value.

Walt Whitman expresses the same thought in an equally beautiful manner, yet with different words in his first stanza of "I Sing the Body Electric":

I sing the body electric,
The armies of those I love engirth
* me and I engirth them,*

They will not let me off till I go with
* them, respond to them,*
And discorrupt them, and charge
* them full with the charge of the*
* soul.*

[Leaves of Grass (N.Y.: Avenel Books, Crown Publishers, 1961), p. 46.]

Bruner suggests that to do this, we must first investigate the nature of what it is we *do* know, and that out of our understanding of this knowledge, we can then proceed to ask what it is that we would *like* to know.(19) And the emergent artist does not begin this search for values entirely in the dark. Much of our past knowledge is stored, both as common good sense and in the printed, drawn, cataloged, library repository. Furthermore, each artist receives a cultural inheritance from his society. With historical perspective he can see that in the past, all great architecture has successfully dealt with social and functional needs for shaping space while at the same time making a statement about cultural values.

And the very fact that we do not at this moment in time have a specific shared set of social and cultural values is indicative that our society is pluralistic, fragmented, complex, and multileveled. This begins to suggest that today's society cannot teach or give us any *single* all-embracing aesthetical value system. What we need today may well be to arrive at a value system that is multileveled, with different values for different specific situations: a value system that is both shared and individual.(20)

But this conclusion should not precede the acquisition of tools and methods by which one may investigate knowledge: the study of a philosophical base upon which one may build. The next chapter will examine first the philosophy of the Greeks and then some of the modern tools (including pragmatism) by which one may get at the truth.

A brief personal conviction remains — it is a conviction that I cannot prove, but one that is felt deeply: This is that architecture has its greatest value when it attempts to enrich the life of every individual who experiences it. For if architecture moves toward expressing the group values of a social humanity, but in the process becomes unlivable for the individual, then it is not an architecture worthy of the artist's serious creative input.

IV INHERITED PHILOSOPHY
AND OUR PHILOSOPHY TODAY

Like don't give me that stuff about how I'm here to learn. I'm here because I have to be, so if I have to be here against my will, why shouldn't I have a say in running the place?(1)

(1) A member of Students for a Democratic Society (SDS); quoted from the New York Times, *Sunday, December 14, 1969.*

... I would certainly go to the barricades for any movement that wants to sweep away the Pentagon. Time *magazine and frozen French fried potatoes. But what is to take its place? The New Left not only have no blueprint, but they don't want a blueprint.(2)*

(2) Gore Vidal in an interview with Playboy, *1969.*

I am he as you are he as you are me and we are all together.(3)

(3) The Beatles, "I Am the Walrus" (1967).

These three statements all deal with the sweeping political and social changes that took place in the United States during the late 1960s and the beginning of the 1970s. And while their conclusions are markedly different, they also have something in common — for they all relate to change and speculation — in short, they are all philosophic statements.

What precisely *is* philosophy? The classic definition says that a philosopher is literally "one who loves wisdom." Some 500 years before Christ, Socrates tells us that the philosopher loves the vision of truth.(4) It would never have occurred to Socrates that there might be any difference between a vision of truth for art, for science, or for morality, since for him these later differentiations simply did not exist. Thus, the philosopher loves beauty in itself, for he is searching for knowledge — knowledge that leads to wisdom. Indeed, Socrates accepted this argument and took it to its logical conclusion.

(4) Quoted in Bertrand Russell, Wisdom of the West; *(New York: Crescent Books, 1959). Much of the Greek way to truth discussed in this chapter has been well stated in this superb book.*

In Plato's *Apology*, he has Socrates argue that what makes man sin is lack of knowledge. If he only knew, he would not sin, and therefore to teach *good* we must have knowledge; so good is knowledge.(5)

(5) A good critique of this argument may be found in Russell, Wisdom of the West, *p. 52. Note the syllogistic argument, or logic, which is described later in the chapter.*

Thus, for Socrates and his immediate followers, philosophy was the most important study for man. Searching for and discovering truth led to knowledge, beauty, and goodness in art, in science, and in man's moral life. This is a profound thought, for it establishes humanism, the belief in man and his capacity to search for truth and goodness in himself, as a base for later Western philosophy.(6)

(7) *Russell,* Wisdom of the West, *p. 7. It is obvious that we all practice philosophy each time we make a value judgment as to goodness, morality, beauty, etc. Thus, the argument "Let philosophers worry about philosophy" is a nonstatement, since we are all philosophers whether we wish to be so or not.*

To search for truth, man must speculate, inquire, and question. Philosophy does not seek, in itself, to resolve our everyday problems, to tell us what we have to do — in philosophy precise answers will never be as important as the act of asking the correct questions. Bertrand Russell tells us that "the only way to find out what philosophy is, is to do philosophy."(7)

(8) *There is a danger of being too simplistic in approaching any study of philosophy, but so critical is an understanding of the Greek idea of* Logos *as the basis of our language reasoning that a discussion is necessary even though oversimplification will occur.*

There are many good books on philosophy, certainly among the best being the writings of the Durants.

It is the principal intent of this chapter to outline some of the obvious roots of our philosophy, so that the reader may better understand how our society presently practices philosophy — specifically how we practice that special branch of philosophy we now call aesthetics.(8) For our general purposes, the study of philosophy began with the Greeks approximately 2500 years ago, when they became interested in the idea of *Logos. Logos* may not be translated directly into English, but we can say that it is roughly equivalent to the idea of the combined terms *word* and *measure.* Through *Logos,* things may be both described (using words) and measured (using some system of measurement or qualification).(8) This process of *Logos* helps us identify things and place them within some established order. We may paraphrase this process as:

Logos = word and measure = a description of what things are, and then measuring their quantity and quality.

Out of the application of *Logos* grows the first study of knowledge — the process of *logic,* by which we may reason to arrive at the truth. In order for classical logical reasoning to occur, there must first be: 1. a few terms (or things) that are agreed upon as being true; and 2. a system for measuring.

It is the Greeks who formalized a measuring system of dual polar differences: good to bad, right to wrong, etc. This may be outlined:

measure = polar scales =

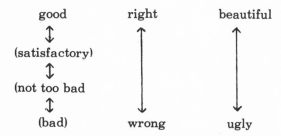

Two important points are worth remembering about this scalar system of measuring, which is still one of our basic tools for learning. First, the Greeks emphasized that each individual had both good and bad qualities within him simultaneously (in other words, all humans were both good and bad, never simply good or bad). The Greeks sought harmony, through which each man understood and balanced these qualities within himself. Second, this polar system of dual opposites does not exist in classical Eastern thought (thus, in Eastern philosophy, one cannot ask if an ancient Hindu was rational or irrational).

When the Greeks began the use of logic, they naturally applied the idea of measure to all fields of inquiry, including mathematics — leading to the beginnings of mathematical theory. Among the first discoveries was that of Pythagoras: that in all 90° triangles, the square of the hypotenuse is equal to the sum of the squares of the other two sides.(9) Geometric proportions so fascinated the Greeks that they rapidly became a base for the rational (i.e., reasoning via logic) study of aesthetics in buildings.(10)

By the end of Socrates' time, the art of philosophy had already progressed to the point that two widely divergent schools of thought — the dialectic and the sophist — existed in opposition to each other.

(9) The Pythagorean proof is usually demonstrated with a triangle of 3, 4, 5 sides because with these measurements, the mathematics are easily computed.

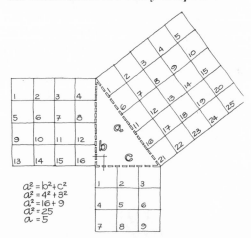

$$a^2 = b^2 + c^2$$
$$a^2 = 4^2 + 3^2$$
$$a^2 = 16 + 9$$
$$a^2 = 25$$
$$a = 5$$

(10) One of the more interesting proportional systems is the "golden rectangle" or "golden mean," which later, during the Renaissance, became almost holy as design dogma.

The golden mean proportion, represented

by a rectangle with sides of 1 to 1.618, can be constructed from the pentagram, as shown in drawing (a). Pythagoras believed that this construction had mystical properties, since it can also be described as a helix that expands at a constant rate (see drawing b). The rate of increase very closely approximates the mathematical progression 5:8, 8:13, 13:21, 21:34, etc., in which the new number is always equal to the previous ratio numbers added together (for example, the number 34 in the last ratio is equal to 21 plus 13 — the previous ratio). This can be rapidly checked by dividing 34 by 21. (The answer is 1.619, or very close to the golden rectangle ratio of 1.618).

Palladio in particular used the square and the golden rectangle as a basis for design. In diagram (c), diagonals of some of the squares in the Villa Rotunda are shown. In diagram (d) diagonals of some of the golden rectangles are shown. This rich interplay of squares and golden rectangles was also used in the facades of the Villa Rotunda.

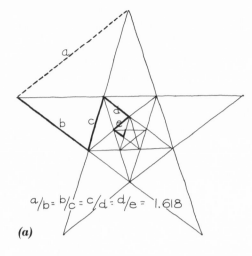

$$a/b = b/c = c/d = d/e = 1.618$$

(a)

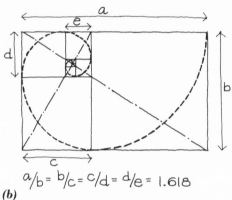

$$a/b = b/c = c/d = d/e = 1.618$$

(b)

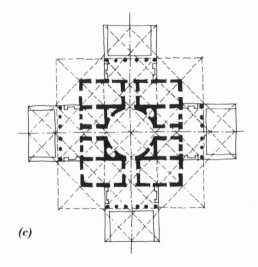

(c)

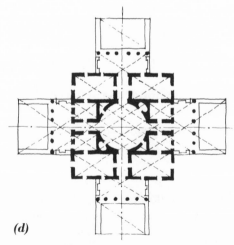

(d)

The dialecticians argued that life could only be examined by *questioning* the premises of meaning. This group, led by Socrates, emphasized *discussion* as the means of arriving, after long inquiry, at the discovery of truth. (We saw earlier that Socrates accepted the tenet that possession of knowledge was goodness in itself.) The second group, the sophists, were led by Protagoras, who argued that since knowledge or truth is different for each man, there cannot be any universal truths, and that what one should strive for is the acquisition of useful opinion. The sophists argued that one acquired knowledge in order to sway other opinions and win the debate (rather than to participate in the discussion of the dialectics).

Protagoras said that the practical test was best, and he thus introduced the first pragmatic doctrine into Greek thought. And it is Protagoras who first said, "Man is the measure of all things."(11)

Following Socrates, Plato and his student Aristotle brought ancient Greek philosophy to its flowering. In 387 B.C. Plato founded the academy, a small school outside Athens in which the dialectic method of education was stressed. Each student through participation in a series of small seminar groups learned, through questioning and under the guidance of a teacher, *to think for himself*. The universal truths were searched for through diverse questions — a *uni*versity of wisdom through a *diversity* of interests.(12)

Aristotle has been called both The Father of Classification(13) and The First Semanticist. At the heart of Aristotle's studies in logic is the syllogism. Technically, a syllogism is an argument with two subject-predicate premises that have one term in common. This may be stated more easily in mathematical language as:

$$A = B$$
$$B = C; \text{(thus)} A = C$$

In this case the first subject-predicate is $A = B$; the second subject-predicate is $B = C$; and the one term in common is B. Using logic, we can drop the common middle term and state $A = C$.

(11) Russell, Wisdom of the West, p. 47. There is a famous story concerning Protagoras that illustrates the inner dilemma of pragmatism that was discussed in the preceding chapter. One of Protagoras's students was too poor to pay his tuition for gaining a legal (or debating) degree from the school. Protagoras told him to pay later, after he had won his first case in court. Upon graduation, the student decided not to practice law and did not pay Protagoras his fee. Protagoras sued, arguing: If he wins this case he must pay me because of his previous bargain. If I win, the court must award me payment by its judgment. The former student argued in return: If I win, the court must rule that I do not have to pay. If Protagoras wins, then I shall not have won my first case in court, and so am not obligated to pay.

This story (which can be found in Russell's Wisdom of the West, p. 47) does not relate who won the case.

(12 The idea that knowledge is inter-related often seems lost in the multitude of separate university disciplines, each fighting for their own slice of the research grant pie.

(13) And thus also, the father of scientific inquiry.

Let us take a common, but different, example, a diagram.

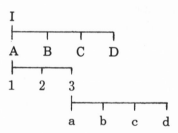

we might say that
y is x
y is z
x is z and z is x

But this last statement is not true. We should have said "part of x is also part of z," or better yet, "x and z each has a part in common, and it is called y." In this example, I have (purposely) not stated the original syllogism correctly to illustrate that even at a basic level of logic, we must take care. We have reasoned illogically.(14)

(14) This diagram might be properly stated in syllogism form, as:

all of y is part of x
all of y is part of z

therefore: x and z have a part in common called y.

There are a number of architectural parallels. For example:

x equals bank
y equals columns
z equals Greek temple

If we state (incorrectly) that x equals z, we employ the logic frequently asked of us by banks — i.e., that banks are equal to Greek temples with columns (implying stability, beauty, oldness, security, permanence, etc.)

Actually what we should say is that the facades of some banks (b) look like the

We can also diagram in a basic way Aristotle's ideas on classification

```
I
├────┬────┬────┐
A    B    C    D
├──┬──┬──┐
1  2  3
      ├────┬────┬────┐
      a    b    c    d
```

(d) is a part of 3, which is a part of A, which is a part of I.

also (b) and (d) are interrelated in that they are both subcategories of IA3.

facades of some Greek temples (a) — or that cosmetics are only skin deep.

A much more serious question then begins to emerge — we often do judge architecture by what we first see, perceiving a greater whole that is frequently not there.

(a)

(b)

Using such processes of classification, Aristotle codified language and greatly developed reasoning via logic.

In any serious inquiry, we have to remember that there is always haze and imperfection that is not resolved until the problem is solved (or truth is discovered). Furthermore, logic does not tell us whether our result is true. Logic is a means of reasoning that tells us the validity of an argument. Only if the premises are themselves true can the logic (properly performed) validate the truth of the conclusion.(15)

(15) For example: All United States presidents have been blacks; Abraham Lincoln was a president; therefore, Lincoln was a black. The reasoning is valid, but the conclusion is not true since one of the premises is not true. The only truth that logic guarantees is that if the premises are true, and if the logic is validly carried out, the conclusion will also be true.

It is, of course, also possible to have a true conclusion when the premises are false. For example: All blacks have been president; Abraham Lincoln was a black; therefore, Lincoln was a president. In this case, the term that was dropped was the false term, leaving the conclusion correct.

For example, if we consider that pigs (P) are mammals (M) and that mammals do not fly (F), we can say:

P = M

M ≠ F

∴P ≠ (F), (Pigs cannot fly.)

Diagrammed, this is —

(P) pigs

(M) mammals ≠ (F) flying

In *rare* cases, however, mammals *can* fly — consider the bat (B) — thus a better (or a more relative) diagram would be

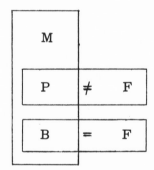

(16) Again, there are innumerable architectural examples — such as, most railroad cars are on railroad tracks, and railroad tracks are not normally found on beaches. Nonetheless, it may be possible to find a railroad car on a bathing beach when it is used as a diner or a snack bar. In this case the shock recognition may increase sales inside the diner (that is, the car is acting as a startling sign), but it does not automatically follow that this use for a railroad car should always be the correct use.

Now: all parts of M similar to P ≠ F.

But it may be possible for some part of M (in this case B) to be able to fly.(16)

We might end this very basic introduction to Greek thought by suggesting that as the areas of philosophy grew more complex, they were broken down into categories for separate study — these categories are likewise with us today; ethics (good and evil); logic (truth and

Stated another way: One Las Vegas may be exciting, stimulating, and interesting — but one Las Vegas may be enough.

falsehood); epistemology (real and apparent — the theory of knowledge); aesthetics (beauty and ugliness); and finally ontology (the theory of being and nonbeing). These areas of study have all grown a great deal more complex as man's cultural history has progressed — but the Western way to knowledge owes a particular debt to ancient Greek thought: the concept that truth may be discovered by questioning, and then testing the consequences of the answers.

This Greek process of reasoning, or Aristolelian logic, is of course not the only way to discover truth. Among other approaches are mysticism, ritual, belief, and experience.(17)

Mysticism emphasizes an absence of organized thought, nonclassification, and sudden inspired revelations. If one meditates long enough on what a frog means, the answer may intuitively appear in a flash of understanding. The same may be said of an architectural design process — those who argue "I design it that way, because I like it, and I know it is right" are, in fact, arguing for an intuitive, revelatory approach to values.(18)

Mysticism is related to ritual, in that a continued practice of ritual will put one in the proper attitude for relevation. The brilliant haiku poets of Japan (as quoted in chapter 1) spent years practicing the discipline of their craft before they were able in a few lines to capture an inner meaning in their poetry.

The philosophy of the Far East — specifically Hinduism and, later, Buddhism and Zen Buddhism(19) — stresses mysticism as a basic way toward understanding the oneness, the underlying order of the universe. A Hindu today in India might describe a milk cow as "our friend who gives us life-milk." An ancient Greek (or an American farmer) would be more likely to say "a four-legged vertebrate animal — a mammal who feeds her young on her milk; milk that we can also take to sell and drink."(20)

(17) Two other possible ways to truth that are not discussed are instinctual and learned or acquired habit. These two ways raise complex questions that are interesting but not germane to our argument — which is simply that there are many ways to truth besides Aristotelian logic.

(18) This attitude is related to the discussion of Issa's haiku poem found in chapter 1.

To demonstrate that this attitude is with us today, consider the critique: "The Kennedy Performing Arts Center in Washington is a Fascist Manifesto!" This is an emotive, felt reaction and while it calls up an immediate imagery, it is difficult, if not impossible, to defend in a reasoned argument.

(19) Zen Buddhism was a particularly attractive way to truth for college students during the 1950s. But Zen has since given way to both militant and pacifist activism — at least in part because finding oneness with Buddha demands disciplined ritual.

(20) If the farmer thought seriously about his description, he would also differentiate (after Aristotle) between a milk-producing cow and a beef cow.

(21) Modern students of semantics are fond of telling us that we cannot ask a question that cannot itself be framed in codified language. But this is a priori truth — if one accepts that reasoning can only occur when we rearrange codified symbols. What if one wishes to redefine reasoning to include any conclusion reached by the mind after some form of stimulation? In that case, intuitive thought would then be possible. (see chapter 5, note 9.)

(22) Which is one reason it is difficult in designing to locate where the fireplace should go — the living room? The dining room? The family room?

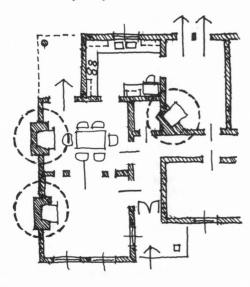

(23) Even after direct experience, Americans tend to think of French Gothic cathedrals as being pure with their height aspiring upwards toward God or pointing heavenward, full of grace and light and air. Spanish cathedrals of the same Gothic period are often thought of as being dank

Another means to truth is through belief. One may believe through faith in a god, or through faith in a respected interpreter (The Bible tells us so). We might buy a car from someone in whom we trust; we might also take a respected art critic's word that a new building is, or is not, beautiful.

The terms — mysticism, revelation, ritual, intuitive thought, inner meaning, and belief — are all interrelated. A religious experience has obvious connections with a mystic revelation. One of the difficulties in discussing all of these ways toward truth is that our Aristotelian-based language is not itself constructed to express nonrational thought. Our Greek process of reasoning by definition excludes the possibility of truth arrived at through mysticism and revelation.(21)

There is, however, one other way toward discovering truth that is in fact, the most important of all — direct experience. We learn about a hot flame by burning our hands as a child (whether we codify the word *hot* or not). Likewise, if we remember a pleasurable childhood experience of sitting in front of a cozy fireplace, we tend to prefer that our future houses also have a fireplace — even if we may never build a fire in it!(22)

These memories and associated learning experiences are so important to our emotional well-being and are so self-evident that we frequently forget that our responses to direct experience are not identical. One child remembers a dark, cool, mystical church as being a pleasurable retreat during hot summer days — another child remembers it as being a hated place in which he was forced to sit once a week. The spatial qualities of dark, cool places probably will be evaluated differently by these children throughout their later lives.(23) The point here is that while direct experience is certainly our most important teacher, it is by no means a perfect way to truth nor will it produce infallible results. In fact, each person is influenced, and influenced differently to some degree, by all of these ways to truth when he constructs value systems for his life and for his aesthetical judgments in art and architecture.

In the preceding chapter, I argued that pragmatism gives all artists particular problems in finding any common set of values in our present society. It was further suggested that present technological pressures are so complex and numerous that artists are frequently tempted to look for avenues of escape from their own difficult personal search for values.

The period since 1960 has been called the first technological age and the transistor age.(24) Consider some of the everyday occurrences that are only now possible after the development of transistor, or energy-controlled miniaturized, systems — moon flights, instantaneous TV reproduction, music in the desert via a hand-held radio, desk computers for use by beginning calculus students, and automatic typesetting machines for newspaper printing.(25) It is no wonder that pragmatism, with its inner problem of lacking a true test of values, cannot cope philosophically with this avalanche of technological (not to mention sociological) change that besets us today.

Of course, philosophy, like all fields of human inquiry, has progressed since 1900, and there have been serious and studied reactions to pragmatism. Two of these are existentialism and symbolic logic (leading to operational process).(26)

In its simplest terms, existentialism states that the meaning of life may be found in its being lived. Thus the action of life — or the process — is more important than the result. Existence has its own inner truth.

As a philosophy, existentialism has had a peculiar impact on fiction. Two good examples are Ernest Hemingway's classic novel *The Sun Also Rises* and Andre Gide's deeply disturbing book *The Immoralist*, which questions the very basis of Western civilization.

Existentialists say that the will to do is before the intellect or reason to do. Rationalism, they say, tackles the world from the outside but does not do justice to the experience of living — this can only come existentially from within.

and too big, too mystical or cluttered up with too much gold and decoration.

The real reason for such feelings are so complex a part of our inherited culture that it is probably impossible to analyze the direct emotional experience. Could it be our puritanical religious heritage? Our preconditioning from history books? Our love of structural honesty? Or our English rather than Spanish heritage?

(24) The visionary-architect Paolo Soleri discusses miniaturization as the key to future cities. Soleri's visions include beehives of human settlement thirty stories underground, with transistorized control systems. Agreeing with Soleri demands a high degree of mystic faith. It is debatable if society will ever want to live in a beehive, no matter how efficient our miniaturized control system is.

(25) In his book Theory and Design in the First Machine Age *(London: The Architectural Press, 1960, p. 9), Reyner Banham goes to great lengths to discuss the impact on our lives of the technological revolution.*

(26) There are obviously other modern reactions to pragmatism besides the two mentioned. Among the more important are the writings of Lévi-Strauss, the behaviorist movement (treated in the next chapter), and political radicalism (which, although it is not a pure philosophy, has certainly influenced value judgments in the twentieth century).

The modern architectural movement has been profoundly influenced by existentialism, although this has never been seriously investigated by theorists. Consider some of the oft-quoted statements of Louis Kahn:

> The sun never knew how great it was until it struck the side of a building.

> I asked the brick what it liked, and the brick said, "I like an arch."

> A city is a place where a small boy as he walks through it, can see something that will tell him what he wants to do his whole life."(27)

Any building by Kahn reflects these existential thoughts. About his Hurva Synagogue plan for Jerusalem, he says: "I sensed the light of a candle plays an important part in Judaism. The pylons belong to the candle service and have niches facing the chamber. I felt this was an extension of the source of religion as well as an extension of the practice of Judaism."(28) This is a heady philosophy, and it requires the practiced hand of a master — for it cannot be learned in a fortnight.(29)

(27) *Quoted from an interview with Louis Kahn found in* Architectural Forum, *July / August 1972, p. 42.*

(28) *Ibid., p. 42. Shown are sketches adapted from Kahn's design for the Hurva Synagogue. Note that Kahn was searching for an idea about the meaning of the form — he was* not *trying to convey a constructional interpretation.*

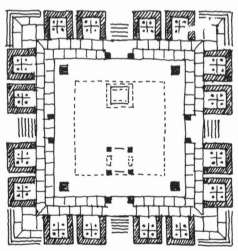

(29) *Kahn's description of the thought behind the design is equally interesting: "I came to a statement that 'order is' because I could never write what it is. I made a long list of what I thought it was. And when I threw the list away, 'order is' remained. It sort of included everything by*

One of the dangers of existentialism is that it may appeal too much to our emotions and feelings. (Its relations to mysticism as a means of truth are obvious.) In the minds of naive followers who are not prepared to search diligently for what a building wants to be, existentialist architecture tends to be romantic, facile, purposely willful, and indulgent of moods (Man should do what he pleases, because it brings him pleasure).(30) Nonetheless, existentialism at its best is a serious approach to finding an alternative to pragmatism.

Another group of philosophers who seriously question pragmatic thought are the symbolic logicians. Susanne Langer (quoted earlier in chapter one in the discussion of creativity) is an important member of this group, and although her book *Philosophy in a New Key* is difficult reading, it still remains a significant contribution to understanding art from the view of symbolic logic.(31)

Symbolic logicians begin by stating that logic as a method of reasoning is still valid but the language we now use is so confused that we no longer understand the symbols employed. Symbolic logicians thus argue for extending Aristotelian logic (not denying it). They warn that our older Aristotelian symbols are based on phonograms (i.e., are related to the sounds of language and only indirectly related to the concepts that lie behind the verbal language), and that what we now need are symbols based on ideograms (i.e., symbols directly related to ideas, or concepts). Such a symbol-language, of course, already exists in pure mathematics (we have alluded to it earlier by using A = B; B = C; ∴ A = C), and it is no accident that symbolic logic has, in fact, grown out of modern mathematics.(32)

The symbolic logicians state that we use symbols (in a codified language) to relay information to our minds, where the symbols are then rearranged, and through the use of logic, transferred into rational thought. This process of stimuli-to-symbol-to-thought is called symbolic transformation. If this statement is correct, then naturally we should examine closely the symbol-images with which we start any argument or discussion, for if the symbols are not related, we can never hope for a reasonable resolution.

not trying to say what it is. That word 'is' has a tremendous sense of presence" (Architectural Forum, *July / August 1972, p. 42).*

(30) *The quintessence of existentialist movies — The Last Tango in Paris — demonstrates that pleasure is not the point (or the result) of all existentialist action. In the movie, Paul wills himself a new life, but in destroying the memory of his old life, he also destroys himself.*

(31) *Susanne K. Langer,* Philosophy in a New Key *(New York: Mentor Books, The New American Library of World Literature, 1958).*

(32) *Leibniz (1646-1711) is usually thought of as the father of symbolic logic (as well as being the father of differential calculus). It is interesting to note that modern mathematics has become so specialized that one group — applied math — usually has a department in engineering schools (and deals with computers, higher forms of calculus, etc), while another group — "pure" mathematics — usually is found either in mathematics departments or in philosophy departments (and deals with philosophy, symbolic logic, and experiments in new math forms. This last group is usually small, dedicated, and introspective.*

For a good introduction to symbolic logic see: A. H. Basson and D. J. O'Connor, Introduction to Symbolic Logic *(London University Tutorial Press, 1970).*

(33) Symbolic logicians are not arguing for any simplistic reduction that removes the richness of our language. As Susanne Langer says: "Codified knowledge is a clearly defined field, governed by the requirements of discursive projectability. Outside this domain is the inexpressible realm of feeling, of formless desires and satisfactions, immediate experience, forever incognito and incommunicado." She suggests that this is not a good field for linguists or philosophers; and then continues, "[But] intelligence is a slippery customer, . . . If one symbolism is inadequate, it seizes another; there is no eternal degree over its means and methods. . . . there is an unexplored possibility of genuine semantic beyond the limits of discursive language" (Philosophy in a New Key, p. 81).

This is such an important point in an understanding of the possibility of an architectural language that another quotation, this one from the historian Sinclair Gauldie, seems appropriate. Gauldie is saying much the same thing as Langer, but in different terms:

> *The essence of a language is that it includes a range of signs which connect with a multiplicity of referents. The usefulness of such signs lies in the possibilities which they offer rather than the discipline they impose; they are capable of acting as bridges or links which bring together whole areas of associated ideas and experiences. It is this associative potential which stimulates an inventive activity on the part of the sender and an imaginative activity on the part of the interpreter. And these activities are the very life of*

Two short examples will illustrate this point. If we say, "Some animals are cows; cows eat grass; therefore, some animals eat grass," we shall probably have a high degree of agreement on the language-symbols (animals, cows, and grass) we have used, and further reasoning is thus possible. However, if we say, "The Catholic cathedral of Chartres is beautiful because of its lightness and grace, which come from its beautiful windows — windows that are true testaments to faith in God," we may find that the total symbol-image of a man who is French, a Catholic, and has been to see Chartres, is quite different from that of a Lutheran farmer who grows wheat in Kansas. Consider simply the primary images: "Catholic cathedral," "windows," "testaments," and "faith in God." Add to these the qualitative words *beautiful, lightness, grace.* Our chances of any meaningful reasoning are unlikely when symbols that have few areas of basic agreement are used.(33)

There are of course symbol-transformation processes (or languages) in fields other than those for verbal-written languages; we have mentioned mathematics, music, ritual, and myth; and while pure symbolic logicians will exclude natural form and art form as languages, since they have no codified areas of agreement, we cannot ignore these symbolic areas, because they do communicate to us.

And while symbolic logicians are concerned with the structure of language (and thus epistemology: the study of knowledge), they understand that outside formal language, it is possible to construct value systems, such as an emotionally perceived language for architecture. Attempts to define these noncodifiable languages will always prove difficult, however.

As an example of this difficulty, Langer shows us two drawings: one of a cat, the other of a rabbit.(34) The two drawings convey two distinctly different symbol-images, yet in our verbal language we would have to say that as drawings, the lines have identical weight and only slight variation as to form. If we pretend, however, that these drawings were photographs instead, think of the minute variations and shades of meanings the symbolic transformation would possess. A symbolism such as this, with so many elements, could not be deciphered and classified, and thus photography has no formal language vocabulary.

One final example will show how symbolic transformations help us to understand architectural meaning. If we see a box(35) with a peaked top (drawing 35a), we might assume it is a child's building block, an abstraction of a house, or even simply a geometric figure. If we add an opening and smaller windows (drawing 35b), we might assume it is a house; if we add to this further (35c), we might assume it is a church-house. The final addition of a figure and the rearrangement of a few lines (35d) transform the church-house into a toy box. If, however, we were to reverse this process and say, "Describe via a drawing a toy church-house for children," the results would be fascinating, rich in metaphorical meaning, and with the distinct possibility that no two drawings would look alike.

language, for they have made it the tool by which man perpetually enlarges the boundaries of his experience. (Sinclair Gauldie, "Language and Code in Architecture," Modulus 9, University of Virginia [1973]; p. 66.)

(34) Drawings (a) and (b) are similar to those found in Langer, Philosophy in a New Key, *p. 68.*

(a)   *(b)*

(35) Sketches (a-d) show how the symbolic-transformation image will change by the addition of only a few lines.

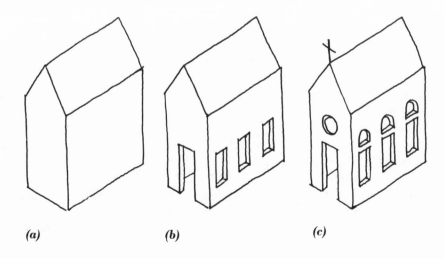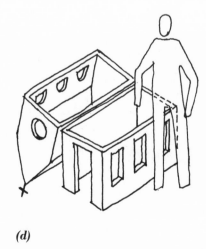

(a)   *(b)*   *(c)*   *(d)*

(36) Langer says: "The Kantian challenge 'What can I know?' is shown to be dependent on the prior question 'What can I ask?' " (Philosophy in a New Key, p. 78).

(37) In the broadest context, this is a very large group, with diverse interests and wide differences in philosophy. What allies them is their concern with the meaning of languge, specifically 1. how we communicate, and 2. How we reason using communication as a tool.

Some people who might be included in the group are: Marshall McLuhan and all of his Medium Is the Massage *readers; the symbolic logicians, linguists, semanticists, and communication theorists; and even the architectural thinker Buckminster Fuller.*

(38) The "sweeping conclusion" might also be called "the little truth to big lie" technique. A good exposition of the semanticists' work and their resultant process can be found in Anatol Rapoport, Operational Philosophy. (New York: International Semantics, 1969)

The importance for architectural theorists in considering the work of symbolic logicians is that through their study of the symbolic structures of language, they have opened new possibilities for studying the nonverbal language of architecture.(36)

Another group questioning pragmatism, and a group obviously closely related to symbolic logicians, are the linguists, semanticists, and semiologists,(37) who study the meaning of words, signs, and symbols. For want of a better phrase we might say that this group is concerned with an "operational process" for discovering what it is we actually mean when we say something.

In 1941 a large number of distinguished linguists, led by the brilliant mathematician Alfred Korzybski, fled Poland ahead of Nazi persecution. Many of this group had a major interest in both higher mathematics and philosophy. Their direct experience with the persuasion and opinion-making techniques of Joseph Paul Goebbels, however, turned much of their semantic interest toward how Goebbels was able to use language as an opinion tool to convince the German people that the policies of the Third Reich were correct. How could Goebbels say one thing, but cleverly imply another? How did propaganda work? Two of the many semantic techniques employed in propaganda might be called the glittering generality and the sweeping conclusion.(38)

A glittering generality makes a general statement that throws damaging expository adjectives and adverbs into the statement — qualifiers that have nothing to do with the argument — in order subtly to alter one's opinion. For example: "Senator Fulbright was typical of many old-fashioned southern senators who opposed the progressive ideas of the present administration's farsighted program." (While Senator Fulbright *was* from the south, was he typical? Do southern senators really oppose new ideas? What is old-fashioned? What is progressive?) The statement is so general as to mean nothing, yet it implies a great deal about Senator Fulbright — and in an uncomplimentary way. Or an architectural example: "The new World Trade Center in New York is so grotesquely huge that one cannot even find the toilets — obviously the toilets are not in the right place, and the scale is absurd.'' (In actual fact, toilets and scale have little to do with each other — and finding a toilet has little to do with the bigness or size of the building.)

The sweeping-conclusion technique starts with a small example that is true and then asserts a preposterous and uncheckable lie. For example: "President Jefferson lent many architectural books and plans of European cities to Major L'Enfant. In fact, without Jefferson's help L'Enfant could never have produced his plan for Washington, D.C."(39)

As a means of combating propaganda, the semanticist group has suggested a return to direct experience, or an "operational process."(40) This process suggests that to discover the truth, one should set up an experiential method by which the consequences of action may be tested. For example, if one wanted to discover if Jefferson (and not L'Enfant) actually designed the original plan for Washington, D.C., an operational process would suggest:

1. Study (read directly) the plans, letters, and correspondence of L'Enfant

2. Study (read directly) the correspondence of Jefferson to L'Enfant

3. Study (search out directly) the prevailing thought of L'Enfant's day (neoclassicism, baroque plans, L'Enfant's education, etc.)

(39) In this case, the statement can be checked — while Jefferson did loan many plans of cities to L'Enfant, the plan of Washington, D.C., is definitely L'Enfant's own creation — his debt to Jefferson is only one among many to outstanding thinkers of his day.

All of the examples given are fictitious — however, a dip into any recent architectural journal should provide more than ample real-life examples for any one.

(40) See note 37 above.) Semanticists *is used here in its broadest sense and is not meant to imply that operational process is subscribed to by all — certainly not by the followers of Carl Jung.*

Operational Process *is also different from operational philosophy, which is the term used by A. Rapoport. What I am suggesting is that the process* can lead us to our own philosophy.

A final operational process would probably be to go personally to Washington, D.C., to study the resultant physical reality.

From the above, it is obvious that as a method, operational process is related to pragmatism in that it suggests direct inquiry into the consequences of action — but operational process does not insist that the answer be pragmatically useful. The process as described has no value system built into it, but one may add one if desired. If, for example, one finds on visiting Washington that the Mall is (in his opinion) overwhelmingly beautiful and awe-inspiring, he can reverse this process and inquire, "Why is it beautiful for me?" In his resultant study, he will discover (probably) that scale, order, Renaissance thought, Jefferson, L'Enfant (among others), Neoclassicism, tree planting, and architecture of grand intention and design are all involved. Somewhere along the way, he will also probably alter his original value judgment, for better or for worse, that the Mall is beautiful. In short, the quality of his value judgment will be affected by his guided direct experience, the operational process he establishes for discovering the truth.

This chapter — as a short discussion on general philosophy — has tried to suggest that the Aristotelian rules are still in use today, and that while pragmatism as a philosophy makes it particularly difficult to form value systems in art, we do have new tools and methods for helping us that are more significant than simplistic avenues of escape. And that among those are existentialist thought, symbolic logic, and operational process.

Using these tools, a method by which one might today construct an architectural aesthetic could be:

1. *Ask what it is we would like to know.* What is it our symbolic framework (our architectural language) will allow us to ask? On what levels and in what manner may we frame our question? What conceptual idea lies symbolically behind the architectural form?

2. *Examine how the question has been answered in previous cultural history.* How has the conceptual idea been reflected in earlier architectural form? What are the interconnections between what a society believes and what it builds?

3. *Establish tentative criteria.* How should the conceptual idea be expressed for our present society? What can we architecturally test using symbolic logic and rational reasoning? What must we test using experimental process? What can we state intuitively?

4. *Reexamine what it is we would like to know.* Is our original question still appropriate? If so, are our criteria valid insofar as we can possibly establish them for this time and place in cultural history?

If the answer to the last question is yes, then we have the beginnings of a shared architectural aesthetic — an aesthetic with which we can build, and then test, the value of our work.

Above all, those who would discover any kind of responsible aesthetic must be prepared to return again to the beginnings, and to question and question again. To Socrates' statement that "The unexamined life is not worth living," we would have to add, that, for the architect, unexamined architecture is not worth building.

V CONCEPTUAL IDEAS:
THE GATHERING PLACE

In preceding chapters, I have suggested how one may begin to evolve his own theory of architecture through an analytical approach. Using a shared basic terminology, he can take any physical environment and study it in relation to a series of determinants — functional, technological, sociocultural, and artistic-personal.(1) Combining his analysis of these determinants with his own felt reaction, not only can he begin to make reasoned value judgments about architecture but he can begin to understand how those judgments have been formed. This, as I have suggested, is a methodology based on Aristotelian logic. It leads to a shared language of architectural form that stresses analytical research, description, classification, and detail, and it is the shared language most used in architectural discussion today.(2)

In chapters 3 and 4, mention was made of the difficulties of using pure Aristotelian logic as a process in our complicated present cultural age, and in particular, attention was paid to our more recent inherent difficulties in using pragmatism as a philosophy. At the close of the last chapter, the suggestion was then made that a method involving both symbolic logic and operational process might allow us to examine architectural form in a way that would help us construct a shared felt language. Although noncodifiable, that language would allow us to communicate through similar symbolical spatial experiences.

The question naturally arises, How might such a process be applied to a formal study of our architectural environment? One such method would be to look directly at the conceptual ideas themselves: i.e., to select a conceptual idea and then to study it directly and in depth to see what implications that idea has for architectural form.(3)

By *conceptual idea* is meant an idea that, when applied to architecture, has generating symbolic importance. If it is a powerful conceptual

(1) It should be stressed again that the number of determinants is not as important as the idea of their classification.

(2) The danger of misused Aristotelian analysis is that it leads to that educational philosophy that states "the product is not as important as the process." As noted in chapter 3, note 18, process and product cannot be separated in architecture — understanding the process is important; yet in the end there must also be a physical reality.

(3) The reader may wish to refer to those discussions in the text and notes that build the argument for using a shared felt architectural language. See chapter 3, note 20 and the text at the end, then chapter 4, note 33 and the text at the end. Finally note 5, below, considers intuition as one of the ways for discovering truth.

(4) *As another example, try defining neighborhood — or even better, neighborhood school. The sociocultural conceptual idea is changing so rapidly that precise definition is impossible.*

(5) *The advantages of studying concepts in order to build a shared, intuitively felt language become obvious — over a period of cultural time, we can see how the architectural response has changed corresponding to the symbolic change in the cultural concept.*

(6) *This point is also discussed in chapter 11, note 2.*

(7) *Consider front doors on marble telephone palaces that are full of equipment but no people; fake mansard roofs at the front of hamburger stands, but flat roofs at the sides; "colonial" filling stations with chimneys, but no fires (one hopes!).*

(8) *This is a complex issue, but an important one. It involves existentialism, operational syntax, and intuition — as well as an awareness that our moods and feelings actually influence the questions we ask.*

(9) *In chapter 4, the semanticist approach was discussed; however, the problems of codifying (or analyzing) experience, as opposed to codifying language symbols, is of sufficient importance to warrant mentioning another group, generally referred to as the*

idea, it will have a lasting effect on men's minds, stimulating intellectual thought and requiring a long period of time for development. In fact, there are conceptual ideas of such power that they can never be fully resolved, for they are always in the process of *becoming.* For example, if we consider the sociocultural conceptual idea of shelter / habitat, we can see that it is an idea always in the process of change — for the society is constantly reevaluating, reforming, and regenerating its life-style.(4)

As soon as such a conceptual idea is translated into architectural form, it takes on symbolic connotations for each of us — through symbolic transformation, we endow the shaped space with our own meanings, often beyond the original cultural intent.(5) If we take the cave house as an example, we see that as soon as the first one is built, the second cave house has a symbolic tradition to draw upon — it has an inherited cultural tradition.(6) Thus, we see cave houses being built today in Turkey and Spain, even though it is obvious that the people know how to build regular farmhouses above ground. They continue to live in cave houses because of the immense sociocultural importance of what began as a simple conceptual idea.(7)

How can one study such conceptual ideas? Essentially by experiencing them, either through studying history or, preferably, through an actual visit. By first asking oneself: What has the concept meant in cultural history? What does it mean now? How has the symbolic form changed? Why? In the case of the cave house example just discussed, one asks, What idea about living has this architecture expressed in the past? Finally, one visits, walks through, touches, feels — or experiences — the architecture of the cave house today, using his felt symbolic language of architectural form to construct his own mental conceptual image of what the cave house today means.(8)

Obviously it is difficult to study an architectural conceptual language within a book format, when what is needed is an experiential process, followed by serious thought. Discovering the right approach for asking, "What does it mean?" requires intuitive ability.(9)

And yet a general discussion is needed, even if the conceptual ideas will be few in number and the discussion will suffer from lack of language syntax. For great artists have always had an understanding of the conceptual ideas of their day, and their work has always shaped these ideas into artistic form, often with astounding clarity. Indeed, as stated earlier, *understanding* conceptual thought is the first step in creativity.

In a broad way we can isolate two general areas of conceptual ideas in architecture: those that deal with form itself and those that deal with sociocultural issues.(10)

behaviorists. This group is well represented by Christian Norberg-Schulz, who says:

> *The most basic insight into the problem is due to "operationalism." One has simply asked the question: "under what concrete circumstances are we allowed to use a particular word?" . . .*

> *Modern science, however, has been forced to realize that the meaning of the words lies in the relationship between language and experience. [*Intentions in Architecture *(Cambridge, Mass.; M.I.T. Press, paperback ed., 1968), p. 575; italics mine].*

One sees immediately the close relationship between behaviorist thought and the "symbolic transformation" of Suzanne Langer, discussed in the last chapter. Norberg-Schulz proposes to codify experience through psychological studies of human behavior. He states that our visual perception is conditioned by our attitude.

Through operational process, behaviorists propose to study how our attitudes toward things (objects) influence our perception,

and thus our aesthetical value system. Norberg-Schulz calls these personal value systems, our schemata.

Carried to its logical conclusion, behaviorism objectively analyzes each individual's psychological schemata and thus rules out noncodifiable thought, or intuition. As Norberg-Schulz says: "We should also repeat that 'intuitive' methods to gain knowledge are illusory" (ibid., p. 82).

An interesting refutation of behaviorist theory occurs when one disagrees with the idea that experience must be necessarily related to things, or objects. Experience can then be felt intuitively without object-based perception schemata. In this case, rather than being a process of knowledge acquisition, intuition would instead be one of the ways in which we master or structure knowledge into wisdom.

At least it is debatable if a felt language can ever have a syntax that is codified. And is that really necessary? Can we not agree that humans are complex, that they often react to physical phenomena (both individually and as a society) in culturally predictable ways. And that by the same token humans sometimes react (both individually and as a society) in culturally unpredictable ways? One of the pleasures of architecture may be that to be shared, its felt language must be physically experienced, rather than simply talked about.

(10) This division is, by its very nature, not precise, but is chosen for convenience.

(11) Ways to fit stairs within a floor plan: — Sketch plan (a) places stairs within the structure and on axis, symmetrical and balanced (a solution popular in the Renaissance); (b) shows stairs half in, and half out of the structure (popular with 1960 form seekers); (c) illustrates stairs outside the basic form (used by Louis Kahn at Richards Medical Research building — removing service elements allows complete freedom with interior partition arrangement); and (d) represents a combination — while this might solve a specific functional requirement, however, it would not be consistent as a building form.

(12) This special vaulting, called a pendentive was discussed in chapter 2 as an example of a technological determinant.

(13) The typical grid pattern of American cities demonstrates the usual dependence on geometry of additive forms used in architecture. The grid is used because it is an easy configuration both for surveying and for recording on a formal written deed. In the western United States, entire states were laid out in square sections of 640 acres each, with one-fourth sections given to settlers under provisions of the Homestead Act.

While an additive grid form works well in terms of country courthouse records, it often does not correspond to social living patterns (nor to topography either; consider the street grid of San Francisco).

(14) Even worse, is the thought that three towers represent the Holy Trinity.

Study in the first area usually concentrates on natural form, and the biological or physical laws that govern how such form is joined or added to, or how it may grow. One example would be fitting together the stair and the volumetric space it serves. Each historical period has resolved this problem in a manner that is unique to its society and to its technological ability, yet is consistent to natural, or organic, form principles.(11) Another example is the placing of a sphere on the landscape. If one places the sphere over a cylinder, the resultant form is technologically simple. To place the sphere over a square (or a cube) base, however, is complex, and requires a special form of vaulting.(12)

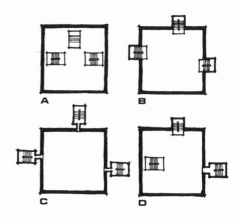

In recent years architects have become increasingly concerned with additive forms and the "rules" by which such forms may grow.(13) Since these rules usually have a mathematical base, one soon finds himself thinking (unless he is careful) that there is something sacred about numbers themselves — carried to an illogical conclusion, this leads to housing proposals that suggest that apartment designs with three towers are preferable to two or four-tower schemes, because of the balanced tension or the structural equilibrium inherent in three pointed configurations.(14)

While additive forms usually involve geometric configurations, growth forms are derived from biological or environmental configurations found in nature, such as a growing tree, or a river and its tributary system.(15)

Of final conceptual-form interest is the fact that similar forms grouped together are often more powerful as a visual image than the single forms individually. Nature is full of such examples, such as contrasting each petal of a flower with the power of the total form of the flower, and architects have not missed the architectural implications of these phenomena.(16)

Although these form studies are extremely useful in considering materials, construction methods, service lines, utilities, and growth patterns, it is important to remember that while form for its own sake is interesting, it is not architecture.(17) Or that a tree is not really like a city; nor is a city *really* like a tree.

(15) A tree grows from ground to trunk to major limb to minor limb to leaf. This analogy is often used in discussions of city traffic patterns (the critical points being the joints, or traffic lights). The C.I.A.M. movement (Congres Internationale Architecture Moderne) was particularly fond of this example in the 1930s; one must be careful, however, of too literal a translation. Streets with traffic also have ebb and flow, peak loads, and noise and pollution.

(16) An architectural example would be the placing of a group of theaters around a central space, shaping this space into a gathering place for theatergoers. (See also Fumihiko Maki, Investigations in Collective Form *[St. Louis: Washington University School of Architecture, 1964] pp. 54-55).*

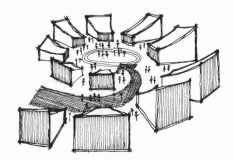

The idea that the whole is greater than the sum of its parts is a cornerstone of Gestalt psychology, which has heavily influenced both the behaviorist and the metabolist movements.

(17) Basic design courses (as differentiated from architectural design) normally concentrate on fundamental, conceptual-form ideas as a means of beginning. Well-taught basic design courses emphasize

that form orders or structures content, and is not the content itself.

A book that deals almost exclusively with form is Some Roots of Modern Architecture *by Heinz Rasch (London: Alec Tiranti, 1967). Rasch proposes that after 1922, five new architectural space precepts grew. In chronological order these were: first, space as* direction; *then,* resistance *(1924); then,* distance *(1927); then,* perception *(1929); and finally,* path *(after 1945). Rasch's book treats space as an issue of conceptual form, divorced from any societal concern. Nonetheless, thinking of architecture as pure spatial form produces magnificent diagrams.*

(18) See Desmond Morris, The Naked Ape *(New York: McGraw-Hill, 1967), for a good discussion of this issue.*

(19) Sketch (a) shows aborigines sleeping in a circle around a fire. Each aborigine sleeps so that his eyes are facing toward the "territory" he comes from — an example of ritual gathering: see Amos Rapoport, House Form and Culture *(Englewood Cliffs, N.J.: Prentice-Hall, paperback ed., 1969), pp. 63, 66.*

Example (b) is of Stonehenge, England, where stones are arranged for ritual in accordance with astronomy.

Let us now turn to the second broad area of conceptual ideas found in architecture — those ideas that are the result of sociocultural needs or desires. These ideas can never be resolved by any single architectural solution, because (as mentioned earlier) the ideas themselves are always in the process of evolution: the shelter / habitat, the landmark, the market, the entertainment center, to name a few such ideas.

Among the most important of these sociocultural ideas is the *gathering place* — used here to denote that place in cultural time where a people desire to meet, discuss, and socially mix as a group. The gathering place is a sufficiently important conceptual idea that we may use it for the remainder of this chapter to demonstrate how an architectural felt language that is shared may be built through studying cultural history.

There is considerable disagreement among anthropologists as to whether this desire to meet, discuss, and socially mix is an instinctive or an acquired need.(18) We do know, however, that all societies — even the most loosely organized — have gathering places, often closely linked with ritual and religion.(19)

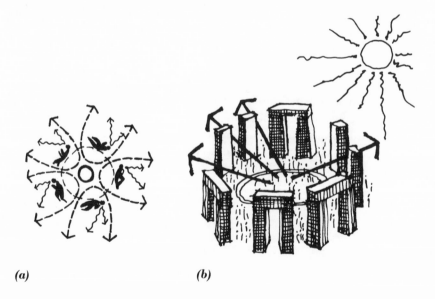

(a)   (b)

We also know that as societies grow, change, and reorganize, their cultural image of what constitutes a gathering place also changes. The Greek market, or agora, evolves into the forum, the cathedral plaza, the commons, the courthouse square, the Boston City Hall Plaza. The shopping bazaar evolves into the supermarket.(20) A brief discussion of two historical types of gathering places — the square and the street — should demonstrate the lasting power of this sociocultural conceptual idea, as well as the intuitive architectural symbolic response.

The square (or piazza, plaza, or place) is the most obvious of gathering places. It is most frequently a shaped outdoor room, although the shaping of the form may be extremely subtle, as with the main plaza at Avila, Spain.(21) In this case, the plaza forms naturally just outside the entry gates to the older city — that place where the older city and the newer city meet. Opposite the entry gate is the important mother church of Santa Teresa, Spain's greatest woman author. The south side of the plaza is purposely nondescript. It lies in shade and has less importance as a meeting place for people.(22) The north side of the plaza has a wide sidewalk and is completely arcaded. This area is filled with cafes and outdoor tables. In hot weather, the tables are pulled back into the shade of the arcade; but in the many wonderfully crisp and sunny spring days of Castile, the plaza is alive with coffee and sherry drinkers, passersby, and waiters. The architectural lesson is direct, but important — the plaza works because each of its parts contributes properly to the architectural whole.

(20) The bazaar also lives on as a viable form in itself, as the Cannery in San Francisco demonstrates.

(21) The plan of Avila, Spain (a), and a sketch of the plaza as seen from the walls (b) shows how cars are parked in the shade while pedestrians have their choice of sun in the plaza or shade under the arcade.

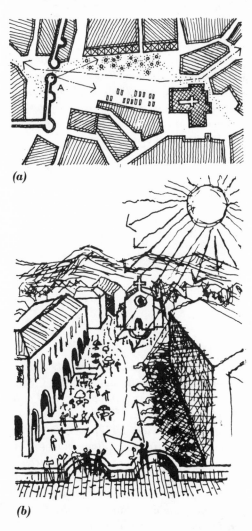

(a)

(b)

(22) To create a subservient building within a larger whole is an ability greatly

needed when too many buildings are individualistic ego-trips of the owner and his architect. An example is the tobacco factory just south of Richmond, Virginia, on I-95. In this case the factory buildings themselves are straightforward, functional (and symbolic) buildings. The main research building, sitting forward on the site with its strident insistence on monumentality, is another matter.

(23) A medieval town plan: plazas occur at churches, entries to town, and the marketplace. Adapted from Paul Zucker, Town and Square *(New York: Columbia University Press, 1959) p. 70; this book is an excellent examination of the historical evaluation of the square.*

The medieval and early Renaissance city was characterized by innumerable small squares in and around the town's parish churches. Just as the parish church was the interior gathering place for its district, the small square or entry place for the church was the district's symbolic outdoor center.(23) Indeed, these squares, together with their linking street system, were discretely organized spaces for specific activities — and one knew where he was by the activity around him.(24)

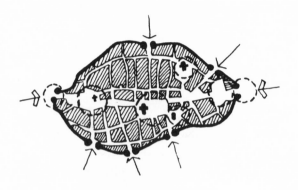

(24) Two examples of a discretely shaped square for a specific activity: the Piazza Armeria, Italy (a) (adapted from Paolo Favole, Piazze D'Italia *[Milan: Bramante Editrice, 1972] p. 187), and a typical Greek fishing village plan (b). At the edge of the harbor, a small church is fronted by an open-ended square. A bar and café opens into the square — the patrons, seated at tables, ideally located in the middle of activity.*

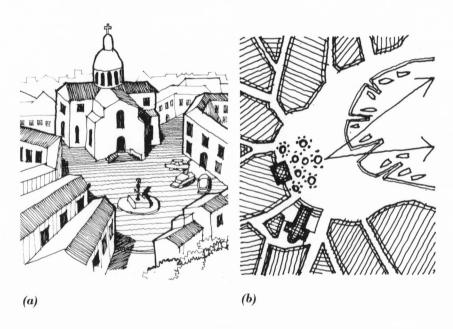

(a)

(b)

Among the reasons for the square are the desires to meet and visit, to identify a special symbolic center (as at the Boston City Hall plaza),(25) to conduct business, to sell produce, to be seen (as at the church plazas in South America, where girls promenade around the central park area), and to mark an important circulation interchange (as at the Arc de Triomphe in Paris). That many of these reasons are still valid will be shown after a brief discussion of *the street.*

(25) Architectural criticism has rarely discussed the Boston City Hall as part of a larger plaza concept (see 25a). The original conceptual section (b) shows that the City Hall was intended as a landmark through which the plaza "flows" into adjacent streets.

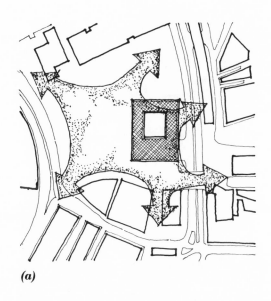

(a)

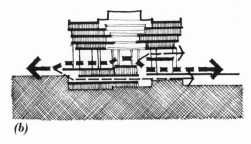

(b)

The street is another type of gathering place, similar to but distinct from the square. It is a unique form of gathering place because not only does it serve as a place to meet, shop, and visit, it also serves as a place to pass through.(26) The most successful streets as gathering places recognize this duality, whether they be streets for people only, as at the Galleria in Milan, or streets where people mix with cars and transit systems.(27)

(26) The street can also be thought of as a theater. Consider: "[Street theater] is the visual, audial and psychic experience of street life; . . . the pageantry and dynamics of people, their movement, dress and color; . . . street decor and architecture; and occasionally conscious efforts to heighten street intensity through 'stage' dramatics." (Gus Ardura, "Street Theater," an article published in Modulus, *vol. 9, University of Virginia, 1973) p. 106.*

(27) Bernard Rudofsky, in his book Streets for People *(New York: Doubleday, 1964), makes a strong argument for the pedestrian street. What is missing is the acknowledgment that often streets are also properly for simultaneous use by cars and pedestrians.*

(28) The Ramblas, Barcelona — The plan (a) shows how the street links the Plaza Catalun with the harbor front; the section (b) shows pedestrians in the middle of the street with traffic at each side.

The most powerful example of the street as a gathering place occurs when the street links two or more intense generators of human activity. A skillfully handled example of this is the Ramblas in Barcelona.(28) This street literally rambles from the major square, the Plaza Catalun, to the city's harbor front. Along the way, the street connects the city market and the opera house, while bypassing the cathedral and the Gothic quarter. Underneath the Ramblas runs the rapid transit.

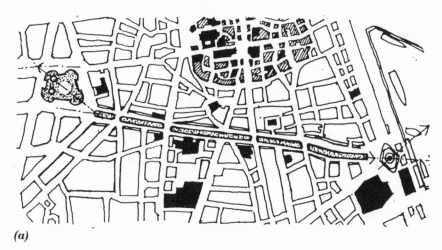

(a)

(b)

Given such generators of traffic, How does the form of the street emphasize its role as a gathering place? By placing pedestrians in the center of the street! As the street section illustrates, a flow of human traffic uses the central esplanade, screened off from the car traffic by trees — and between the trees are flower stalls and lottery-ticket sellers. The noise level here is high — for this is the circulation artery of Barcelona and the meeting place of all its citizens.

In this general discussion of outdoor gathering places, I have tried through limited examples to illustrate a single point — that the gathering place, like all strong sociocultural conceptual ideas, can, if properly translated, result in architectural images of enduring quality. One can infer that if they are also to succeed, the architecturally formed gathering places of the future must similarly reflect the cultural desires of our future society.(29)

(29) The possible adaptation of a small-town American Main Street to reaccommodate the pedestrian. The north lane

In today's age — where rapid transit take us from housing community to shopping district to work factory to housing community again — the older image of medieval linked plazas, which were discrete and easily understood, can no longer work. While design predictions beyond ten to fifteen years are never very accurate, certain directions are discernible, both in our emerging social life-styles and in our recent architectural form. We can postulate that our society will be pluralistic with an intricate social stratification. (See chapter 3.) We can see this occurring in mini-suburbias (or mini-communities) that are homogeneous in social class but are interconnected via highway systems to heterogeneous, larger political units. Further, we know that within the dense city centers, overlapping of circulation, use pattern, and design form will occur in multilevels; e.g., a subway level may be layered by service, pedestrian, and office levels — an interlock of stacked functional uses formerly separated by zoning laws.

One design result of this is that, at the smaller residential grouping, our society already is demanding a personal sense of identity — frequently accomplished through a small gathering place such as the cul-de-sac with fifteen surrounding houses;(30) the swimming pool in a courtyard, enclosed by apartments;(31) the residential square (as at Charles Center in Baltimore); or the restructuring of residential

(only) of parking is removed, the sidewalk is widened, trees are planted, and benches are added between trees; street traffic is left open, and signs on buildings remain. Each block may take on a special character (shown here are advertising kiosks — which may be changed, relocated, or moved).

(30) The paved circle (at left) is used not only by cars but also by children and adults as an area of social mix. Note: Each house also has a private yard, and there is no through traffic.

(31) The pool becomes the gathering place for an apartment complex.

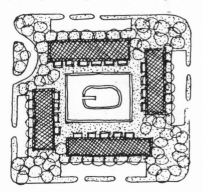

(32) Saint Marks Place, Bedford-Stuyvesant area, Brooklyn — an existing street is converted into a private place. Note: cars have not been eliminated, only reorganized into new diagonal parking space areas. Through traffic is prevented by placing a playground in the middle of the block.

(33) One must take care in a pluralistic society to see that the range of these intimate residential places satisfies the social mores of the people directly involved. (E.g., basketball courts must be for children, not dope pushers — a tough assignment.)

(34) I.D.S. Center in Minneapolis — in the sketch plan (a), the central courtyard is enclosed by buildings and roofed over with a glass skylight. At the second-floor level (b), the pedestrian corridors actually span over the streets to connect with pedestrian levels in adjacent blocks.

streets into closed private places.(32) All of these examples seem worthy of encouragement in a society where alienation is a problem — and their relative success when tried demonstrates that they satisfy a real social desire for a smaller and more intimate community.(33)

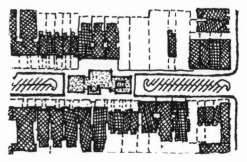

One of the more fascinating aspects of emergent urban design is the gradual disappearance of the formal monumental public square. As the grand gathering place is moving indoors into arenas and astrodomes, the more personal civic space is rapidly becoming a transparent, or translucent, half-indoor and half-outdoor place within the city-block structure. Man as a social animal still desires to gather, but with the rapid pace (and literal speed) of his present life, the form of his gathering place changes. A simple example of this is Paley Plaza in New York City, a small place to rest, seated on a chair, within sight of a busy urban street.

A more dramatic example of this new direction is the I.D.S. Center in Minneapolis,(34) with its great glassed-in crystal court. Also in-

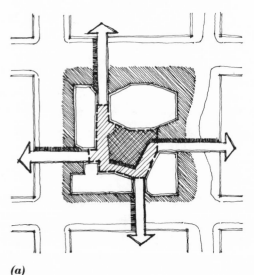

(a)

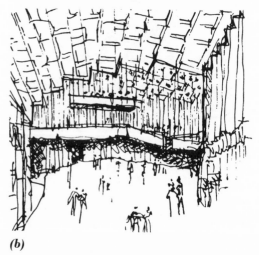

(b)

teresting is how this room connects with civic pedestrian streets both at street level and at a first level above the ground. Philip Johnson has said this spatial arrangement illustrates "turning the Seagram Building inside out"(35) — meaning, of course, that the former's outside plaza has now been moved inside. The comment is not as irrelevant as it might first appear, for the social gathering functions are, in fact, inside the crystal court and thus turned inward, away from the street noise and traffic. The pedestrian street moves through the building, widens, and becomes a gathering place.

Other recent U.S. examples of plazas inside buildings include the hotels of John Portman, the Citicorp Building and the Ford Foundation Building in New York City, and the Disney World hotel — where the visitors' train penetrates and moves through the hotel lobby.

The combined interaction of pedestrian movement (street activity) with courtyard (social and symbolic center) also can be seen in countless examples of commercial malls, such as the Shopping Gallery in Philadelphia.

This return to an understanding that first there must be a sociocultural need for a gathering place before there is an architectural reason for shaping one is a healthy sign. One last example will show how complex this interaction may become. A plan for unbuilt Staten Island housing by I. M. Pei and Associates emphasized a series of levels, with services, cars, pedestrians, public places, and commercial spaces all mixed (yet controlled) and oriented toward the water.(36) Rising above these multileveled public gathering places were to be a series of residential towers — the generators of the human traffic necessary for the success of the public areas.

At the beginning of this chapter, I suggested that studying conceptual ideas was another way of developing an architectural value system, even though our formal language favors analytical, or Aristotelian, process. The very real reason for conceptual study is that when we ask the inner meaning of an idea, we go beyond analysis, no matter how thorough that analysis has been.

(35) Philip Johnson, Architectural Forum, January-February 1973, p. 35.

(36) Staten Island housing proposal — the two plans show how public space (shaded darkly) interacts with service space (lightly shaded) and apartment towers (heavily outlined). The plan at water level (a) has an open plaza next to

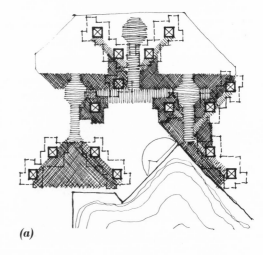

(a)

the water, surrounded by commercial, restaurant, and boating clubs. Parking is behind, near street access. The second *plan at a higher level (b) has public space interlocking apartment towers. The section (c) shows both the lower, stepped plaza levels and the interconnected level.*

Choosing the gathering place as an example for discussion of a sociocultural conceptual idea has also been purposeful, for it is apparent that our society is changing its attitude as to why and how it wishes to gather. Unless one questions and begins to understand this change, he may, as an architect, find himself designing an empty plaza or a mall that no one needs, wants, or can enjoy.

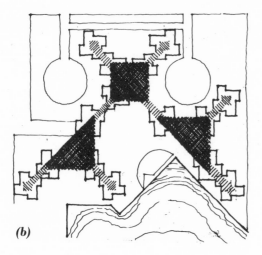

(b)

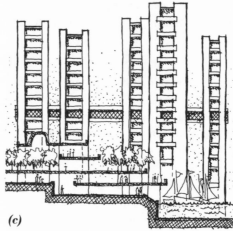

(c)

That is why this discussion has centered on the power of the sociocultural conceptual idea itself to generate architectural form rather than on the construction details of how the spaces should actually be shaped.(37)

(37) Space may better be analyzed using Aristotelian logic; place connotes feeling, mood, and sense. (The sensitive architect, of course, will use both deductive and intuitive reasoning.)

(38) Ben Shahn states this idea well: "and remember that you are trying to learn to think what you want to think, *that you are trying to coordinate* mind and hand and eye." *(From* The Shape of Content *[New York: Random House, Vintage Books, 1960] p. 131; italics mine.) Note the existentialist philosophy inherent in the advice.*

The discussion has also remained general in order to introduce the notion of conceptual study as a way toward understanding architecture. The next two chapters on shelter / habitat will carry this notion much farther as a means of developing a shared intuitive architectural language.

The best way to study a conceptual idea, however, remains to experience it. To discover a successful gathering place, one should visit gathering places until he finds one in which he feels comfortable. He should then pause and ask, Why? Why do people use this place? What is its meaning? Its future? What makes the form of the place work? And finally, he should sketch, draw, diagram(38 — and think, resketch, and question again, "What does this place mean?"

VI   THE SHELTER / HABITAT I:
SINGLE FORM

This chapter and the one that follows are, first, about the individual family dwelling, or the house and, second, about groups and patterns of these dwellings, or housing.

The term *house* conjures up such powerful emotive images, however, that a new term — one with less preconceived response — is needed for discussion.(1) I have chosen the combined word-term *shelter / habitat,* since it contains two generic concepts inseparably linked. The first concept — shelter — implies both physical protection from the elements, be they climate, animals, or other humans, and *physical enclosure* for spatial needs. The second concept — habitat — implies cultural involvement in a place where cooking, eating, sleeping, and living activities occur.

(1) Apropos is the famous statement A house is not a home. *In this case* house *implies shell, structure, and materials to enclose, and* home *implies warmth, fireplaces, and familial love and care; in common usage, however,* house *and* home *are interchangeably used.*

Throughout history, as each society has changed its attitudes towards these twin needs of shelter and habitat, the resultant architectural conceptual idea has evolved, changed, and produced an infinite variety of physical form.

As suggested in the last chapter, this may be stated another way: Shelter / habitat is an idea about living place that is always in the process of becoming. By studying this process of becoming and by asking the conceptual question, What does this living-place mean? we can continue towards building a shared architectural language.

(2) This is not always true, however. Certain Polynesian societies have lived in such excellent island climates that shelter needs have always been minimal. One result is that their cultural and technological ability has been best expressed in their boat designs rather than in their house construction.

Some social historians carry the argument of beneficial environment further, claiming that dominant societies only emerge in climates where conquering and overcoming the environment is important. The argument is that such environments produce inventive and dynamic cultures, while more benign environments produce a more docile culture.

Early historical examples of family dwellings demonstrate a greater concern for the concept of shelter than for that of habitat. A hostile environment, a preponderance of natural enemies, and limited technological knowledge made the simple task of building a shelter difficult in itself.(2)

(3) Amos Rapoport, House Form and Culture (Englewood Cliffs, N.J.: Prentice-Hall, 1969), states that when they migrate seasonally to the coastal plains, Indians from the mountains of California nonetheless still construct (for cultural reasons) snug and tightly built huts that are more properly suited for snow protection in the mountains than for the warm winds of the sea coast.

(4) The plan of Hadrian's Villa (a), outside of Rome, is open and meandering and implies a courtly life-style. The opposite is true of Manzanares Castle (b), outside of Madrid, which is walled and closed and implies a protected and inward-oriented life-style.

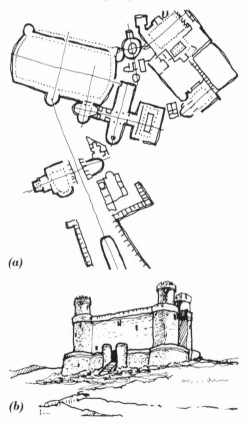

(a)

(b)

As a general rule, however, we can state that as strong cultures with their correspondingly complex life-style have emerged, the concept of habitat has also increased in importance until we have innumerable examples of shelter / habitat form in which little concern is shown for shelter itself. The main form determinants are then determined by cultural attitudes.

For example, the modern suburban house is often sited on a floodplain; built with insufficient foundations, poor bracing of its framing system, and too little insulation; and planned so that its picture window faces the western sun.(3) The result — when there is a flash flood, a tornado, an energy crisis, or even a long, hot summer — is always an unpleasant living experience, and often a difficult one. This rule — that as cultures emerge, the habitat concept increases at the expense of the shelter concept — must, of course, be treated as a generality, for cultural needs can also revert back to shelter needs, as happened in the early Middle Ages, when defense and protection reemerged as critical issues. The gracious Roman villas and country estates with their gardens and open plans give way to powerful, walled feudal strongholds.(4)

The final architectural form of shelter / habitat will thus always reflect both physical shelter needs and cultural habitat attitudes. Nonetheless, for purposes of this study, we shall examine these needs and attitudes separately, returning later to their interaction in the final, built form.

To begin with shelter needs, the most obvious one is probably protection from daily weather change. For example, intense rain calls for overhead protection, along with means of getting the rainwater away from the foundations. In areas with only occasional rain but intense sun, however, another kind of overhead protection is called for. In the Punjab area of India, which has both a long hot and dry summer and a short but intense monsoon season, villagers build their roofs out of twigs, thatch, and mud and then remove the thatch during the summer — so that the sun is screened out, but air movement can occur. Just prior to the rainy season, the villagers will replace the thatch and then cover the roof with tin sheets held down with sundried bricks. Large American Victorian-period houses in the Midwest resolved a similar problem by having porches that often surround the entire house. During hot weather the family changed indoor living place for outdoor place, including a second floor screened-in sleeping porch.(5)

On the one hand, a village society with limited building technology must continually change the physical condition of its one room shelter/habitat. On the other hand, Victorian America, a society that had ample building means, often changed one set of rooms for a totally new set.(6)

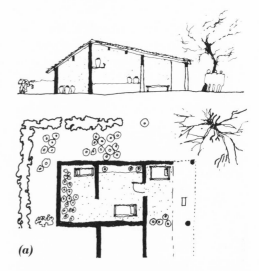

(a)

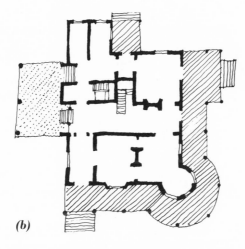

(b)

(5) A potter's house in Vastrapur village (a), outside Ahmedabad, India, has no windows, but does include a large verandah where all family life — cooking, sleeping, and socializing — takes place. The inner rooms are used for storage and for sleeping during the cooler months. When air circulation is needed, roof thatch is removed.

This Victorian house (circa 1890) in Missouri (b) has a porch for every occasion. During hot summers (punctuated by heavy rains), much of the family's life remained outside the formal interior of the house.

(6) More affluent members of society have also often opted for a seasonal change in location itself. Wealthy Romans, such as the Emperor Hadrian, had country villas; the British in India fled to hill-station cottages during the summer; many Americans now own a second home.

Besides rain and sun, other changing weather conditions that call for shelter responses include wind, heat, cold, and dampness. Shelter / habitat form will reflect each of these conditions depending on whether the climate is beneficial or harmful. For example, in some areas wind is a pleasant breeze to be enjoyed, while in other areas, wind is a fierce blizzard to be kept out of the dwelling. One should not expect a farmhouse in North Dakota to look very much like a house on the Florida beach.

(7) An interesting problem that faced the early planter settlers in humid Brazil was how to keep their pianos in tune!

(8) Two examples of cliff construction: the "hanging house" in Cuenca, Spain (a), which cantilevers out from the cliff edge through the use of wood bracing, and the Lovell House in Los Angeles by Richard Neutra (b), which utilizes a steel frame anchored into the rock.

This raises a shelter-need issue that is related, but not identical, to weather change — *location.* Shelter / habitat north of the equator will call for different orientation from that south of the equator. Specific locations may call for earthquake protection, as in San Francisco; for foundation protection, as on the shifting sand beach at Cape Hatteras; or for extreme weather protection, as in the northern Alaskan oilfield areas. Some locations have such severe environmental problems that even today they cannot be made into suitable areas for habitation. Large portions of the Amazon jungle are still constantly flooded, subjected to intense heat, overwhelmed with mosquitoes and termites, and inaccessible except by difficult boat passages.(7)

The most fascinating facet of location, however, occurs when an unusual and often difficult site makes possible a dramatic view. Cliff sides, mountaintops, ocean dunes — all provide the opportunity for orienting living space to capture such views, but at the same time these sites also demand skillful adaptation to provide protection from the elements. Cliff-edge dwellings, for example, not only must be anchored firmly into rocky outcroppings but must also be designed to protect the inhabitants from strong wind forces, usually coming up-cliff in gusts.(8) Shelter needs, of course, are not solely concerned with

(a)

(b)

climate and location. Another need is that for *defense*. Although earliest man's primary need was for protection from animals, it was not long before protection from other men became paramount. Historical examples range from fortified, isolated farm dwellings to the full-scale castles of the Middle Ages. (As pointed out in chapter 2, with the introduction of sophisticated artillery, the castle ceased to be effective defensively, and soon disappeared as an architectural shelter / habitat form.)

There are also other special defense forms that point out the interaction between cultural attitude and shelter need. One of these is the chapel. During certain periods of the Middle Ages, monastic chapels were recognized as being places of refuge, to which citizens could retreat. (Many were also well-fortified in case the attacking parties did not honor this cultural convention.) A present-day example of this attitude is the embassy, where shelter may be taken from local law enforcement. (Most embassies are also well-fortified for the same reasons that existed in the Middle Ages.)

Another example, and one of the most interesting historical shelter / habitat forms, is the Japanese teahouse. The Shokintei, located in the gardens of the Katsura Villa at Kyoto, illustrates shelter need based on defense, as well as cultural attitude.(9) Forced to leave his sword outside, the Samurai warrior had to crawl through a narrow opening to enter another world where he was thus protected from attack, and was nourished with tea in a quiet and carefully constructed shelter / habitat.

A final category of shelter need is the simple requirement for space in which the family unit may cook, eat, sleep, and socialize. These needs are often programmed as so many square feet for the kitchen, the dining room, etc.; this is a dangerous attitude, however. FHA requirements, for example, state that the first bedroom must be at least 120 square feet, the second bedroom must be at least 100 square feet, and the third bedroom must be at least 80 square feet. The result is predictable. Developers' houses have bedrooms that are exactly 120, 100, and 80 square feet — rooms any larger are considered excessive (as well as being less profitable!).

(9) The interior plan of the Shokintei Teahouse (a) is eminently functional, with the tea-preparation area the dominant architectural feature. The entry facade (b) has only a small opening — through which guests had to stoop, leaving swords and other cumbersome clothing outside.

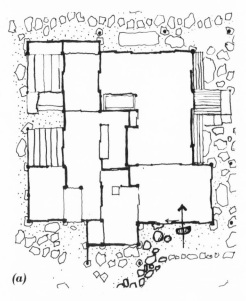

(a)

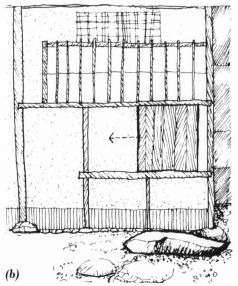

(b)

*(10) So dense are Hong Kong's New Set-
tlement housing blocks that each building
has its own primary school on its rooftop.*

*(11) A plan (a) and a section (b) of a
typical French Louisiana plantation
house, illustrates how complete air movement cools the interior. Veranda
overhangs also help control the sun.*

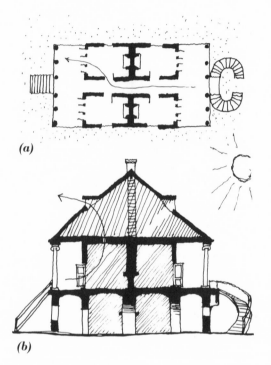

(a)

(b)

*A similar generic house (although vastly
different in scale) is the well-known
dogtrot farmhouse often found in
Alabama and Mississippi (c). An open
hallway area in the middle serves as the
principal social and living area. The
plan's name comes from the implication*

The danger in this type of programming is that it never asks the basic
question, What kind of place is required to satisfy the human shelter
need? For sleeping needs, even in the United States, do not have to be
resolved by building three individual bedrooms.

In addition, different societies *do* have different cultural attitudes
towards spatial requirements. In Hong Kong, the shelter / habitat
apartment units in new high-rise buildings are filled to a density of
one person per 20 square feet. In American terms, this would mean
that a typical suburban home of 2,000 square feet would accommodate
100 Chinese at Hong Kong density!(10) This example points out that
although there are very basic human dimensions — such as the length
and height of a human while sleeping and standing — that must be ac-
commodated in planning a shelter / habitat, beyond these basics, each
society will shape and size the dwelling-unit form according to its own
cultural attitude.

To conclude this introduction to shelter needs, let us look carefully at
one specific, sophisticated example of shelter / habitat — the French
Louisiana plantation house.(11) No dwelling type more clearly shows
the influence of climate, location, and specific shelter requirements.

Louisiana's climate is hot, rainy, and extremely humid. The early
French farmers soon evolved a plan that raised the main living space
one floor above the ground (see section, fig. 11b). This allowed the
lower floor, constructed of heavy brick, to be used for farm im-
plements, food storage, work space, and the kitchens. More importantly, it placed the main living space above damp and muggy ground
heat. A very high attic then served as insulation space and kept the
lower areas cooler.

In addition, the middle living space was left open as a wide hallway
that tunneled the prevailing breezes. This hallway, along with wide
verandas, became the real principal living space. The verandas also
kept the sun from hitting the building's sides, as well as providing protection from the often driving rains of Gulf Coast storms.

There are several subtle aspects of this form that should be mentioned. One of these is the fact that constructing the lower floor of brick
helped prevent water deterioration of the upper-level wood framing
members, as well as protecting the house from termites. It also meant
that when rivers rose rapidly (as they frequently did), the living space
was above flood level. Finally, the flexibility of the plan meant that
during the farming seasons, when extra workers were needed, the living space was open and occupied all of the veranda spaces, but that
when the short winter season came and farm operations were more
limited, the family could retreat into the four interior rooms, which
each contained a fireplace.

The French Louisiana plantation house — evolving over a period of
some two hundred years — is a superb example of shelter needs affecting the final architectural form of shelter / habitat.

Let us turn now to cultural attitudes and examine how they affect
shelter / habitat. Cultural attitudes are always difficult to isolate, for
they are integrally bound up with how the society views itself
philosophically, and they are always complex and interlocked in
meaning. For purposes of the following discussion, therefore, three
rather broad and general areas of societal concern are taken as starting points, and the many varied cultural attitudes will then be related
back to these three areas insofar as possible.

These areas are:

1.   the family, and the society's conception of how it regenerates
and protects itself within a social structure;

2.   the land, and the society's conception of how it lives in relation
to nature;

3.   the government, and the society's conception of its political
structure.

*that dogs can run in a figure eight
through and around the house.*

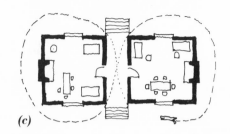

(c)

(12) . . . builders and developers never build houses, they build homes. The dream home is surrounded by trees and grass in either country or suburb, and it must be owned, *yet Americans rarely stay in it more than five years. It is not a real need but a symbol.*

This symbol means a free-standing, single-family house, not a row house, and the ideal home is aesthetic, not functional (Rapoport, House Form and Culture, *p. 132.)*

(13) Two concepts of cultural life-style: the freestanding archetype (a) with physical distance separating each shelter / habitat; and the shared-wall archetype (b) in which density makes street life an important cultural consideration.

(14) The Georgian house plan, found throughout colonial eastern America (and in a modified version, throughout modern suburbia), has much in common with the French Louisiana house discussed above.

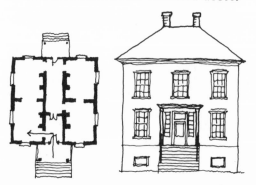

The concept of inward family and that of extended family are two examples of cultural attitude towards the *family.* For example, the farmer in the early American West lived inwardly, in isolation with his family in a wilderness, whereas today's Puerto Rican in New York City lives as a member of a larger family group, with apartments throughout the city and extended contacts via plane with San Juan. In the first case, the ideal architectural model, or archetype, is the freestanding self-contained home sitting on three acres of land.(12) In the second case, the ideal archetype is a mild climate with a high degree of street life, such as actually exists in Puerto Rico.(13) The American concept of family life also means noise control and visual privacy have traditionally been obtained through physical separation. The greater the spatial distance, the happier the family. Puerto Ricans and other societies that place greater emphasis on the extended family are less concerned about these issues and lead a more active public life.

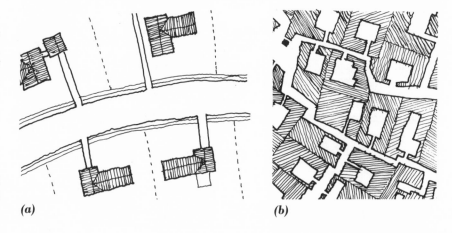

(a)   *(b)*

Cultural attitude also determines whether family life will be formal or informal. The classic formal plan is frequently referred to as Georgian and has a central hallway with rooms equally balanced on each side.(14) This plan allows rooms to be sealed off from the others for privacy, entertaining, etc. Such an attitude leads to separate formal living and dining rooms, with personal bedrooms on a second level. (In the example shown, note that although all the rooms are identical, the entries off the hallway are not — a clear public path exists to the left.)

A more informal life-style leads to an open plan such as a typical Usonian house designed by Frank Lloyd Wright.(15) In this plan, the kitchen is at the activity center of the house, controlling entry, bedroom extension, and living space. The dining alcove and living room are open and connected.

Initially, it appears obvious that present-day informal American life favors the open plan; nonetheless, many new suburban houses are built with central hallways and Georgian and Colonial facades. A society that is in change, often fragmented and diverse in its attitude, will cling to older established forms while still espousing change.

At one extreme, this results in a shelter / habitat that has a Colonial facade with a modified Georgian plan that preserves the central hallway but cuts up the remaining space into breakfast alcoves, powder rooms, TV rooms, etc. At the other extreme, the result is a shelter / habitat with an open plan, but which preserves a small formal front parlor (although it is labeled living room) containing a piano and reserved for important guests.(16) The ranch-style home often has two front doors — one, a formal entrance, leading into the living room, and the second and more important entrance leading from the parking area into the open-plan family spaces. This second entrance is used by family and friends alike for everyday visiting, parties, bringing in groceries, and garbage removal. The formal entrance is so symbolically important, however, that it is still called the front door.

These examples point out that the American concept of family is undergoing change, which, since 1970, has been accelerating — large numbers of youth living together but not in marriage, a decrease in the birthrate, the construction of commune shelter / habitats, and the difficulty of financing the ideal home are all related to this change in the concept of the family. While it is impossible to predict with accuracy how future cultural attitudes will view the basic family social unit, it is not difficult to see that the change is fundamental and that shelter / habitat form will likewise be fundamentally affected.

(15) The Jacobs House by Frank Lloyd Wright (see chapter 8 for a discussion of this Usonian house idea).

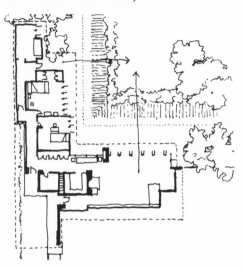

(16) A typical suburban house plan. Note that the kitchen — oriented to the family room, the outdoor patio, and the garage entry — is the center of family activity, but that a formal front door remains.

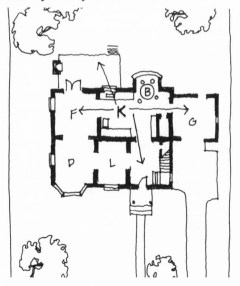

Cultural attitude towards family is of course closely connected with attitude towards land. We can also examine the two earlier examples of formal and informal plans from this aspect. The Georgian example sits above the land; it dominates and controls space, looking down on the surrounding ground. The open-plan example extends out and is part of the land. These two opposing cultural attitudes — being independent and free from the land and being integrated and attached to the land — have been with us since early history. The ancient Greeks, struggling with poor soil, soon placed their houses on craggy rock outcroppings above their valley farms. Man was viewed as being independent, conquering nature, and having visions toward other islands with more fertile soil. The house of the gods was made timeless as a stone temple — raised on a platform, serene, and eminently rational.

(17) Rapoport, House Form and Culture, *p. 133.*

A more recent example of independence from the land can be seen in a study of the cultural attitudes of the Viennese, where 61 percent of the people wanted apartments in the center of town.(17) Carried to its extreme, this attitude leads to the high-rise apartment or the stacked archetype in which there is no contact with the land. This architectural model has been favored in situations where urban amenities are highly valued (such as living in the center of Rome or Paris) or when economic considerations make land costly and the units are stacked to save ground area.

(18) Pruitt-Igoe is a favorite example of sociologists who claim that architects don't properly understand the real clients' needs. (See chapter 3, note 5, for a rebuttal.)

However, we have to remember that in the more than twenty years between when Pruitt-Igoe was constructed and the time in which it was altered, we have tended to forget how wretched the rat-infested slum was that it replaced.

That this second reason can be dangerous can be seen by considering the infamous 1950s public-housing project, Pruitt-Igoe in St. Louis, where newly arrived blacks from the lower Mississippi Valley were housed in large new high-rise blocks. In this instance, the blacks, who had always lived at ground level tending small gardens, raising chickens, and using outdoor privies, were given no advance social preparation for living in an urban high-rise apartment complex. An instant slum was created: plumbing was ripped out of the toilet rooms, and violent crime existed in the stairwells. A partial solution employed was to dynamite some of the buildings and thus reduce the density.(18)

The American attitude towards land has always been ambivalent. On the one hand, the culture has always demanded that the land be conquered, carved up, subdued, mastered, and owned. Land has been treated as a natural resource to be used.(19) Horace Greeley's famous advice, "Go west, young man, and grow up with the country," is indicative. If opportunity no longer existed in New York, then the young should go west — where land was plentiful, and fame and fortune awaited those who could tame it. On the other hand, Americans have always had a deep sympathy with the land, feeling a strong identification with the soil. This feeling can be traced from early English settlers through the transcendentalists and Thoreau's Walden Pond,(20) to today's Kansas wheat farmer who does not live in town, but rather prefers a solitary existence surrounded by his fields.

A survey conducted in a subdivision showed that when asked, "What would you most desire to improve your environment?" more than 90 percent of those questioned replied, "Have more land."(21) Yet free, developable land can no longer be obtained merely by going west. Just as the new changes in cultural attitude relating to *family* are affecting shelter / habitat, so too its form is being affected by land scarcity. And again, while prediction of future cultural attitude towards land is impossible, we do know that the architectural change will have to be profound and far-reaching. In many areas of the U.S. where land is expensive, materials are scarce, and density is high, shared-wall and stacked archetypes are already replacing the older ideal freestanding archetypes.

Society's conception of its *government* and the political structure that supports it is a third example of a powerful cultural attitude that affects shelter / habitat form. In totalitarian states, there is usually a rigid hierarchy of housing — workers and slaves are housed in repetitive and identical shared-wall archetypes, such as row-house blocks. Those higher on the hierarchal scale live either in larger shared-wall units or in more individually designed villas. Feudal society, which depended upon the local baron for protection, clustered housing around the castle. The same type of hierarchal pattern can be found in early Virginia plantations, where the master lived in a grand

(19) As long as the land is vast and untamed, this is a reasonable human assumption. However, as E. F. Schumacher has pointed out in his important book Small is Beautiful, *natural resources, once used, are no longer natural resources; i.e., the land is limited, and once destroyed, it cannot be replaced.*

(20) The importance of the transcendentalist movement will be more carefully explored in the next chapter and in the later chapter on the work of Frank Lloyd Wright.

(21) Johnson Village, Charlottesville, Virginia, on file at city assessor's office (1974). See chapter 2, note 23, for a plan of this subdivision.

(22) Two examples of hierarchal patterns: A Cameroon village gathered around the headman's house and walled in for protection and George Washington's orderly plantation at Mount Vernon.

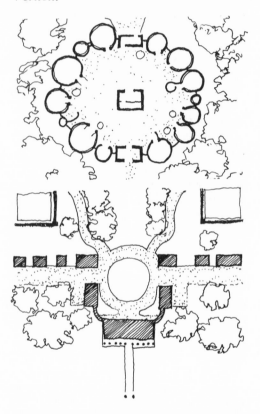

house supported by the surrounding slave quarters, barns, stables, and working sheds.(22)

Societies that view themselves as more open and egalitarian stress individuality and choice. Of course, housing choices are also dependent upon land availability, plenty of materials for construction, and an equally "open" market. Some new fashionable housing communities actually are surrounded by fences with armed guards at the entries — many of the affluent residents are afraid for their possessions.

Another example of concentrated wealth can be seen in the courtyard archetype found in many Mediterranean countries. Behind a blank wall, the courtyard unit may be small, or large, ranging from one-room dwellings to palaces. Present-day Marrakesh is typical. Social life is carried on in narrow, twisting streets and in the market; family life is hidden behind stuccoed brick walls; and one must know the housing district in order to know how to find a friend's house.(23)

There are as many cultural attitudes toward housing as one wishes to list. To attitudes related to *family*, *land*, and *government*, we could add those concerning *religion*, *recreation*, *education*, etc. More useful, perhaps, is to take one house example and investigate it in depth to examine how cultural attitude has affected its form.

(23) This same concept can be found today in Kyoto, Japan. The Imperial city was founded with housing districts laid out in large gridded blocks. As houses were built within each gridded district, they were numbered as they were constructed. Thus, when one visits in the district, he must now stop and ask where the family lives, since house numbers are not consecutive.

Let us look at a typical Victorian house found in a small Illinois town and built in 1885.(24) The plan perfectly demonstrates the American cultural ideal of both dominating the land and being closely related and a part of it. Consider the following:

1. The house sits in the middle of a large one-acre plot. Although it is located in a small town, it still commands its position within space.

2. There is a formal and impressive front entry, and the parlor and living room face the front side; the kitchen and barns are at the rear.

3. The plan is carefully linked functionally with the land. The parlor views the front; the living and dining rooms face the semiprivate side yard; the dining room extends out into the yard via a terrace and a rose garden off of the terrace; the kitchen has its own service yard, with barns and a vegetable garden. In short, the land is developed in integration with the house spatially.

4. The interior of the house reflects the same duality. There is a formal hall with public spaces on one side and service and family spaces on the other, yet there is nothing rigid in the plan. With plenty of space — bedrooms and maids' rooms being above — it is possible to seal off the parlor and living room in winter while still leading a good life within the family areas.

5. Finally, the well-worked-out transitions reflect a satisfactory acceptance of public-to-private spatial hierarchy. Note that from the street one crosses through a public planting strip, then a public sidewalk, through a gate (with an open fence), to the family sidewalk that rises slightly before an entry porch, to a front door, to a hallway that still modestly screens off the family living space. Throughout this sequence, there are clear architectural clues to tell the visitor that the street, the land, and the house are comfortably integrated within a larger concept.

(24) *A plan (a) and a sketch (b) of a Victorian house built in Illinois in 1885 demonstrates the integration of the house with its outside landscape, while the house still makes a mark upon the land.*

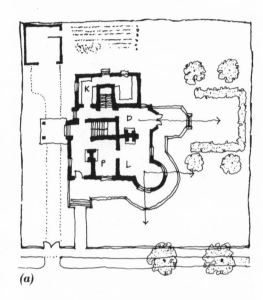

(a)

(b)

(25) It may be argued, of course, that insofar as stylistic differences are related to significant changes in cultural attitude, there is an important reason even at the conceptual level for studying style.

Such an argument refers to historical cultural style, which is a broader definition than I have intended here. My reference is instead to individual artistic style, which changes frequently — often within an artist's lifetime. In the chapters on Wright and Le Corbusier, I hope to illustrate that they were great artists both at the conceptual level (and thus within the cultural style of their time and place) and at the individual-artistic-style level.

To carry this point further: There is a group of architects who are frequently called the New York Five. In their book Five Architects, *which deals with the subject of the individual house, one of them, Peter Eisenman, discusses at considerable length artistic concerns of cubist space, formal proportions, implied or missing columns, and ambiguity.*

While Eisenman argues these concerns well, they are, in the main, issues of sculpture rather than of architecture. Neocubist ideas of sculptural form certainly have architectural implications, but architecture also involves human participation within the spatial creation: i.e., families who want and need a place to gather together as a family.

The resolution of these cultural ideas within the final architectural form (see sketch 24b) tells us a great deal about the family. The use of brick, the substantial size of the house, the mark upon the land, and the carefully built fence tell us that this family feels secure within society and has worked out a happy relationship with its land. The house reflects pride but not arrogance, and it is a house most Americans could still live in with a comfortable feeling about their place in society.

Throughout the preceding discussion of shelter / habitat, no specific mention has been made of materials, structure, and construction technology. While these factors certainly influence the final form, they are modifying rather than primary in conceptual terms. That is, while they help us to express our conceptual idea in a built form, they occur, as a rule, after the need and the cultural attitude, and are thus modifying.

By the same token, no reference has been made to style. Conceptual idea precedes style, and although stylistic differences between, for instance, the house designs of Frank Lloyd Wright and of Le Corbusier are indeed significant, they are not germane to this particular discussion. Fashions and styles change with surprising frequency, but the basic human needs for shelter and the cultural attitudes towards habitat evolve more slowly and at a deeper and more profound level.(25) This is why quick stylistic changes in suburbia will not solve housing needs. Paste-on Colonial, Georgian, Spanish Mission, and Cape Cod facades do not deal with the issues.

If we accept the notion that present-day American society is in the midst of rethinking and restating, at a conceptual level, its attitudes about shelter / habitat, then we are left with a perplexing question. How may we identify this change and properly express it in our house designs?

The answer must lie in further developing our shared, intuitive architectural language. By asking again, "What does the building want to be?" — or, as stated earlier, "What idea about living place do we want this specific shelter / habitat to express?" — by restating the problem at a conceptual level, we can then strip away our surface preconceptions, relying on our intuition, honed and sharpened through our shared architectural experience.(26)

(26) This refers back to the argument presented more fully at the end of chapter 4.

Let us apply this process to a common shelter / habitat problem currently prevalent throughout the U.S. — the design of a vacation house. Let us assume that a family of two adults and two children owns twenty acres of land in the mountains and desires "a cabin to get away from it all." How should we proceed?

First, we should interview the family and visit the site with them — hiking with them in the mountains and living with them (if necessary) — and then we should restate the problem so that it answers the question, "What do *they* mean by a cabin to get away from it all?" What we shall likely discover is that it is *not* a vacation house (with 3 bedrooms, 1½ baths, living room, family room, etc.) that they want, and need, but rather a "retreat place."

Philosophically, what they may desire is a place to rest, relax, and have dreams again; to rediscover the American hope of communion with the land; or perhaps, simply a quiet place from which one backpacks into even more rugged wilderness to sit beneath a favorite oak. Functionally, they may need a place to cook, but perhaps not formally, as in a kitchen; to entertain two friends with wine in the still evening (to entertain fifty friends with a party, but without having to "clean up"); to sleep, although perhaps on a cot?; to bathe, although maybe in a stream?; a place to drive to, but maybe to park 100 feet away, with the car hidden in hemlocks and brilliant poplars? A retreat place implies a small, peaceful activity, not a house loudly proclaiming "I am," but rather a simple form stating "Here I am," in respectful silence.

(27) A shelter place: One roof form covers terraces of activity.

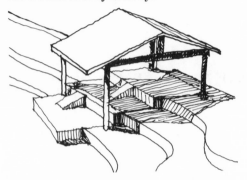

(28) A pavilion place: A single form opens up to the land.

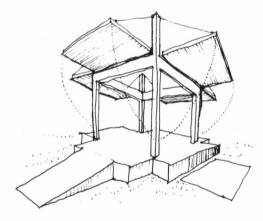

(29) A hearth place: The act of gathering together becomes the generator of the form.

The careful consideration of these and other such issues can result in an intuitive understanding possessed by the sensitive and trained architect of what makes this specific site special for this family's need for retreat. The architect must then take this intuitive understanding, combine it with rational analysis, and *think a concept*: He must shape spatial form so as to create a place where occasion may occur and man may remember; he must create architecture, and he must not be afraid, at a conceptual level, to dream.

Following are three conceptual dreams of retreat places:

1. A shelter. One roof form over stepped terraces — the roof establishing place, with each terrace opening out into the land. A simple mark.(27)

2. A pavilion. Walls fold up to make an open place, and like Whitman, we test our philosophy under sky, sun, and moon. Ultimate respect.(28)

3. A hearth. Fire is the core towards which we turn for warmth. Platforms off from the chimney mass create zones of activity. The form itself sits minimally upon the land. The hearth becomes winter place; the garden, summer place.(29)

From such dreams, architecture may evolve. It is an awesome task, however, for when we ask, What does it mean to make this mark upon the land? we must be prepared to discover that a tent alone may suffice. Or the land itself, left alone.

> Till rising and gliding out I wandered off by myself,
> In the mystical moist night air, and from time to time,
> Look'd up in perfect silence at the stars.(30)

(30) *Walt Whitman, "When I Heard The Learn'd Astronomer," from* Leaves of Grass *(New York: Avenel Books, Crown Publishers, 1961), p. 86.*

The architectural answer to a retreat place lies in understanding how to look up in perfect silence at the stars.

This chapter has dealt with the perplexing conceptual issue of the single shelter / habitat. But what happens when these individual units are combined into a group form? When the family becomes part of a larger social complex, the neighborhood? When houses become *housing?* The next chapter will deal with these equally difficult conceptual issues.

VII THE SHELTER / HABITAT II: GROUP FORM

In the last chapter, mention was made of four archetypes or models that frequently reappear in history when functional needs and cultural attitudes are appropriately fused in the concept of shelter / habitat: the stacked unit, the shared-wall unit, the courtyard unit, and the freestanding unit. This chapter will take these single-family models and examine what happens when they are multiplied and joined into a larger group form.

Doing so will show that concepts for *house* cannot be separated from concepts for *housing*. The attitudes of each single family on how it should live are an integral part of how a society or a group of families lives. Therefore, the examination of each group form will concentrate on a study of those ideas that suggest guidelines for further development — ideas that help us discover possible better ways to live together.

In this light, the last archetype to be investigated in this chapter, the freestanding-unit group form, will be given special attention. The common manifestation of this group form is suburbia, and no present architectural issue is of more significance than the questionable future of these neighborhood environments, in which some 70 percent of Americans now reside.

The apartment is the best known example of the individual *stacked-unit* archetype, and the apartment tower is its most common group form. The obvious advantage of the apartment tower as a group form is that it provides a large number of housing units with minimum ground coverage. In theory, this allows for higher family densities where land is scarce and for more open space. As the towers rise, each apartment can receive light, air and a view. In addition, town planners can argue that the tower is cheaper to build, because circulation networks and service systems are all consolidated and shortened in length.

Where green space is actually preserved and an open vista is left, the result can be a magnificent urban environment, as along the east side of Central Park in New York City(1) or beside Lake Michigan in

(1) These luxurious apartments facing Central Park are among the most expensive in New York City. As condominium units they frequently sell for $500,000 or more.

(2) Inhabitants of the Lake Shore Drive Apartments by Mies van der Rohe (also shown in chapter 3, note 2) argue that the views back toward the city of Chicago at night are as dramatic as the views of the lake during the day.

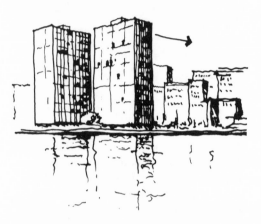

(3) In the Lake Shore Drive Apartments, Mies designed all the outside drapery fabrics so that every unit would appear the same, although the occupants could use their own materials and colors on the drapery linings facing the inside.

(4) The Unité at Marseilles — one of the more important architectural concepts of the twentieth century — is fully discussed in chapter 8 as an evolution of Le Corbusier's ideas on housing and city form.

Chicago.(2) The disadvantage of the apartment tower as a group form is that it seldom is built with open space around it. The sketch of the Central Park towers is a good case in point. Those apartments facing the park have light, air, and a view, but what of the apartments on the sides of the towers, which face each other? Or those in the buildings that lie behind the towers?

Another disadvantage of the tower group form is that it is not easy to personalize the individual space, i.e., once the shelter / habitat unit is divorced from the land and stacked in repetitive and identical building shells, it becomes difficult for the inhabitant to paint his window a different color, to grow his own vegetable garden, or to hang his own particular draperies.(3)

The architect Le Corbusier dealt with this issue by suggesting that community spaces be placed within the apartment block itself — the roof devoted to gardens, a swimming pool, and recreational space; the building raised off the ground so that open space could flow through; and a mid-floor level devoted to a street-in-the-air. In so doing, Corbusier hoped to create a living environment for a total community.(4)

Corbusier's ideas have been developed by other planners and architects. In particular, the street-in-the-air concept has been used as at Park Hill (1961) in Sheffield, England, where an attempt has been made to provide house-to-house neighborhood interaction by providing an entrance into every apartment from a raised pedestrian walkway. These walkways, referred to as streets-in-the-air, are also used for small-milk-truck deliveries. They are not, however, the organizer of the neighborhood community life, as was intended.(5) For, once the shops, ground-level access, play space, and meeting areas (such as park benches) have been removed from the pedestrian street, it becomes, apparently, a corridor, and not a meeting place.

This same problem exists at the later Robin Hood Gardens development (1972) in London by Peter and Alison Smithson. In the housing here (as at Park Hill) no living activity faces into the raised walkway, and without any private place on the street-in-the-air itself, there exists no reason for the family to *want* to be there.(6)

Interestingly, there is an earlier project, Spangen Housing (1922) in Rotterdam by Van der Brock and Brinckman, that serves as a clear model for the street-in-the-air concept. At Spangen, the living spaces face into the street. In addition, each unit has a private sitting area — which overlooks an interior green space below on the street itself. Potted plants, furniture, and street life make the street-in-the-air a successful place for neighborhood interaction(7).

(5) Due to a sharp rise in the adjacent land form, each "street" at Park Hill eventually reaches a ground access; thus, small trucks may use the streets for deliveries.

(6) A typical deck-level plan for Robin Hood Gardens illustrates that the "street" has no individualized outside social areas (living rooms are actually on levels below and above each street). An excellent review of Robin Hood Gardens, as well as a perceptive discussion of streets-in-the-air, can be found in Anthony Pangaro, "Beyond Golden Lane, Robin Hood Gardens," Architecture Plus, June 1973, p. 36.

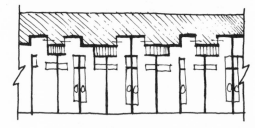

(7) The Spangen Housing has both a private family area on the street and a bedroom balcony above the street and overlooking it. The entire environment appears as a series of row houses on a street and not as a series of stacked apartments.

(a)

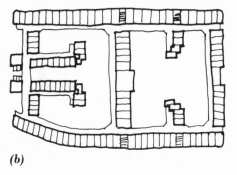

(b)

(8) See also the discussion at the end of
chapter 5 on the I. M. Pei design for
Staten Island housing.

(9) The original form at Taos also
possessed defensive capability in that lad-
ders could be drawn up at night to protect
the upper dwellings from sneak attack.

(10) The Foundling Estate in
Bloomsbury steps its apartment units
back, so that each family has an attached
prefabricated greenhouse module. While
each unit looks down into the central area
(see section a), the circulation towers lead
directly to street level, bypassing the
shops. Despite problems, the Foundling
Estate (plan b) remains one of the rare attempts to provide a more varied and personal environment within the city.

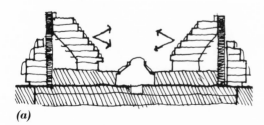

(a)

Whatever the problems of Park Hill and Robin Hood Gardens, they
are nonetheless recent and important attempts to create more
humane environments within a high-density group form by utilizing
the street-in-the-air concept.(8)

Another interesting idea that frequently is suggested as a means for
improving the group form of stacked apartments is that of building
stepped-units, each with an outside private area. The stepped-unit concept is certainly as old as the hanging gardens of Babylon, but
perhaps the finest existing example is at Taos, New Mexico, where the
roofs of lower Pueblo Indian dwellings form a platform for a smaller
number of dwellings above.(9) Each higher level is slightly smaller,
and the result produces not only terraces off of each unit but also a
group form that resembles a stepped mountain — a powerful symbol
for the Indians of their former cliff-dwellings in the mountains.

A recent attempt to make a stepped-unit neighborhood is the Foundling Estate (1960) in Bloomsbury, London. This project, much
maligned by critics, was nonetheless a serious effort to create a complete and cohesive neighborhood form.(10) The most frequent
criticisms of Bloomsbury are, first, that the vertical circulation occurs on the dark underside of the building and is divorced from the
shopping area in the middle (meaning that residents come and go
without passing through the commercial center) and, second, that the
plan is linear and does not recognize the block grid of the city.

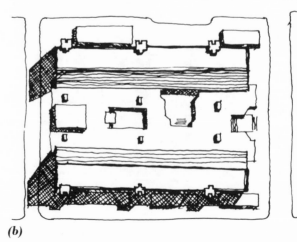

(b)

These criticisms lead one to speculate about what would have happened had the stepped-unit form been reversed and the plan made square and inward-oriented rather than linear. The interior courtyard that would then be formed could be roofed over with a skylight, and shops, pedestrian circulation, and public facilities could be concentrated in an active central core. The roofs could be linked with pedestrian bridges and an open green park provided.(11)

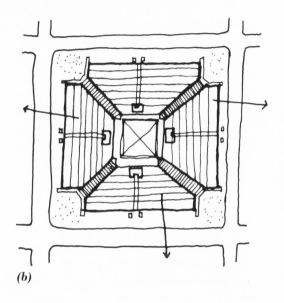

(b)

(11) This stepped-unit model (section a and plan b) would concentrate human activity within the center of the form. While no housing group-form has been built to this concept, John Portman's San Francisco Hyatt Regency Hotel, with its seventeen-storied central atrium, demonstrates the potential of the idea.

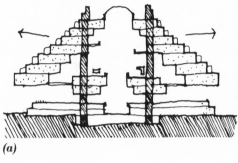

(a)

(12) Two books that deal with issues of housing form are: Martin Pawley, Architecture vs. Housing (London: Praeger Paperbacks, 1971); Charles Abrams, Housing in the Modern World (London: Faber and Faber, 1966).

All of these ideas — the pedestrian street-in-the-air, the stepped-unit, the roof garden, the integration of housing with shopping — suggest that the group-form potential of the stacked-unit archetype has been but barely explored as a viable means of living within the city.(12)

The second general shelter / habitat model — the shared-wall unit — has as its common group-form the row-house neighborhood. So popular did this group form become that during the Industrial Revolution, large housing districts — actually cities in themselves — were added to existing European cities.(13) Since it is possible with shared-wall units (as opposed to individual units) to obtain a higher density of dwellings per city block, developers naturally favor this group form. In addition, the long and narrow lot maximizes privacy and provides through-ventilation.

(13) An aerial view of Fulham, a district of London, illustrates the vast extent of its rapidly built row-house developments.

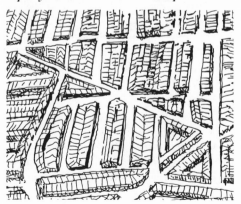

(14)   The sketch shows a typical city block with twelve single-family detached houses on twelve equal plots.

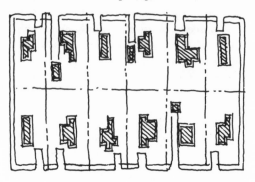

(15)   This sketch shows the same city block as in note 14, but with twelve single-family houses grouped into two shared-wall forms. The open space "saved" would allow for an 80 foot by 120 foot common park or play area.

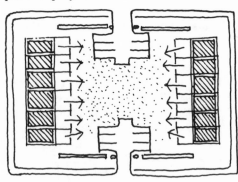

(16)   The sketch demonstrates the more typical developer response when using row houses. The density has been increased from twelve units to twenty-two, in two shared-wall forms.

And just as long as the typical block group-form does not exceed the normal densities of individual detached houses, there is a clear spatial advantage to the shared-wall model. For example, a typical city block of 200 feet by 240 feet might be divided into twelve lots, 40 feet by 100 feet, each containing a detached dwelling.(14) A shared-wall, or row-house, arrangement, using the same density of twelve units, could easily provide individual yards, while still saving an 80 foot by 120 foot parcel of land for use as a community play space or park. The advantage of this layout is obvious: It provides a variety of space and a hierarchy of neighborhood use. Interaction among the twelve families is encouraged, and possible walkway linkages to adjacent city blocks are provided.(15) Unfortunately, such potential advantages of the shared-wall group form are rarely realized. More frequently, land speculators insist on filling in the open spaces of the typical freestanding individual group form, thus using the shared-wall units as a means of increasing profits through raising family density (from twelve units to twenty-two units in the example shown).(16)

Largely for this reason, the shared-wall unit has never been popular in the United States. The great mass of Americans associate the row house with high densities and older, unfashionable areas of the inner city where immigrants are held in European enclaves until they can become Americanized and can move out into their own individual suburban homes. Thus, today's shared-wall units are never referred to as row houses but are instead called garden apartments and town houses, and they are always grouped into villages, glens, forests, etc.

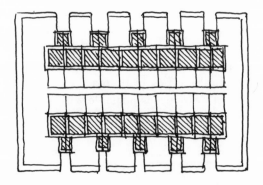

The potential of the shared-wall group form remains, however. At Chatham Village (1931) in Pittsburgh,(17) the row houses were grouped in such a way as to provide a continuous interior greenway, with changing perspective and scale. By placing the vehicular circulation around the periphery, the architect-planners Wright and Stein were able to create a car-free environment and one that has never had a vacancy since the housing association was first formed.

(17) Chatham Village, at Pittsburgh, was designed and developed by Henry Wright and Clarence Stein. Cars have been grouped into garages and held along the periphery service road. Chatham is built on a narrow land spur with steep and sharp drops on three sides. The interior greenway is thus higher than the service roadway, and openings in the housing forms provide frequent distant views over and above the car level.

(18) A partial closing of the street creates a public park or place at Bedford-Stuyvesant in Brooklyn. (See also chapter 5, note 32.)

And there are other encouraging signs. The revival of row-house areas in Alexandria, Virginia, and Georgetown in Washington, D.C., are examples of a new awareness of shared-wall potential. Equally encouraging are the scattered attempts by some cities to reclaim neighborhoods in older urban areas through closing streets and forming neighborhood block associations. A prime example of this attempt is the Bedford-Stuyvesant project, mentioned above in the discussion on gathering places.(18) The possibility of revitalizing large areas through a new and more careful look at shared-wall group forms is one of the more exciting architectural challenges within our existing cities.

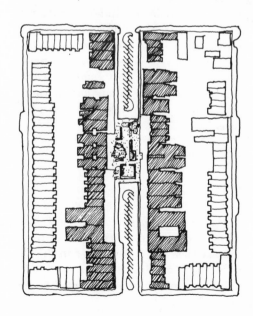

The third general shelter / habitat form, the courtyard unit, has never been utilized on a large scale as a possible group form in the United States. The public's image of such a form has always been that of a Casbah, where Mediterranean Moslem mysteries occur down dark, dim alleys, behind blank walls. Marrakesh, Morocco,(19) well exemplifies this view.

Such a form does suggest districts rather than gridblocks and an organization more closed and tightly knit than the open vistas preferred by a car-oriented society.(20) Nonetheless, the courtyard unit as an archetype has much greater potential. A fascinating and little-known German book, *A Wanderer in the City*, published in 1957, explores some of these possibilities.(21)

Through the use of *walls* as a form determinant, it is possible to create plots of varying sizes and shapes. This allows the plots to fit the slope and the unusual characteristics of the site. In addition, the walls delineate walkways and public places, much as the walls of the medieval city outlined city space as separate from open space.

(20) This has been shown to be true through eight years of testing with beginning architecture students at the University of Virginia. In a simulated walk, via slides, through the Alfama districts of Lisbon, more than 50 percent of the students each year have felt that the tightly knit area of shared-wall row houses and courtyard units was "dingy and too narrow," and "without sufficient open play space."

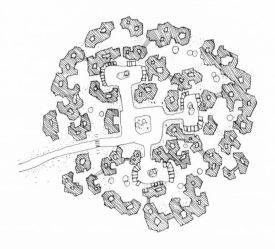

(21) This courtyard-neighborhood concept, adapted from Walter Schwagenscheidt, A Wanderer in the City (Berlin: Hans Bruntsch and Co., 1957), p. 117, has never been attempted in the United States.

Within each courtyard, the shelter / habitat unit may be built and may grow as needed. Whether Americans will ever realize the potential of the courtyard-unit group form is, however, debatable. For a cultural insistence on building houses that dominate the land directly contradicts the use of walls that blend and tie hidden units together into a single, larger neighborhood form.(22)

This brings us to consideration of the fourth group form, the freestanding unit — and in particular the neighborhood environments we know as suburbia. Passing reference has been made in this chapter and the preceding one to the uniquely American housing dream that includes the strange dichotomy that demands that the land be cleared, conquered, and dominated by a freestanding single-family house, while at the same time demanding that the land be nourished and lived upon within natural surroundings. This conflict between conquering the land and living with it is basic to the dream. How did this come to be? For the most part, this country's early settlers were fleeing from crowded European conditions. Entering a wild, heavily forested, and often harsh environment, they were forced to clear land, plant meager crops, fish, and hunt game in order to survive. And yet, paradoxically, there was always plenty of land, and plenty of fish and game. The result was a vision, powerful in the minds of these settlers (who were often persecuted even after arrival in the new country), of a house sitting within a hundred acres, possessed by the family, free and *protected by ownership*. The vision proclaimed that as time passed, the family would grow in importance until the modest farmhouse was replaced by an imposing mansion.(23)

It was not until the transcendentalist movement, however, that this vision was brought to philosophic fruition. The fact that the American transcendentalists skillfully brought together and joined the deep concerns and aspirations of an emerging country with a dominant transcendentalist European philosophy meant that their impact on culture, art, and architecture was profound and long-lasting. Indeed, the American transcendentalist dream of a free man possessing his land and living in harmony with nature still exists today and is the idea of the idea — the powerful reason for the form of suburbia.

(22) At the gardens of El Pedregal in Mexico City, the architect Luis Barragan has demonstrated how walls, color, and water can create a poetic vision of a unified architecture.

(23) The dream begins with cutting out of the wilderness a sufficient plot to build a rough-hewn cabin.

Transcendentalism (in the American sense we are interested in) was the early-nineteenth-century religious, ethical, and philosophical movement centered around the teachings of Ralph Waldo Emerson. Transcendentalists believed that the Divine exists within each man. And while man may not directly experience God face-to-face, he may nonetheless, intuitively consider Him, and in this *inner* manner, may communicate. If we but open our thoughts to God, He will intuitively lead us to the right action. These beliefs were outgrowths from the ideas of the German philosophers Hegel and Kant, who argued that transcendental thought cannot be derived from experience, but exists a priori, or before experience. Our intuitive thought thus "transcends" our conscious experience. Emerson's philosophy was more loosely formed than its German counterpart, but the particular emphases of the American movement are important in understanding how it led to a distinctly American housing dream. Some of the movement's beliefs were:

1. Since God exists within each man, each man communicates directly with God.

2. Since God exists within all of nature, man must be respectful of nature.

3. Each man must intuitively find his *own* way through action. Discovery by oneself keeps us free.

4. Through education, continual searching, individuality, and self-betterment, we shall attain a "true" aristocracy, a democratic aristocracy.

These beliefs were particularly realizable in a country that was rapidly expanding and that had plenty of land. With the Homestead Act (1862) the federal government openly encouraged development by giving a quarter section (160 acres) of western public land to any settler and his family who would occupy the land and build a farmhouse.

Thoreau's *Walden* embodies all of these transcendental values — a fierce love of freedom, individuality, a trust in nature and intuitive values, a deep and serious love of the land itself, and a hearty distrust of institutions, laws, taxes, and organized society.

But it is in the emotive poems of Walt Whitman that we best find many transcendental values exalted.

I celebrate myself, and sing myself,
And what I assume, you shall assume,
For every atom belonging to me as good belongs to you.

You are also asking me questions and I hear you,
I answer that I cannot answer, you must find out for yourself.

Now I re-examine philosophies and religions,
They may prove well in lecture-rooms, yet not prove at all under
    the spacious clouds and along the landscape and flowing cur-
    rents.

Here is realization,
Here is a man tallied — he realizes here what he has in him,
The past, the future, majesty, love — if they are vacant of you, you
    are vacant of them.(24)

In the preceding chapter, a typical Illinois Victorian single-family house was discussed as an example of the impact of American transcendentalist values on architectural form (see chapter 6, note 24). When such houses are grouped together, the resultant form can often be strikingly beautiful — as indeed many small towns in Illinois still are.(25) Unfortunately, the beauty of such small towns is all too frequently lost when the houses are crammed together and mixed with industry and the higher traffic levels of the city.

(24) Walt Whitman, "Song of Myself" (pp. 1, 40), and "Song of the Open Road" (pp. 66 – 67) from Leaves of Grass (New York: Avenel Books, Crown Publishers, 1961).

(25) *A typical plains town in Illinois, circa 1900, has a careful order in its overlaying grid street-pattern with one main street. The commercial area often changes to a residential scale abruptly — stores close to the street giving way to houses set well back from it, with trees in front. The overall impression is one of a small, tight core, surrounded by open land and dotted with grass, trees, and houses of different sizes.*

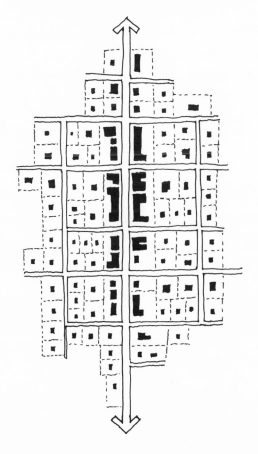

(26) *The layout of Parkview Place, St. Louis, shows 253 houses within a curved-street neighborhood. The private-street district is surrounded by a regular gridiron city pattern. Note that the area is enclosed within continuous fences and walls with gates. Only the gates to the east are kept open; thus, through traffic is prevented from going through the neighborhood.*

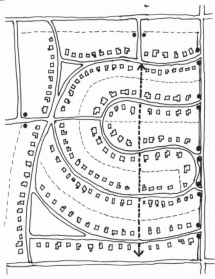

Parkview Place also contains two small triangular parks and a pedestrian crosswalk leading from a commercial street on the north to Washington University on the south.

(27) In later developments, the security offered by the gates also included protection from other social classes, although this does not appear to have been an intent of Pitzman's original idea.

(28) The figure shows Howard's diagram for a garden city. Note that a railroad line encircles the town and helps restrict

An early American reaction to the industry and crowded noise of the expanding city was the private-street neighborhood: a planned area, screened off from the surrounding city by gates, in which the streets were privately owned and maintained. The city of St. Louis has more than fifty such private-street areas, all of them laid out and planned by one surveyor, Major Julius Pitzman. Beginning with a single private street in 1867, Pitzman's work culminated with Parkview Place, designed in 1903.(26) This idea — a neighborhood enclave, secure from city noise behind gates, with tree-lined private streets, open green space, and single-family houses — was soon adapted for use throughout other American cities.(27)

Other reactions to crowded city conditions were also occurring, and perhaps the most influential of these was the 1898 book *Tomorrow: A Peaceful Path to Real Reform*, by the Englishman Ebenezer Howard.(28) Howard's principal contention was that "Garden Cities" of finite size (32,000 inhabitants) should surround larger metropolitan areas to which they would be connected by railway. Each garden city was to have its own industries and a rich mix of housing densities, parks, and open farm land.

Howard's ideas were immediately seized upon, and soon large housing estates — garden suburbs — surrounded metropolitan areas. In the United States, regrettably, these suburbs contained no industry,

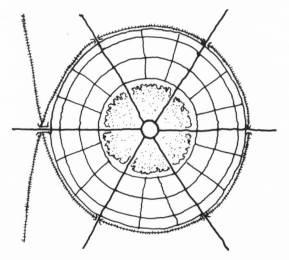

and rather than being set off from the city, they were simply added to it. This fact — coupled, first, with the amazing growth of the car industry, and second, with the development of a subsidized roadway network dependent upon automobile use — has hastened the building of suburbia.

Frequently referred to as bedroom or dormitory communities (since the absence of industry and of most commercial establishments means that one must leave the neighborhood for work and shopping) suburbia nonetheless reflect a life-style that most closely resembles the transcendental housing dream.(29) And, there have been many continuing efforts to improve both the physical form and the architectural context of suburbia. Mention has been made earlier of the architect-planners Henry Wright and Clarence Stein, who at Chatham Village in Pittsburgh and at Radburn, N.J., did much to suggest means of rational form improvement. Wright and Stein's ideas were natural extensions of planning concepts from both Pitzman's private street and Howard's Garden City.

Crucial to all of their planning was the separation of the car from the pedestrian, so that community space and schools could be reached and enjoyed from each household unit.(30) Their concern that the grouping of houses should produce more than simply a collection of boxes (i.e., that the whole should be greater than the sum of the parts) is rarely shown in the typical suburban neighborhood, where the streets wander across the land and the houses are planned in a pattern that maximizes the density allowed by zoning requirements.

population to 32,000 persons. Two cities, Letchworth and Welwyn, were both built following Howard's guidelines — Ebenezer Howard, Tomorrow: A Peaceful Path to Social Reform *(London: Faber and Faber, 1898).*

(29) An excellent description of what happens when a small town becomes engulfed in suburbia may be found in Suzannah Lessard, "Reflections — The Suburban Landscape: Oyster Bay, Long Island," The New Yorker, *October 11, 1976, page 44.*

(30) The superblock is achieved by grouping several normal blocks together and removing the cross streets. Through the use of the cul-de-sac, an interior greenway is created with a rich variety of safe outdoor places suitable for walking, for play, and for community social planning.

(31) This partial plan of Terra Granada at Walnut Creek, California, demonstrates basic PUD goals — the housing units are clustered into tight cul-de-sacs with three-story apartments inside the cul-de-sac and two-story town-house apartment units around the outer edge. Greenways then lead to the golf course.

Although there is a spatial openness in the plan, Terra Granada contains some six-thousand condominium apartments at a density of twenty-four units per acre.

(32) The next chapter will deal directly with the evolution of Frank Lloyd Wright's Prairie house — the apogee of the transcendental housing dream.

A recent innovation, the Planned Unit Development (PUD as it is called within the development profession), has taken Wright and Stein's idea of the superblock and institutionalized it as planning law. Simply stated, a PUD is a large assemblage of land, usually 100 acres or more, in which single-family houses are mixed with higher density apartments and are clustered around cul-de-sacs. Through such clustering, the PUD proposes to leave open land for recreation and walking.(31)

Finally, although the PUD does leave open land, it invariably also proposes a much higher housing density than that allowable under the existing zoning law, the argument for this being that the higher density will produce a land-tax benefit to the city.

Unfortunately, too often the open space provided is only leftover land, not meaningful space. One must always ask, Does the open space lead to a school or a playground? To shopping or to community activity? Or is it merely undevelopable marsh or rocky soil on which a profit could not be realized in any plan?

Furthermore, higher density of development, with its higher land taxes, does not automatically mean financial benefit to a city. When several thousand persons are added to a city, one has to ask, What happens to the school sytem? The regional traffic pattern? The sewer and water networks?

The PUD is certainly a start towards rethinking the American suburban housing problem, but it is not enough. Certainly we must accept the evidence that something has gone wrong. Indeed, as developers have milked ever more profit out of smaller and smaller pieces of land (helped by architects and civil engineers), the transcendental spirit behind suburbia has continually eroded. What was once a noble ideal of man living gently in relation to his land(32) has degenerated into concerns about good schools, having a yard, and owning one's own home. The result is often tasteless — endless single-family houses, each planted exactly in the middle of one-fourth acre plots. Furthermore, the much-touted suburban alternate to the single-family house — the garden town-house — is, almost without exception, mean in concept, destructive of the land, and cheap in execution.

At some point in our history, we have apparently forgotten that our desire for a freestanding single-family house on our own plot of land is a philosophical dream — a dream that can never be fulfilled as long as the physical reality consists of:

1. The construction of detached houses on such small plots that one looks directly from his bathroom into a neighbor's bathroom, ten feet away

2. The destruction of land, the building of ever-wider new roads, the spreading out of suburbia — all having made us so dependent on the car that we have forgotten that the car was meant to free us (Rather than designing houses for two-child families, we now design them for two-car families!)

3. The cutting down of all trees, the leveling of the ground, and the killing of all the wildlife, so that we have lost our contact with nature

4. The establishment of uniform requirements as to street widths, property setbacks, and open side-yards, which — combined with uniform aesthetic tastes — have killed our individual ability to discover the land, the air, the dependence that transcendental values once implied.

And yet, the transcendental dream persists in the minds of a vast public. As Amos Rapoport says: ". . . builders and developers never build houses, they build homes. The dream home is surrounded by trees and grass and must be owned. It is not a real need but a symbol. . . . The popular house is based on the ideal that one's home is indeed one's castle and on a belief in independence."(33)

If what Rapoport says is true, then perhaps what is wrong is, not the *idea of the dream*, but the way in which the dream has been manipulated and taken out of context.

(33) Amos Rapoport, House Form and Culture (Englewood Cliffs, N.J.: Prentice-Hall, 1969), p. 132. Another substantiation of the continuing belief in the housing dream can be found in a poll published by the magazine Professional Builder, December 1977. This poll of those interested in purchasing a house showed that 97.4 percent wanted a single-family house on a single lot. Attached homes attracted only 2.2 percent, and low-rise condominiums, only 0.4 percent!

(34) This may be stated another way — it is only through vigorous and effective social and political action that the dream can be changed in a meaningful way. The thought that by changing the entry facade, we allow housing choice is hypocritical. What is wrong with suburban housing form is that, rather than reflecting a philosophic dream, it reflects instead a profit-oriented speculative idea — that is, that land should be used for making money. As one begins to understand this underlying economic reality, the fallacy of architectural determinism, which states that social behavior can be controlled through architectural form, becomes evident. Society determines architectural form, not the other way around. And while rearranging entry facades may help one find his front door and rearranging kitchen corridors may help the housewife see who is at the front door, there is no evidence that real choice will have been obtained through looking different, or that the crime rate will be reduced through better surveillance. When there is choice, the society will move in the direction it sees fit.

The architect and planner's role must be to design an environment that recognizes past, present, and predicted future housing goals, and then restates these in a physical form that allows for this choice and the potential for change.

If America wished, it could return, at least partially, to the dream. But in order to do so, serious changes would first have to occur in our societal goals, planning, and political laws. For example, families within our society would need to have fewer children, with correspondingly less pressure for land development. Alternative transportation systems preserving landscape would have to be accepted. Cluster houses — saving real, open (and unmowed wild) areas — would be mandatory. And home choice would have to be guaranteed through political and social laws that stress individual renewal of cities, so that urban alternatives could exist. Taxation policies as regards one's home and the land it is on would have to be changed.

America would also have to break the present speculative grip now held by a few on land itself. For it is *land policy*, not *housing policy* per se, that is the critical issue of the social dream. As long as those who control land can make a profit on it without improving it, and without helping one have a better life upon it, then exploitation is inevitable.

These are serious issues, and they are only a beginning. Must freedom be symbolized by ownership? Why not by possession instead: a possession held in trust and based on how one lives upon the land, protects it, and cares for it?

While we cannot return to transcendentalism (for Thoreau's way is not ours, nor is there any reason for wanting it to be), there is much that is honest, uniquely American, and still relevant in a dream of a free man in harmony with his home and land. Suburbia has become the habitat of Everyman. Only Everyman can alter and improve the dream. When Everyman does, he will forever sweep out master bedrooms, 3½ baths, rec rooms, snack bars, indoor-outdoor carpet tiles, and two-car-width driveways.

He will start afresh: with land, with a life on the land, with children, with a new housing dream that is part Whitman, part transcendentalist, part Wright, part new aspirations, new needs, and new opportunities.(34) It is then that Everyman may begin to discover again how to live happily with his own dream on the land he possesses.

VIII FRANK LLOYD WRIGHT

When the materials are all prepared and ready, the architects shall appear.... I swear to you they will understand you and justify you. The greatest among them shall be he who best knows you, and encloses all and is faithful to all.

Walt Whitman, "A Song of the Rolling Earth," *Leaves of Grass.*

It helps to think of Frank Lloyd Wright as the last Victorian, for although he is frequently acclaimed as being the first (if not the greatest) modern twentieth-century architect, it is, in fact, the ideals of nineteenth century America that are best embodied in his marvelous work. He is probably the finest artist of the transcendental dream described in the preceding chapter, and the architect destined to fulfill Whitman's prophecy. Also it is principally through a study of, first, his Prairie houses, from 1900 to 1911, and later, his Usonian houses, from 1935 to 1950, that we can see not only how he realized this transcendental dream in architectural form but also how he set the standards for what remains the best in American suburbia.

To understand how Wright was capable of originating the idea of the Prairie house, it helps to see him in his proper cultural perspective. To begin with, his birth in Wisconsin in 1869, four years after the end of the Civil War, places him near the end of the transcendental movement, in an area and near a city (Chicago) that were literally booming. The discoveries of balloon wood framing in house building and of skeletal iron framing in office construction helped spur even more development in the most American of the country's cities. With continued railroad expansion and limitless fertile western lands, the future of Chicago seemed secure.

(1) The Froebel blocks (a, b, c) were a set of children's building toys in geometric shapes, that could be arranged into forms highly suggestive of much of Wright's later architecture. Grant C. Manson, in his book Frank Lloyd Wright to 1910: The First Golden Age *(New York: Reinhold, 1958), has an excellent summary of the Froebelian influence on Mrs. Wright and, through her, on the young architect-in-training.*

Furthermore, both Wright's mother and his father were strongly affected by transcendental thought. Its influence, through them, upon Wright include his mother's dreams (before he was born) that he would become a great architect; her private training with him, using the Froebel games — a series of blocks, paper cutouts, and organic relationships;(1) and his father's ministry in the Unitarian church, which believes in the unity of God rather than in the Trinity. Wright grew up in a home where Emerson, Thoreau, and Whitman were read; where music was revered (he was later to become an excellent pianist), and where the virtues of work on the land with one's own hands at harvest time were extolled.

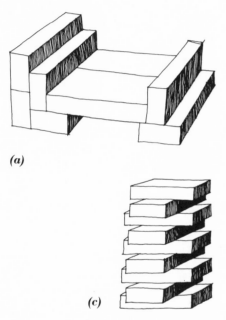

(a)

(c)

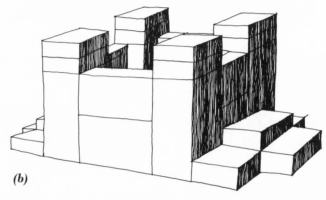

(b)

Finally, Wright's maturation in a city of highly visibly self-made men, and his training under the skilled eclectic architect Silsbee and then later under the master, Louis Sullivan, were to stamp him as the last of the Chicago School architects.

In a certain sense, Wright was premodern. Twenty-two years older than Corbusier, he predates futurism, cubism, and de Stijl. And his first important work, the Winslow House, was built in 1893, some seven years before the twentieth century.(2) The plans and elevations of this work are a marvelous blend of Victorian solidarity and the emerging thought of the then twenty-four year old Wright. Already the roof has become a great shelter that floats above the living space. The house is functionally zoned (as are the best of all American Victorian homes), and the spaces begin to flow and interlock in that sense of plasticity that he was later to defend so stoutly.(3)

(2) The Winslow House is half Victorian and half emergent Prairie house. While the front of the house remains solid and respectable, the rear has already begun to become plastic, extending into the landscape.

(3) See chapter 6 for an analysis of a typical Victorian house.

His progression as an architectural designer was rapid, and in 1902 we see the first full-blown Prairie house, a home designed for the Ward Willits family.(4) A careful look at this plan is sufficient to demonstrate how Wright's creative idea reflects transcendentalism superbly. The core or center of the house is the fireplace mass with a hearth in both the living room and the dining room. Thus the warmth of a natural fire is the focal point, and man turns *toward* this fire for comfort, security, and social gathering.

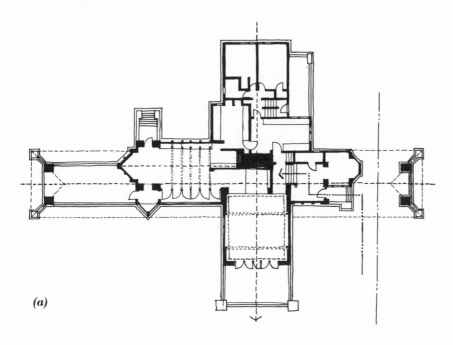

(a)

(b)

(4) The Willits House clearly shows a modified cross plan, (a) with each arm extending outward. This plan motif was to be used many times by Wright. The perspective sketch (b) illustrates how each arm of the plan is composed of horizontal lines and planes that "flow" outward into the land.

(5) While similar in outward appearances in its plan form, the Villa Rotunda by Palladio is totally different in concept from Wright's organic Prairie house.

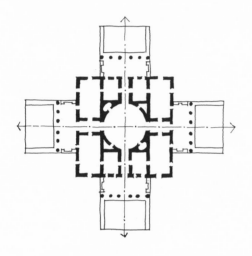

(6) Frank Lloyd Wright, The Natural House *(New York: Horizon Press, 1954), p. 44.*

This concept of the inner mysticism of nature (fire) is in direct contrast to Renaissance thought, which placed man at the center — frequently under a dome, as at the Villa Rotunda by Palladio, where man controls the space that radiates outward.(5) In Wright's Prairie houses, it is always the hearth that is the center, the most inner recess. Harking back to rugged colonial times, Wright's fireplace cores are always massive and serve to anchor the house at a particular place on the land. All the rooms of the house then explode outward from the core. Each series of rooms, grouped according to function, becomes a wing extending out into the land: porches, terraces, overhangs, low walls — all help destroy the outer walls, so that no clear distinction occurs between outside and inside. Wright said: "A sense of architecture is the sound of the 'within.' We might call that 'within' the heart. Architecture now becomes integral, the expression of a new / old reality: the liveable interior space of the room, itself. The room must be seen as architecture, or we have no architecture. We have no longer an outside as outside. Now the outside may come inside, and the inside may, and does, go outside. They are *of* each other."(6)

In the Prairie houses, Frank Lloyd Wright brought the transcendental dream to full maturity — man is free, independent, and possesses his own house, his own land. The land has become part of the house, the house, part of the land; and both have become part of man, integral with him.

It was Wright's belief that every citizen deserved such a house. His vision was of a land filled with one-acre to five-acre plots containing Prairie houses in which the dream could be fulfilled.(7) Of course, the

(7) Perhaps the most famous Prairie house is the Robie Residence (1909) in Chicago. In this house, the transcendental promises of an organic architecture composed of planes of space are fully realized.

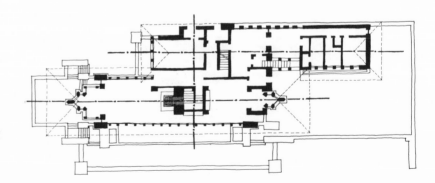

actual development of American suburbia has happened quite differently from the ideals of that dream. Far from allowing man to be in harmony on or with the land, present suburbia housing-form offers little real choice for those who can afford to live there — and no choice at all for those who are not financially secure, or for those who are not allowed in.

Wright was aware of this potential problem. Even as early as 1902 he was providing designs for simple $5,000 houses for publication in the *Ladies' Home Journal* — houses that might be built by what he felt was the newly emerging democratic aristocracy: rugged individualists who would work hard to improve themselves, creating better lives and a true American culture.(8)

It was not until the late twenties and thirties, however, that Wright (alarmed at what he saw happening in the orthodox architectural scene) began to spend serious time on the problems of mass housing. At his student workshop, the Taliesin Fellowship, the apprentices worked on a huge model for a theoretical city, Broadacres. In 1934 the first plans were published. (The best exposition of the ideas behind Broadacres may be found in Wright's own book *The Living City*.)

The name Broadacres is itself descriptive since the plans called for a horizontal, decentralized, anti-city. Likewise, the population density called for was more suitable for village life than for city hustle and activity, and the basic land unit was one acre per family. Indeed, Broadacres was designed to be lived in by a new idealistic society who together would destroy the mobocracy (Wright's term) of bankers, lenders, and middlemen (in his eyes, parasites) who were keeping us from rediscovering land, light, and air.

(8) This 1902 Ladies' Home Journal *design by Wright is remarkably similar, albeit scaled down, to the Willits House (see note 4).*

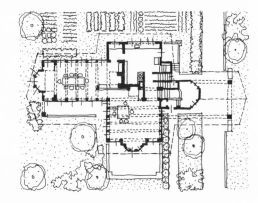

Despite the impossibility of realizing such a utopian city — for by this time Broadacres was already a protest, a reaction against unchecked suburban growth and high-rise inner-city housing — Wright's designs are both imaginative and thought-provoking. Complete with public baths, athletic clubs, arboretum, vineyards, public and private gardens, music halls, theaters, and nine sectarian temples arranged around a larger building for "central" worship, Broadacres is a true vision of a better life, where a cultured agrarian society would, as in Thomas Jefferson's idealized society, create a truly American aristocracy.

Comes to our American view, then, the highest form of aristocracy yet known — the highest because *innate*; Aristocracy natural as the quality of the man himself, no longer *on* him, but *of* him: aristocracy his, not by way of privilege nor inheritance, but truly his; a quality developed from within himself. Unique, . . . Thomas Jefferson prophesized the democratic Aristoi. We his people must not only meet the radical changes in our political and social systems but face no less these changes in the basis of our culture.(9)

(9) F. L. Wright: A Testament *(New York: Horizon Press, 1957) p. 62.*

(10) This typical four-plex house scheme was realized later by Wright at the Suntop homes (1939) in Ardmore, Pennsylvania.

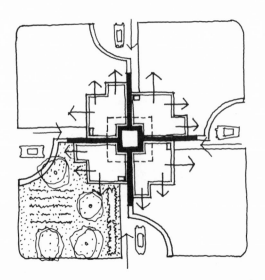

Broadacres was Wright's last great attempt to reimpose transcendentalist values on the city. And, although the social order he envisioned might be unrealistic, in the house plans themselves, Wright's designs, as usual, were highly pragmatic. A typical city block contained only four houses,(10) grouped toward the center so that a common core could be utilized for all the houses. On the one hand, this made for a close, grouped building form more economical than separate houses. On the other hand, it also grouped the open land into a maximum package for each house unit. (Not incidentally, this also kept the car removed from the house.) The result is that each house unit is set within its own garden.

Wright felt that returning the land to the individual (poor and rich alike) was the means to keep us free: "All together these [houses] would stand among shade trees, fruit trees, berry bushes, vegetables and flowers in gardens — . . . here is a quality home within reach of the artisan properly in the country"(11) And Wright took these ideas far beyond the utopian Broadacres. In 1938 *Life* magazine commissioned him to design one of his Usonian houses for its readers. The term *Usonian* was employed by Wright to connote that which distinguished *us* (as Americans) in *unity*. For Wright this distinguishing characteristic was the transcendental dream of the organic whole of man integrated with his land, the house being a symbol of his freedom.. "To Americans thus came natural, free building. For mankind *the ideal* of man free, therefore his own building humanistic. Both these freedoms I understood then as now to be basic to all our modern art, parallel to the *idea* by which we live and have our being as a people. This is the meaning of democracy."(12)

As difficult as these words may be to fully comprehend, Wright's actual drawings are quite clear. The Rosenbaum House in Alabama (1939) is a good representative; the plan is carefully zoned into separate functional areas, with the living room opening completely onto a garden.(13)

(11)   F. L. Wright: The Living City *(New York: Horizon Press, 1958), p. 153.*

(12)   Ibid., p. 153.

(13)   In plan (a), the Rosenbaum House opens to the rear, while the front of the house has a blank wall to the street as shown in sketch (b).

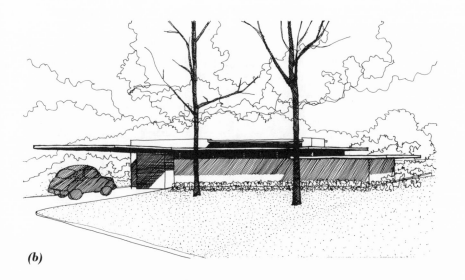

(b)

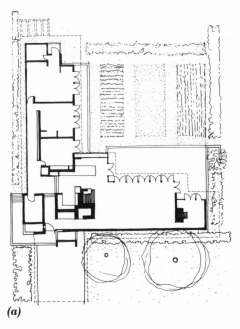

(a)

The plot plan is much smaller than that of the typical Prairie house, but the complete integration of house with land remains. Built on a careful four-foot module, this Usonian house is a model for the open life-style so prized in today's suburbia. The kitchen is an efficient work area close to the living room, while the car is close yet still screened from the family areas. The central-fireplace core remains, but is smaller, more efficient. And while the garden side of the house is open to the land, the street side is closed off and private. Wright designed and built many of these Usonian houses from 1939 to 1950, and they have never been surpassed in expressing the transcendental housing dream.

The preceding discussion has been centered on Wright's attempts to create a uniquely American concept of house, or shelter / habitat. His aesthetic idea of organic and free-flowing space can be seen in all of his work, however — the Larkin building, Midway Gardens, the Imperial Hotel, the Johnson Wax administrative building, Price Tower, the Guggenheim Museum — all buildings familiar to any student of twentieth century architecture. Nonetheless it is through his houses that Wright makes his most important conceptual contributions to architecture. In this respect, no single house is more important than the Kaufmann vacation house, Fallingwater, built near Bear Run, Pennsylvania, in 1936.(14)

(14)   The main-floor plan of Fallingwater illustrates how the house literally hangs out over the waterfall. With its fireplace hearth part of the rock itself, the structure is firmly rooted in the earth.

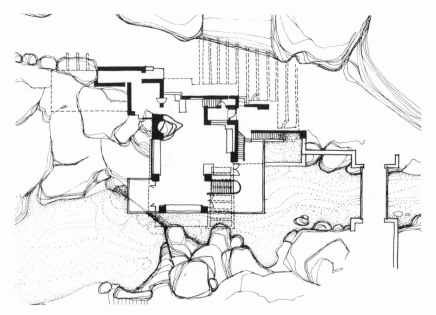

Norris K. Smith, perhaps the most perceptive of Wright's critics, has argued that Fallingwater *best* expresses the concept of the organic and natural house, so crucial to Wright's aesthetic.(15) Smith further argues that Wright's belief in growth and change, a dynamic quality in an informal living style, and in an idealized architecture (as opposed to a historic and intellectualized architecture) clearly link him with Rousseau, Coleridge, Wordsworth, and the romantic outlook prevalent in 1790, as well as with the later transcendentalists and Unitarians of 1830 to 1900.(16) This argument leads to the conclusion that Wright was conservative, and not avante-garde — and that his architectural concepts championed ideals of romantic self in an age already committed to a collective and corporate society.

(15) "It is still the critical consensus, I believe, that Fallingwater is Wright's most imaginative realization of his conception of the 'natural house,' built in Nature for the natural man, who himself 'shall be like a tree planted by the rivers of water.' If ever a house was rooted in the landscape, it is this one." (Norris K. Smith, Frank Lloyd Wright: A Study in Architectural Content [Watkins Glen, New York: The American Life Foundation, 1979], p. 140.)

(16) Ibid., pp. 153, 167, 168. Smith has a

Whatever one's personal interpretation, Fallingwater is a powerful poetic architectural image. Rooted to the rock itself, the house grows up, out of, and above the waterfall below. Seen from below,(17) the house has a vertical fireplace mass (the hearth is the natural rock unmoved), with cantilevered decks hovering over the water. From the side or from above, the house appears to grow out of the hillside.

particularly cogent analysis of Wright's organic beliefs, particularly the metaphor of the tree that continually grows and changes (p. 146).

(17) The fireplace mass at Fallingwater anchors the house.

Frank Lloyd Wright 133

No single architectural aspect better addresses Wright's concepts of organic, natural, flowing space and of plasticity than the symbolic manner in which circulation spaces are treated. On a rock in the stream and immediately adjacent to the waterfall, a ceremonial stairway leads up into the living room. This stair is clearly symbolic, for no one could approach it via the water without being swept over the falls. Within the house, circulation space flows from room to room — a series of informal functional places are created, but as in the larger Prairie houses, each major room extends out onto decks and porches and into the landscape.

The house is tied into the land by concrete beams, which anchor it securely into the hill above. A walkway leads under these beams and up toward the guest house above. Finally, steps lead from the guest house pool up into the woods, where a dirt path disappears into the undergrowth.

Fallingwater is transcendental in its conception of a family place that is united, yet open and in harmony with nature. Experiencing it — for only in walking through Fallingwater may it be appreciated, it cannot be comprehended as a rational and intellectual exercise — one senses both the temporal quality of nature and a unified concept of architecture. No single work by Frank Lloyd Wright better exemplifies his declared creed that "man takes a positive hand in creation whenever he puts a building upon the earth beneath the sun."

IX LE CORBUSIER

The house is a machine for living.

As to beauty, this is always present when you have proportion.

(Le Corbusier, *Towards a New Architecture*)

A town is a tool.

Towns no longer fulfill this function. They are ineffectual; they use up our bodies, they thwart our souls. . . .

A town is a mighty image which stirs out minds. Why should not the town be, even today, a source of poetry?

(Le Corbusier, *The City of Tomorrow*)

No architect has had a greater influence on the direction of twentieth-century aesthetics than Le Corbusier. Believing that man and his society had become enslaved in the crowded industrial city — socially, politically, and culturally as well as aesthetically — Corbusier had a vision of a new collective society that would free man, and in so doing would lead to a new architectural aesthetic.

In these beliefs Corbusier felt the citizens of the city were inalienably entitled to air, light, and a community of parks, grass, and trees, and that architects had a responsibility to participate in the social actions of twentieth century reform by reorganizing the built environment.(1)

(1) *This belief that architecture could help free man (if not, indeed, elevate him) is close to the argument of architectural determinism, which states that our spatial environment can mold and shape our behavior (see chapter 7, note 30). Architecture may express and subtly influence our actions, but it does not directly transform our behavior.*

Like many theorists and prophets, he saw the forces of modern society as inexorably bringing his dreams to fruition, and this belief that he was *right* sustained him throughout his long search for the correspondingly morally correct aesthetic. The means toward this aesthetic was to be industrial technology — one based on standardization, prefabrication, improved building methods, new materials, and finally on one specific material, *béton brut* —rough, reinforced concrete. Through the use of this industrial technology, Corbusier believed he could sweep away the recent architectural past and create new sculptured forms that would reaffirm the Platonic ideal of beauty in architecture — proportion, scale, and an underlying harmony in the physical world through geometric relationships.(2)

(2) "To create as an artist from a preconceived notion of form; . . . Corbusier . . . professes faith in the verities of geometry, not for the sake of geometry itself, but rather for the sake of eternal values." Paul Westheim, from an article on Corbusier in Wasmuths Monatshefte fur Baukunst *7 (1922): 71-73.*

Finally, Corbusier was a poet of architectural form. It is this quality that infuses his rational intellectual and functional approach, that moderates his Platonic ideals of beauty, and that gives genius to his work. And it is the poetical spaces and forms of masterpieces such as the Villa Savoye, Ronchamp, and La Tourette that will continue today and in the future to influence our ever-changing architectural aesthetic.

(3) Corbusier's original name was Charles Edouard Jeanneret, which he later changed when living in Paris to Le Corbusier, after distant ancestors from the south of France. Although Corbusier and Frank Lloyd Wright are often thought of as contemporaries, Wright was already in his twenties when Corbusier was born.

Born in 1887 in La Chaux-de-Fonds, Switzerland, Corbusier by the age of fourteen was attending classes in the local art school, which specialized in the training of watch engravers.(3) His talents for art, sculpture, and architecture were early recognized, and it should be remembered that his later attitudes toward architecture were always influenced by this disciplined beginning that emphasized sculptural form and the interplay of shadow and light.

Following graduation in 1905, he spent the next twelve years in intensive study, travel, teaching, and architectural apprenticeship. During this period he designed six houses and a theater in his native town, but probably the most important influences on his emerging aesthetic were the periods he spent in the offices of Joseph Hoffman in Vienna, Auguste Perret in Paris, and Peter Behrens in Berlin.

Of particular importance was his fifteen-month employment in Perret's office, beginning in 1908 when Corbusier was twenty-one. It was during this period — when Paris was recognized as the intellectual center of modern art — that he was introduced to the newly emergent styles of futurism and cubism, as well as to Perret's striking use of reinforced concrete as a new structural building material.(4)

In 1917, his formative years ended, and at the age of thirty, he settled permanently in Paris. For the next thirteen years he painted; wrote profusely on art, architecture, and city planning; organized and participated in exhibitions; and emerged as a brillant architect with polemic convictions, culminating in the Villa Savoye, built from 1929 to 1931.

In painting, he first worked closely with Amédée Ozenfant, and together they published a manifesto, *After Cubism*, which began to outline directions toward a new aesthetic. Arguing that the latest modern art-world values were confused, they proposed to return to the earlier, rational, geometric foundations of cubism, and they called this new restart purism.

Beginning in 1920, Corbusier participated as an editor and publisher in the magazine *L'Esprit nouveau*, where he argued ever more forcefully, and often with caustic wit, that purism would attain its aesthetic inspiration through the proper use of new technology. In 1923, many of his magazine articles were edited, reorganized, and published in the book *Towards a New Architecture*, which remains his canonical work and among the most influential books in the history of architectural aesthetics. In these writings, Corbusier consistently argued that changing society would demand purer forms, undecorative yet more appropriate functionally to new life-styles.(5) Nature should be left alone, as a counterpoint to architecture — which was the province of man. And man should give beauty to his architecture through the Greek, or Platonic, ideal of proportional geometry.

(4) *Hoffman, Perret, and Behrens were all important in the development of the modern movement in architecture. The fact that Corbusier could find ready employment with all three architects is indicative of both his ability and their respect for his prior training. Of some historical interest is the fact that when Corbusier worked in Behrens's office, he met another young apprentice — Mies van de Rohe — who was later to emerge as an equally famous architect.*

(5) Le Corbusier, Towards a New Architecture *(London: The Architectural Press, 1946). Like Wright, Corbusier championed the idea that the floor plan was the generator of the form — i.e., that the house should grow from the inside out.*

(6) Pavilion de Esprit-Nouveau (1925).

(7) Quoted in The Master Builders *(New York: 1960), p. 46. Alfred A. Knopf.*

These goals were well stated in his design for a pavilion for the Exhibition of Decorative Arts in 1925.(6) This full-scale model of a studio-house emphasized standardized construction, with a nonstructural skin wrapped around a post-and-beam structure with a flat roof. The furnishings were of chrome steel, and the interior had less furniture than contemporary dwellings. Built-ins and storage walls were used, as was the Thonet bentwood chair (so popularized by Corbusier that it later became known as the Corbu Chair, even though he did not design it). The pavilion was truly a machine for living. Corbusier stated: "My intention is to illustrate how, by virtue of . . . *standardization* . . . industry creates *pure* forms, and to stress the intrinsic value of this pure form of art that is the result.(7) The pavilion was filled with useful objects and cubist and postcubist paintings. Clearly Corbusier was addressing a new, radical idea of pure architectural form, and not merely ideas of function.

These new form ideas were called by Corbusier "the five points of a new architecture: "

1. Through the use of reinforced-concrete construction, the house could now stand on *pilotis*, or columns, above the ground.

2. Again through the use of reinforced concrete, a strong, flat roof could allow for a *roof garden*, which would replace the land covered below.

3. With a columnar structure (as opposed to bearing walls), the interior could have a free, or open, plan.

4. Since the exterior skin was no longer needed to hold up the roof, a continuous *ribbon window* could be used wherever light was needed.

5. Finally, the exterior skin itself could be interwoven in and out of the columnar structure, creating a *free facade*. (8)

From 1922 to 1930, Corbusier developed these rational formal points in a series of brilliant machines for living — the Ozenfant House (1922), La Roche (1923), and Garches (1927) are examples — which culminated in his first masterpiece, the Villa Savoye (1931).

Typical of these purist style houses is the Villa Carthage project (1928).(9) Both the section and a sketch for the proposed exterior illustrate all five of Corbusier's points: Reinforced concrete construction allows for raising the living areas and for a roof terrace (in this case covered by a light deck for sun protection); the interior is open both in plan and in section; ribbon windows are used; and the exterior skin is plastically used to create a free facade.

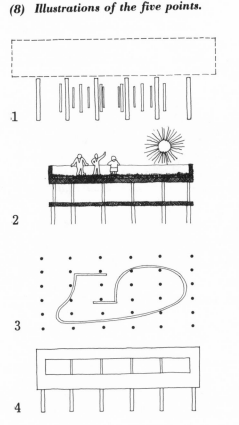

(8) *Illustrations of the five points.*

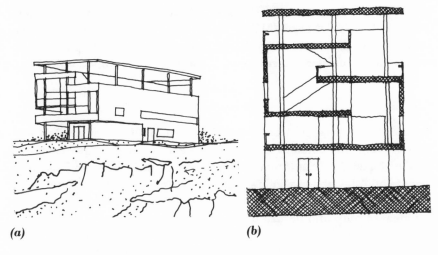

(a)   *(b)*

This project also illustrates two dominant themes, one spatial and one ideological, that run throughout Corbusier's career. The first of these is his use of interlocking vertical space to create a new interior sculptural form. He uses the vertical dimensions in a way that is reminiscent of Frank Lloyd Wright's handling of the horizontal dimensions. Whereas Wright's houses interlock with the land (the outside comes in, the inside comes out), Corbusier's houses spring up *out of the land*, and interior space interlocks from floor to floor up to the roof, where a garden recaptures the space lost on the ground. Time and again, Corbusier uses the vertical elements of stairs, ramps, projecting balconies, and two-story spaces to create this sense of interior spatial freedom.

(9) The Villa Carthage project (1928). The section (a) shows Corbusier's mastery of interlocking vertical space. The perspective (b) illustrates the great freedom used in applying the skin of the facade over the structural frame.

(10) In his book The New Brutalism *(New York: Reinhold Publishing Co., 1966), p. 15, the historian Reyner Banham refers to this as an* objet-type, *a model that could easily have come from Corbusier's own studio.*

(11) Corbusier never abandoned this theme of the single studio apartment as the ideal spatial cell for living. As will be seen later, this model caused severe problems in the Unité d'habitation (for families), but allowed for a masterpiece at La Tourette, a monastery, where the individual cells are logically grouped together in a collective society.

(12) Peter Serenyi, "Le Corbusier's Changing Attitude Toward Form," Journal of the Society of Architectural Historians *24 (March 1965): p. 15.*

Serenyi feels that the years 1928 and 1929 were pivotal for Corbusier in that he still maintained the Platonic ideal, but that his attitude during that time toward form became more personal and less mathematically derived.

For those interested in an overview of the meaning of Corbusier's work, Serenyi's book Le Corbusier in Perspective *(Englewood Cliffs, N.J., Prentice-Hall: 1975) is recommended. For plans, sections, and photographs of the architecture itself, the acknowledged definitive source is a series of books edited by Willy Boesiger and published by Praeger Books.*

(13) The Villa Savoye. The facade sketch (a) illustrates Corbusier's "points" numbered 1, 4, and 5. The first floor plan

This concern for saving ground space by building vertically is most appropriate in the urban environment where land is scarce and the apartment plan is more suitable than the individual house. As many critics have observed, Corbusier's ideological theme for the apartment plan was the Parisian studio apartment.(10) With their high ceilings, often under a garret, these studio apartments frequently had balconies or lofts added for additional living and sleeping space, and skylights inserted in the roofs in order to obtain even lighting for painting. Ideal for the individual artist, the small but spatially exciting studio-apartment plan works well as a model for one or two persons but is not as easily adapted for a family with children.(11)

All of these early ideas were brought together and forcefully stated in the Villa Savoye outside of Paris — "the finest, and indeed, the last house in the Purist Style."(12) More than any of his earlier works, the Villa Savoye expresses the studio-apartment unit, set in apposition to nature, as a pure sculptural form, a white and man-made object, not unlike its ideal counterpart, the Greek temple.(13)

On the interior, the plan is remarkably open. Both a circular stair and a powerful ramp connect the three floor areas. The roof garden is fully developed as an adjunct living space to the salon; and the free facade and the ribbon window are used to express, not the function of the space enclosed, but rather Corbusier's Platonic ideal of beauty — an ideal of man and nature in geometrical harmony.

In its sculptural form, the Villa Savoye is not functional — certainly not from the functionalist aesthetic view, which argues that only function can (or should) determine the form. Not only are the ribbon windows arranged geometrically, but the columns too are placed for

(a)

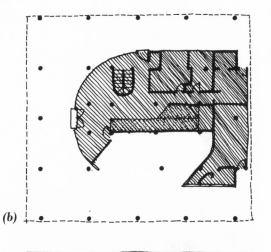

(b)

(b) and the second, or main, floor (c) plans illustrate point 3. The roof terrace sketch (d) illustrates point 2.

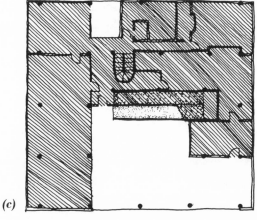

(c)

(d)

spatial effect rather than for function (one column projects through the sitting area of the master bedroom!). And the entry lavatory is located not near the car garage (where it would be most useful), but rather, immediately opposite the front door, proclaiming the architect's role in rearranging functional objects as elements of sculpture.

At the Villa Savoye, Corbusier said he wanted to create something poetical — a machine for living that went beyond function and became geometric architectural poetry.(14)

(14) The noted architectural historian Rudolf Wittkower gives Corbusier full credit — "[he] intellectualized man's intuitive urge. . . . It is only Corbusier who brings to bear on the old problem of proportion a prophetic, unceasing, searching and above all, a poetic mind." ("Le Corbusier's Modular," from Four Great Masters of Modern Architecture *[New York: Da Capo Press, 1970], p. 204.)*

In 1930, at the age of forty-three, Corbusier reassessed his work and started in a new direction by rethinking his attitudes toward society and the materials and composition of his architecture. Having earlier espoused the solitary artist's approach (as in the studio-apartment *objet-type*), he now joined the syndicalist political movement and shifted toward a collectivist theory in which groups of individuals, acting together, could revolutionize city form.

This reassessment had particular impact on his ideas regarding city planning, and in 1935 he published *The Radiant City*, a book that achieved great importance in Europe. As early as 1922 at the Paris Salon d'Automne, he had exhibited a theoretical Contemporary City for 3,000,000 persons, which advocated immense high-rise apartment blocks set in large green parks. In 1925, his *Voisin* plan applied these ideas to the center of Paris. In this plan, which proposed destroying a great deal of the city's center, Corbusier addressed himself to what he considered the four most urgent needs of Paris: apartment homes (to increase density), parks (to provide greater open space), high-rise office buildings (to concentrate activity at the city's core), and multi-leveled highways (to simplify circulation).

His proposed method was not additive or organic, but rather drastic surgery. Francoise Choay points out that he was a rational and sociological logician whose "method consists of *defining, classifying and putting in order* needs and functions."(15) At the 1933 meeting of the CIAM (the International Congress of Modern Architects), these goals of Corbusier were formally stated in the Athens Charter as: living, or habitation; working; circulating, or traffic; and cultivating one's mind and body, or leisure.(16)

Throughout the late thirties the Radiant City plans were attacked by many critics as being unreasonable. What was overlooked was that Corbusier was proposing, *not* a real city, but rather a theoretical one. Just as Wright's Broadacres had expressed a low-density, organic, and natural suburban dream, the Radiant City expressed a corresponding high-density, rational, urban ideal. Corbusier's plans are not for cities in which parks are set, but rather for a totally new type of city that is itself set in one vast encompassing park.(17) Urban dwellers

(15) F. Choay, Le Corbusier *(New York: George Braziller, 1960), p. 15.*

Choay also gives another argument as to why Corbusier was not a Functionalist "[He] never disassociated town planning from architecture; building is essentially a social action aimed at man and the solution of his problems" (p. 18).

She feels three factors may be found in all his work, rationalism (intellectual approach), human concern (man's needs and scale), and poetry — this last factor becoming more important with time: "As Corbusier grows older, each architectural element becomes an opportunity for sculpture, although it never loses its function" (p. 22).

(16) *Two certain influences on Corbusier's thoughts were Tony Garnier's plans for a* Cité Industrielle *(1903) and Sant' Elia's drawings for a Futurist city (1914).*

(17) *This idea is well expressed by Sir John Summerson in "Architecture, Painting, and Le Corbusier," in his* Heavenly Mansions *(New York: W.W. Norton and Company, 1963), p. 191.*

were to live in towers surrounded by gardens; suburban dwellers in row houses, each having a garden; and the whole was to be contained within continuous, public green open space.(18)

From 1930 until the liberation of Paris in 1944, Corbusier continued his intellectual growth, both as a planner and as an architect. With the end of the Second World War in 1945, his mature architectural aesthetic can be seen in its final form. Two startling projects served notice that this mature phase had been brought to fruition — the Unité d'habitation (1948—52) and the chapel at Ronchamp (1950—54).

The Unité was Corbusier's first opportunity to combine and demonstrate his new thoughts on architectural construction and collectivist city planning. Seventeen stories high, the Unité was located on the outskirts of Marseilles and held 1,600 inhabitants in 360 apartment units. With twenty-six kinds of communal facilities, shops on the seventh floor, and a gymnasium and pool on the roof, its overall mass was immense.(19)

(18) The antithesis of Corbusier was the planner Camillo Sitte, whose proposed projects for Vienna stressed cultural continuity and careful organic growth. In his book When the Cathedrals Were White, *Corbusier expressed the thought that Sitte was an intelligent planner who had simply stated the problem incorrectly.*

(19) Unité de'habitation.

The elevation (a) shows how Corbusier attempted to humanize the scale by giving an individual expression to each two-story living unit. In addition, the terrace sunscreens were painted primary colors.

The section (b) shows the roof garden, the apartment massing, and the clear space below created by the pilotis.

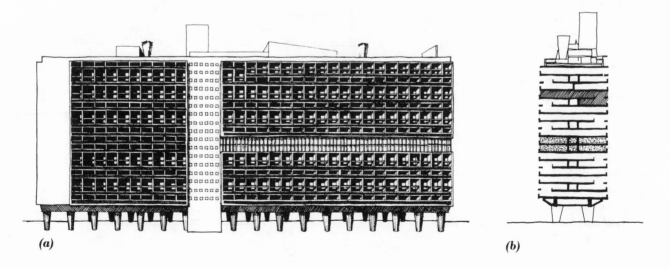

(a)   *(b)*

Constructed of *béton brut*, it was said by Corbusier to be a vertical garden city. Despite this claim, the Unité d'habitation does not really work well either as an apartment block or as a mini-city. With the advantage of hindsight, we now know that the shops are not used (the French preferring to shop in the town's traditional market areas), children play in the park below and not on the roof, and the rooms of the apartments are, in many cases, too narrow (less than seven feet wide in the children's bedrooms). In order to meet the stringent square-footage requirements of the government housing program while still preserving his belief that a two-storied studio apartment was the correct spatial model, Corbusier was forced to sacrifice many functional amenities in his final plan.(20)

Despite these sociological and planning problems, the Marseilles block remains a brilliant tour de force.(21) By interlocking the apartments around a central corridor, Corbusier achieved through air circulation in each unit, and reduced the required corridors to only one for every three floors. Of possibly even more importance, this project signaled that raw concrete used in powerful sculptural masses was to express a new architectural aesthetic. Abandoning his white-box machine aesthetic of the late twenties and thirties, Corbusier had begun a new movement, to be called Brutalism.(22)

(20) Serenyi says the apartment plans are a result of Corbusier's continued belief in the correctness of the monastic cell found in the Parisian studio: . . . "each apartment of the Marseille Block is designed for a single human being living completely alone, while sharing the advantages of a larger collective order" Peter Serenyi, "Le Corbusier, Fourier, and the Monastery of Emma," Art Bulletin 49 (1967): 277-86.

(21) Plans of the Unité apartments.

Three floors (1, 2, 3) are shown to illustrate two typical apartments, (a) and (b), each entered from the middle floor (2). Note that plan (a), which is entered on the living-room level, works better than plan (b), which requires the master bedroom and the living room to be combined as one space.

(22) Reyner Banhan says that the Unité d'habitation is the canonical work in béton brut, looked to by the movement's followers. "To construct moving relationships out of brute materials was to be the central ambition of Brutalism" (The New Brutalism, p. 16).

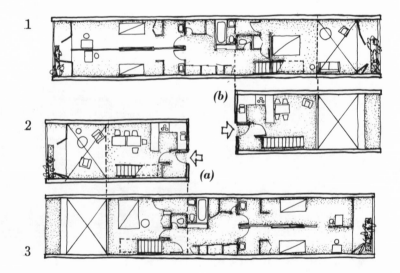

Another work — the chapel at Ronchamp, finished in 1954 — is perhaps Corbusier's most stunning and poetical composition.(23) A pilgrimage chapel, the building replaced one that was destroyed by bombs during the war. Ronchamp is located on a hill, and its form has been likened to a great ship in which weary travelers and pilgrims can rest. It is both the most sculptural and the most personal of Corbusier's work, and it consistently is rated by architects as among the ten most important buildings of the modern movement — which attests to its continuing importance.(24)

(23) Sketch of Ronchamp chapel.

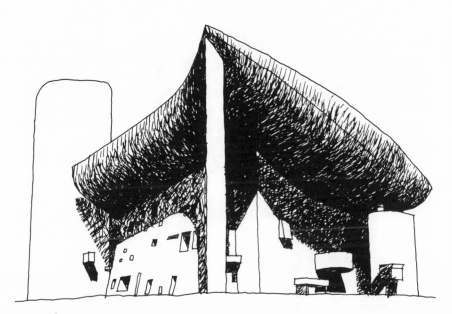

(24) Despite Ronchamp's apparent free form, it employs a careful proportional system, the modulor, devised by Corbusier from 1942 to 1948 — Le Corbusier, The Modulor *(Cambridge, Mass.: Harvard University Press, 1958). The fusion of proportional (rational and functional) thought with intuitive sculptural effect is the hallmark of Corbusier's last and most mature work.*

(25) An important building — between Ronchamp and the later La Tourette — is the mill owner's building in Ahmedabad, India. Here the sculptural qualities of Ronchamp have been regularized into planes and flat surfaces.

A series of important commissions followed Ronchamp, as Corbusier was increasingly recognized as being the most influential architect in Europe and among the foremost artists in the world.(25) Two projects deserve special mention — Chandigarh, India, and La Tourette in France.

Chandigarh, the new capital of the Punjab, was commissioned by Prime Minister Nehru to symbolize Indian control of the area. As a completely new city, it afforded Corbusier the opportunity to construct in built form many of his ideas on town planning.(26) The city is zoned, industry is outside the housing areas, while the government complex is set in a vast park with the Himalayan foothills as a backdrop.

(26) Plan of Chandigarh.

The gridded streets provide for loose zoning, with industry to the right, the government center at the top, and commerce in the center of this sketch plan. The main park follows a small stream from the government center through the town to fields below. Corbusier's actual architectural participation was concentrated on the government buildings.

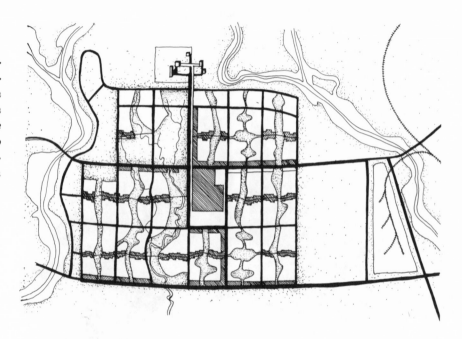

(27) It is beyond the scope of this book to analyze the many sociological and planning considerations that have emerged as Chandigarh has slowly been built. These issues are very complex; however, the great value of Chandigarh is that it not only allows us to observe the many limitations of rational, gridded, zoned planning (as opposed to a more organic, natural, cultural growth), but it also allows us to feel the power of great vision — men dreaming of a powerful city, clean, with light and air for every citizen.

At the town's center is a business and commercial area. With the streets laid out in a giant grid (representing approximately ten square American blocks in scale), parklike green spaces extend throughout, linking all of the spaces together. Chandigarh remains unfinished — still in growth and change, as is typical of all cities. Even so, it is not as revolutionary as Corbusier's earlier Radiant City ideas. The four goals are realized here — living, working, circulating, and cultivating one's mind and body — but the overall plan is less didactic and more humane than the earlier theoretical sketches.(27) One can only wonder what would have resulted had Corbusier lived longer and exercised a greater control over the architectural realization of his ideas.

Among his last projects is probably Corbusier's greatest and most profound work — La Tourette, a monastery near Lyons that was finished in 1960.(28) Here, his vision of single studio-cells joined together could finally be realized. "A building not only perfect visually but also functionally was brought into existence — . . . within the walls of this ideal community, individuality and collectivity were perfectly reconciled."(29)

La Tourette is more clearly rational than Ronchamp, for the Dominican priests had a much more complex living program than that of the pilgrimage chapel. As a result, the monastery is ordered, functional, and cloistered around a traditional courtyard form. In no other building, however, was Corbusier as free in his use of raw concrete. Bell towers, air scoops, clerestories, roof forms, interior stairs(30) — every element is treated sculpturally within the total architectural form; and no building more eloquently expresses Corbusier's final, mature fusion of intellect and poetry.

Corbusier's greatest legacy remains his ability to stir our imagination with new forms that reexpress old ideas. His buildings startled his contemporaries and made them rethink the nature of materials. And whatever one now thinks about Corbusier's social and political beliefs of individuals collectively gathered (for we have come a long way in realizing that collective societies often destroy the individual), we still must admire his vision of a new and better city and his mastery of architectural form as sculpture. Together with Frank Lloyd Wright, who expressed a different philosophy, Le Corbusier has made possible a twentieth-century architecture. It remains for us to understand properly the meaning of this achievement and to build upon its heritage.

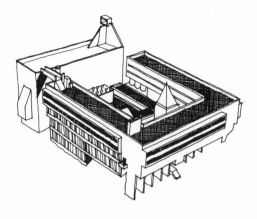

(28) Aerial view of La Tourette.

(29) These comments by Serenyi are from "Le Corbusier's Changing Attitude Toward Form," p. 86.

(30) A sculptural floating stair in the library room at La Tourette.

X   THE MODERN MOVEMENT

There is considerable argument among historians as to when the modern movement actually begins; by the year 1900, however, there were clear indications that a new architectural aesthetic was in the making. The necessity for this new aesthetic was rooted both in the economic, political, and social forces producing cultural change and in the basic perpetual change in view by which man himself altered his understanding of the environment and his own role within it.

In the first instance, the effects of the Industrial Revolution had already accelerated the shift from an agrarian society toward a more densely populated urban one. A large working class was emerging, as well as a prosperous and organized bourgeoisie, which was demanding not only better hygiene, better housing, and better working conditions but also more time for leisure and cultural pursuits — activities implicitly promised by this new technology.

While the early stages of the Industrial Revolution were characterized by machines of great power — the cotton gin, the spinning mill, the railroad — later stages saw the advent of smaller machines in which both the machines and their control mechanisms became more humanly scaled and suitable for everyday use in the home. By 1900, the expanding middle class had great expectations of a better life — just ahead.(1)

In addition to the sweeping economic, political, social, and technological forces acting upon the meanings of architectural form, however, man also was undergoing an equally profound change in his perception of space.

(1)   Reyner Banham, in his book Theory and Design in the First Machine Age *(London: Architecture Press, 1960), argues that the "First Machine Age" began with coal gas for lighting and ended with domestic machines and electricity in every home.*

Banham suggests we are now in a "Second Machine Age" in which highly developed production methods have brought the domestic machine to the masses and not merely to an upper-middle-class elite and in which "television, the symbolic machine of the Second Machine Age, has become a means of mass communication" (p. 10).

One can argue further that we are perhaps today in a Third Machine Age (or a Transistor Age), characterized by the miniaturization of control mechanisms — making possible moon flights, printed-circuit radios, and instantaneous data-printout computers.

Whatever machine age we are now in, it is clear that the turn-of-the-century expectations for the potential of the domestic machine have been fully realized.

In earlier times, man generally had viewed space as being contiguous and conforming to a hierarchal unity. Occupying a recognizable place within the city, he understood his relationship to it *subjectively*. That is, he experienced where he was, and the inherent order was comprehended by walking through streets, plazas, housing districts, and shopping areas and observing directly the spatial meanings of the urban context.

While it is true that the intimacy of the medieval city began to disintegrate during the Baroque period, spatial understanding was still maintained by grand avenues that began and ended at strong landmarks. The Renaissance discovery of the mathematical rules for perspective had helped in the creation of cities with long axial boulevard vistas and landscaped parks of grandeur. The citizen, nonetheless, still perceived the city's spatial order by directly experiencing it. The power of the king-state could be subjectively understood within a system of fixed-point perspectives.

(2) This argument for the rise of objective *analysis over* subjective *understanding is well presented by Francois Choay in her book* The Modern City: Planning in the Nineteenth Century *(New York: George Braziller, 1969). Choay states:*

As for the city dweller, he was unable to assimilate this urban revolution. . . . he was now confronted by a spatial order devoid of its traditional richness of meaning.

. . . those actually experiencing the urban phenomenon came to consider it something alien. They no longer felt inside the process and determined by it; they remained outside, observing the transformation with the eye of the spectator.

. . . this attitude that the city is something subject to examination has been made possible by a simultaneous evolution in the structure of knowledge. Since the end of the eighteenth century, western man has begun to view the entirety of his material and spiritual productions with a certain objectivity. [pp. 8, 9]

This subjective and personal understanding was radically changed by the Industrial Revolution, and from 1850 onward man began to see space as being continually more fragmented and discontinuous, and only casually linked by direct observation. Frequently housed at great distances from his work, the urban dweller began to comprehend space *objectively* via tramway and railway glimpses rather than subjectively via direct experience, as in the preindustrial city.

Furthermore, abstract and analytical means of communication — beginning with the newspaper and the periodical — began to supplant physical space in its older informative role. Intellectually, the social sciences — anthropology, sociology, economics, psychology, social history, and city planning — all emerged as further manifestations of viewing the structure of knowledge (as well as physical space) in a predominantly rational and objective manner.(2)

Between 1850 and 1900, Marx prophesied a new society; Darwin espoused natural selection; Cezanne created a new way of seeing in painting; Wagner composed his *Ring* cycle operas; Freud began his work in psychoanalysis; and Frank Lloyd Wright built the Winslow House. Just ahead lay Einstein, Proust, and Joyce — and the telephone, the electric light bulb, the radio, and the cinema. Clearly emerging was a new world that would need — and demand — a new architecture and a new aesthetic, the modern movement.

As humans within living history, architects were not immune to this ferment, and soon many were calling for the overthrow of the Beaux-Arts, and the academic and Classical tradition. Decrying historical determinism, they argued for a new movement based on democratic social goals rather than on what they felt were the too narrow goals of an academic and cultural elite.(3) The modern movement was thus to

(3) Comparing the plan of the Paris Opera House (1874) by Charles Garnier (a) with that of the Fagus Factory (b) (1911) in Germany shows clearly the differences between academic planning (formality, axiality, and symmetry) and elementalist planning (elements arranged in a balanced, yet functional, composition).

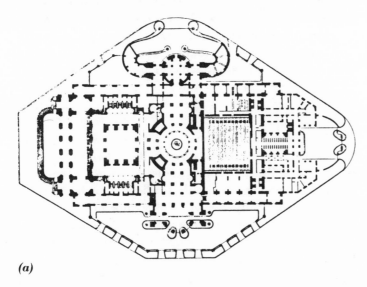

(a)

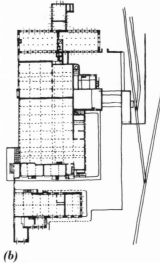

(b)

argue for a functional architecture that solved pragmatic problems and resolved human spatial needs. The environment was to be improved, and every family was to be decently housed and to enjoy clean air, parks, gardens, and open space. A primary goal of architecture was to help in improving society.(4)

(4) The problems with this kind of reasoning that leads to architectural determinism have already been pointed out in chapter 7, note 34, and in chapter 8.

The means toward these goals was to be the new technology — a technology that would master the machine and, employing dramatic new materials, would create useful societal space. Sophisticated steel construction, reinforced concrete, precasting, prefabricating, and assembly methodology were all to be championed. In addition, the plethora of new domestic machines — radios, washers and dryers, electric stoves, refrigerators, even the later car and television set — were to be looked upon as means toward freeing the family from drudgery, and were therefore to be housed and given programmed space within the new, more open, architectural plans.(5)

Underlying these heady goals and dreams were the belief that the new architecture should also express movement, transcience, and later speed in its perceptual form. This continuing change in man's understanding of space / time remains today a basic issue in the expression of all art forms.(6) To state this another way, the emerging modern movement saw the architect as a social servant(7) who, through the use of technology and new materials, would create a correspondingly new and functionally correct architecture — an architecture whose aesthetic also expressed a new objective, perceptual understanding of space / time.

The funcational and rationalist strain of the new movement can probably best be seen in the German *Werkbund* movement led by Peter Behrens and Hermann Muthesius. At the *Werkbund* congress of 1911, Muthesius was to proclaim that rational standardization was a virtue; that technologically derived materials and products could be as beautiful as older, more natural, materials; and that product design should be improved and guided by an aesthetic of abstract form.(8) In contrast with the more academic concerns of the Beaux Arts, this represented a radical change in aesthetics.

The Fagus Factory workshop block designed by Walter Gropius and Adolf Meyer in 1911 (see note 3) has been cited as "the first building of the Modern Movement properly so-called."(9) Hailed for its clarity of plan and its three-storied glazed corners, the workshop block was followed in 1914 by Gropius and Meyer's *Werkbund* Pavilion. As

(5) The championing of the machine by both Wright and Corbusier can be seen as placing them both within the modern movement, despite the great dissimilarity of their work.

(6) Siegfried Giedion goes so far as to say that modern architecture begins with the enlargement of space (as at Versailles in the late baroque period) and comes of age with our awareness of the increase in speed, or the quickness of time-movement. — Space, Time, and Architecture *(Cambridge, Mass.: The Harvard University Press, 1956).*

(7) Seeing the architect as a social servant is similar to John Dewey's seeing the teacher as one. Dewey's 1898 creeds (see chapters 3 and 11) were influential in the evolution of the modern movement's goals.

(8) Muthesius's book The English House, *first published in Germany in 1905, and only translated into English by Janet Seligman in 1979 (Rizzoli of New York, publishers), is one of the classic treatises on social functionalism in architecture. In three lengthy volumes, with 524 illustrations, Muthesius dissects minute issues such as placing the lady's wardrobe and dressing table as close as possible to the lady's side of the bed!*

(9) Banham, Theory and Design, *p. 79.*

Reyner Banham has aptly noted, the evolving factory aesthetic owed as much to Frank Lloyd Wright(10) as it did to the emergence of industrial technology. Nonetheless, such a diverse and talented group of architects as Bruno Taut, Max Berg, and Hans Poelzig — along with Behrens, Muthesius, Gropius, and Meyer — gave the German *Werkbund* a powerful lead in developing a new technologically oriented aesthetic.

However, it lay with another group — the Italian futurists — to best express the new ideas of space / time perception and the excitement of movement, change, and speed, as well as the revolutionary fervor of modern rationalism. Their manifesto, written by Fillipo Marinetti and published in 1909, proclaimed that "the splendor of the world has been enriched by a new beauty — the beauty of speed. A racing car with its bonnet draped with exhaust-pipes like fire-breathing serpents — a roaring racing car, rattling along like a machine-gun, is more beautiful than the Winged Victory of Samothrace."(11)

Throughout this initial manifesto (and the ones on painting, sculpture, and architecture that followed), Marinetti and the other futurists attack the older order — the museums, the libraries, the academies, the inherited culture — and champion the new, the temporal, the fresh, and the short-lived. In combination with their craving for speed, excitement, and change, they announce the annihilation of space and time and proclaim the need for a new aesthetic to match the political changes at last being brought to fruition in Italy.(12)

(10) Banham claims Wright's influence is the result of the German publication of his work, in 1911 (ibid., p. 63). The sketch shown is of the Werkbund Pavilion, which is strikingly similar to much of Wright's early work.

(11) From the fourth proposition from the manifesto published in Le Figaro, *February 20, 1909.*

(12) The Technical Manifesto of Futurist Sculpture *(1912) by Umberto Boccioni is of particular historical interest in that, by that year, Einsteinian space theory has rarely been so clearly stated, either intentionally or accidentally: "Sculpture must bring objects to life by rendering apprehensible, plastic, and systematic their prolongations into space, since it cannot be doubted any longer that one object finishes where another begins." (quoted from* Theory and Design in the First Machine Age, *p. 112)*

Much has also been made of the futurists trip to Paris in 1911, where they met a number of the cubists. While the futurists were certainly influenced by cubist painting technique, however, the futurist goals were more revolutionary and their manner of viewing space more radical.

(13) Adapted from Sant' Elia's drawings for the Citta Nouva, *these sketches display ideas of town planning that are still with us — separated and distinct traffic systems (often several layers deep), step-back apartment floors, glorification of the elevator (vertical speed and movement), and dramatic sulptural forms reminiscent of grain silos, warehouses, and powerful machines.*

Rather than handicrafts, permanence, and the romanticism of the late nineteenth century, the futurists argued for the beauty of the machine itself, a love of impermanence, and a puritanical rationalism. The symbols of the future were to be the car, the airship, machines in motion, the hydroelectric station, the central terminal, and the gigantic structures of the new city. The power of these new images can be seen clearly in the stunning drawings of Antonio Sant' Elia, who in May 1914 exhibited a group of building and town-planning ideas under the title of the *Citta Nuova.*(13)

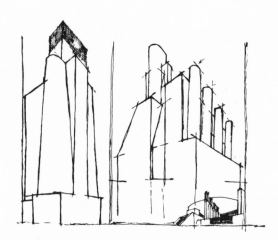

That exhibition was followed on July 11 by the *Futurist Manifesto on Architecture.* So striking is this document that much deserves quoting:

> Lifts [elevators] must no longer hide away like solitary worms in the stairwells, but the stairs — now useless — must be abolished, and the lifts must swarm up the facades like serpents of glass and iron. The house of cement, iron and glass, without carved or painted ornament, rich only in the inherent beauty of its lines and modeling . . . the street which, itself, will no longer lie like a doormat at the level of the thresholds, but plunge stories deep into the earth, gathering up the traffic of the metropolis connected for necessary transfers to metal catwalks and high-speed conveyor belts. . . .

I affirm that the new architecture is the architecture of cold calculation, temerarious boldness and simplicity; the architecture of reinforced concrete, iron and glass, textile fibers and all those replacements for wood, stone and brick.

And finally:

The fundamental characteristics of Futurist architecture will be expendability and transience. Our houses will last less time than we do, and every generation will have to build its own.(14)

Whether this heady dialectic could ever have produced an architectural reality as powerful as the sketches and theoretical ideas, was never put to the test; Sant' Elia was killed in the First World War, and the futurist architectural movement died with him. Nonetheless, the movement's influence became part of the mainstream of modern architecture, and as Banham has observed: "The growing pressure of mechanization made the world seem more and more Futurist, and as men felt this increasing pressure, they found Futurist ideas at hand to channel their ideas and give shape to their expression."(15)

It should not be deduced from the preceding that the origins of the modern movement were all functionally inspired and rationalist in ideology. There was a corresponding antirationalist or empiricist reaction within the movement to the Beaux Arts as well(16) — a reaction that championed individualism, romanticism, and natural organic form and decoration. The first, and best-known, individualistic reaction was Art Nouveau, a movement named after a Parisian shop that opened in 1895.

(14) Alberto Sartoris's book L'Architetto Antonio Sant' Elia (Milan, 1930) contains the text. The passage quoted may be found in Banham, Theory and Design, p. 129. The last thoughts quoted are probably by Marinetti rather than Sant' Elia, although Sant' Elia certainly would have agreed with them.

(15) Banham, Theory and Design, p. 136. The futurists had considerable influence on the de Stijl movement as well as on the constructivists, expressionists, and later town planners in both Europe and America. Their influence on Corbusier can be acknowledged, but has never been formally traced.

(16) Most critics will acknowledge that the modern movement today has a mixture of both rational ideology (i.e., knowledge through reasoning) and empiricist ideology (i.e., knowledge from experience) in its present aesthetic.

One serious problem with understanding the meaning of the modern movement, however, is that the empiricist side of the revolution has always been shortchanged. Critics and historians as diverse as Giedion, Pevsner, Banham, and more recently Kenneth Frampton have failed to understand the pervasive influence of the empiricist tradition — experiential feeling, intuitiveness, and the poetical grandeur of individual creativity.

(17) A cotton print by C. F. A. Voysey from 1888. The Art Nouveau love of sinuousness and stylized natural forms are clearly evident in this pattern half-way between Arts and Crafts and Art Nouveau.

(18) Nicholas Pevsner, The Sources of Modern Art and Design (New York: Praeger Publishers, 1968), p. 113. Despite his inability to appreciate Art Nouveau, Pevsner does devote increasingly more space to the movement with each succeeding book and edition. In the 1968 edition, the chapter on Art Nouveau is the longest, and Gaudí receives more than seven pages — all of this despite the following Pevsner assessments: "excess and artifice," "violent expression [which] tires one soon," and the coup de grace, "it [Art Nouveau] was entirely lacking in a social conscience" (p. 115).

Because of its diverse nature, Art Nouveau is difficult to characterize. In precise art-history terms, its first architectural work is Victor Horta's 1892 house on Rue de Turin in Brussels; however, there are clear antecedents in the arts and crafts movement led by William Morris in England, and in the designs of Mackmurdo, the paintings of Whistler, and the sinuous prints of Voysey.(17) The movement refused the historicism of the nineteenth century and trusted individual inventiveness to shape "objects for *use* rather than with paintings and statues."(18) This insistence on useful (and functional) objects, combined with a love of the potentials of new materials (in particular, iron and glass) keep Art Nouveau, like its more rationalist counterparts, clearly within the origins of the modern movement.

As a style, Art Nouveau became known for its use of stylized and individualistic *decoration*, employing bent and molded wrought iron — its ductability allowing delicate arabesque designs. Those in the movement thus characterized included Van de Velde in Holland, Henry Tiffany in the United States, and Hector Guimard, whose 1900 Paris metro stations will remain to remind us of the lightness and the playful forms possible when an architect / craftsman handles a new material.

Such an assessment, however, leaves out serious and important architects — peripheral to Art Nouveau itself, but frequently considered part of it — Louis Sullivan (whose Chicago Auditorium [1888] and the Carson Pirie Scott department store [1903] employ an organic style of decoration), the young Frank Lloyd Wright, Charles Rennie Mackintosh (whose Glasgow School of Art [1897] uses an interplay of curved and light forms against solid masses behind), and Antoni Gaudí — one of the more interesting architects of all time.

Gaudí was certainly aware of the Art Nouveau movement, and was undoubtedly influenced by it. It has been observed, however, that he employed characteristic elements of the style at such an early date that it is difficult to believe that he did not invent them.(19) His Vicens House (1880) has an iron fence built from both cast-iron and laminated-iron parts bolted together.(20)

A proud, nationalistic Catalan, Gaudí was deeply religious and spent the greater part of his life from 1884 until his death in 1926 working on the great Barcelona church of Sagrada Familia. To dismiss him as an offshoot of the modern movement would be an error, however, for his mature work in Barcelona is at once inventive, individual, and rich in potential modern imagery.

Believing that an intimate knowledge of structural construction, such as that possessed by the Catalan Gothic builders, was essential to architecture, he worked with scaled models, and with craftsmen on the building site, to improvise, change, and mold his buildings. This made him a sculptural architect — and thus a radical against the drawing and classicist styles of the formal academies.

Gaudí's best work goes far beyond the stereotyped image of Art Nouveau as surface decoration. The Parque Güell, the Güell house, the chapel at the Güell Colony (all finished near the year 1900),(21)

(19) James Johnson Sweeney and Josep Lluis Sert, Antoni Gaudí (New York: Praeger Publishers, 1970).

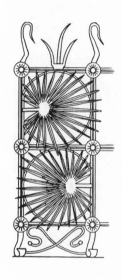

(20) The ornate gateway to the Vicens House (Barcelona, 1880) by Gaudí.

(21) A plan of the crypt of the Güell Colony Chapel, located just south of Barcelona. The irregular spacing of the columns comes from the different and irregular vaulting above. In addition, each column is tilted, to express precisely the actual structural forces from the vaulting. In another of his books, Pioneers of Modern Design, (Norwich, England: Penguin Books, 1960), Nicholas Pevsner calls this church "amazing, fascinating, horrible and inimitable"!! (p. 112).

stamp him as an artist of great inventive abilities and daring structural insight. His work is free in both plan and elevation. At the Casa Milá,(22) built in Barcelona in 1905, each apartment has irregularly shaped walls and undulating balconies with wrought-iron railings. Constructed of cut stone, the building could never have been built with the plans and contract documents now normally used by architects.

(22) *The plan (a) and the facade (b) of Gaudí's Casa Milá in Barcelona.*

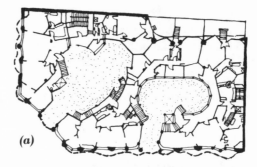

(a)

(b)

Gaudí's greatest contribution — only now tentatively being recognized — was his demonstration that an intuitive, personal architecture was possible within the original tenets of the modern movement. Basing his aesthetic on the organic forms found in nature, Gaudí nonetheless tested his structural innovations with the most sophisticated model techniques of his day, and he demonstrated that the empiricist tradition could produce a stunning new architecture.

The immediate future, however, lay with the rationalist strain of the movement, and in particular the architects of the Bauhaus. Art Nouveau was dismissed as being irrational (and therefore irrelevant).

After the First World War had at last broken down the final resistance of the Beaux Arts tradition, the new values of clear, logical, technical, functional, and "pure" architecture triumphed. What happened is best exemplified by the emergence of the Bauhaus School, and the ushering in of the so-called Heroic Age. Founded in Weimar by Gropius in 1919, the Bauhaus lasted until 1933, when the school was forced to close by the rise of the National Socialist Workers German Party. During the fourteen years of its existence, the Bauhaus stamped a distinctive character on the design methodology of the modern movement.

In German, *Bauhaus* means "to construct" or "to build a house," and the Bauhaus teaching method was one of learning by doing rather than learning from reading or through lectures. While history was not abandoned, it was actively neglected, particularly the recent history of the Beaux Arts tradition.

In regard to the crafts, the Bauhaus taught that the artist and the craftsman were related, and the school's basic design course began from scratch, using folded paper, spools, cardboard, string, and other basic materials. In the more advanced courses, industrial machines were used, and textiles, furniture designs, and car body-work were all studied as being germane to a modern design and architectural education.

Artists and graphic designers such as Paul Klee, Wassily Kandinsky, Josef Albers, Herbert Bayer, Johannes Itten, and László Moholy-Nagy worked together with architects such as Marcel Breuer and Mies van der Rohe. The eventual impact of the Bauhaus's slowly emerging philosophy of functionalism, industrial craftsmanship, and clear rationalism was immense. Typical is the Breuer chair,(23) which symbolized Gropius and Moholy-Nagy's belief in the unity of art and technology.

The Bauhaus move from Weimar to Dessau in 1925-26 signified the evolution of a consistent aesthetic most frequently referred to as the International style. The architect who has clearly come to represent this aesthetic was Mies van der Rohe. His earlier compositions, such as his 1923 project for a brick villa,(24) foreshadow the maturity of his brilliant design for the German Pavilion at the Barcelona International Exhibition in 1929.(25) In this pavilion, Mies lucidly states the functional tenets of the International style: Horizontal and planar walls enclose exhibition spaces that are sparsely, but elegantly, furnished with crafted, industrial furniture. Marble-slab walls are contrasted against thin steel columns and sheets of glass.

(23) This 1920s chair by Marcel Breuer epitomizes the integration of the arts espoused by the Bauhaus. Although Breuer was later to become an architect of considerable note, he remains best remembered for this industrialized chair design.

(24) This 1923 proposed project for a brick villa, owing much to Frank Lloyd Wright and the later expressionist movement, is one of Mies's most famous conceptualizations.

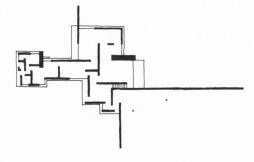

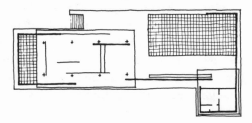

(25) Plan of the German Pavilion at Barcelona, 1929, by Mies van der Rohe.

(26) Hans Poelzig, P. V. J. Klint, and Michel de Klerk all did buildings that fall loosely within the expressionist movement. Klerk's fascinating Eigen Haard Housing Estate in Amsterdam (1921) has, according to Pevsner, "the oddest angular or curved sudden projections, and the oddest roofs and skylines" — An Outline of European Architecture, 6th ed. [Baltimore: Penguin Books, 1960], p. 666. Fortunately for Pevsner, expressionism (like Art Nouveau before it) gave way to a purer rationalism and "the new style, . . . temporarily doped by the fumes of expressionism, reestablished itself"! (p. 667).

(27) The Einstein Tower, Potsdam (1921), by Mendelsohn. This building had an immediate effect on many American designers, who were interested in streamlining locomotive engines, cars, and buildings. There are also interesting parallels between the tower and the work of Rudolf Steiner, whose Goetheanum building is not far in distance from Corbusier's Ronchamp chapel.

(28) Concerning his version of plasticity, Wright said he meant "continuity in which walls, ceilings, floors, now become not

When one compares the Barcelona pavilion with and against the contemporary Villa Savoye by Corbusier, it becomes obvious that by 1930, the triumph of the modern movement — at least in avante-garde architectural circles — was complete. Although the Barcelona pavilion is elegant *functionalism* and the Villa Savoye is cubist-inspired purism, both buildings are industrial, clean in line and form, and technologically oriented, and both use new materials in structure and in construction methodology. And in their conceptions of flowing, interlocked, nondiscrete space, Mies and Corbusier are much closer in architectural spirit than they are apart.

This triumph of a new rationalist aesthetic was not achieved, however, without the interaction — and often the conflict — of many other architectural "isms." cubism, de Stijl, constructivism, and perhaps most importantly, expressionism, all played a role.

Although expressionism as a defined movement was short-lived, lasting only from 1919 to about 1925, its undeclared goal of bridging the gap between rationalism and intuition deserves better recognition. Influenced by the personal individualism of Art Nouveau, the dramatic power of futurism, and the underlying functionalism of the early pioneers, the expressionists created works that fused both the romantic and the rational strains of the emerging modern movement. Equally important, the expressionists demonstrated an understanding of the new spatial concepts of viewing forms as continuously linked and only to be understood through movement. In their best work there exists both a restless mannerism and a personal humanism.(26)

The little-studied architect Erich Mendelsohn called this quality dynamism, and in his striking Einstein Tower in Potsdam (1921), he expressed a curvilinearity rarely equaled in architecture.(27) With its sweeping horizontals, the Einstein Tower has frequently been likened to a great ocean liner, streamlined for movement, and capturing a plasticity in external form reminiscent of Frank Lloyd Wright.(28) In his strivings to achieve a personal, individual style united with a functional program, Mendelsohn exerted considerable influence on younger architects in Europe.

In fact, many of the beginning teachers at Gropius's Bauhaus were influenced by expressionist theory. Even Mies designed in 1919 a glass tower clearly inspired by a romanticism not to be found in his later work.(29) However, as the Second World War neared, a belief in functionalism allied with technology best exemplified the aesthetical directions of the modern movement, and the international style, which was to lay dormant during the war years, was destined to reemerge as preeminent.

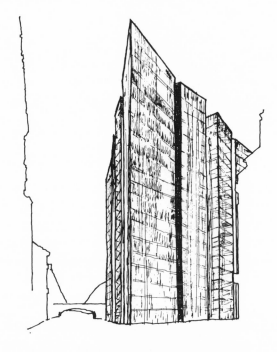

only party to each other but are part of each other. . . *Architects were no longer tied to Greek space but were free to enter into the space of Einstein"* — The Natural House *[New York: Horizon Press, Meridian, 1954], p. 20.*

(29) Project for the Friedrichstrasse station competition, Berlin, 1919, by Mies van der Rohe. Pevsner says that the intense expressionist "fascination with America and the wonderment at American daring, ruthlessness, and tempo . . . can also be regarded as a sign of a romantic rather than a rational frame of mind" (An Outline of European Architecture, *p. 665).*

1946 found much of the world ravaged and in dire need of housing, rebuilt industry, new roadways, and transportation systems. With much of Europe and Japan in ruins, the United States had emerged as the world's dominant industrial and economic power. Their cities undamaged (at least in the physical sense), Americans were free to express unabashedly their love of convenience and technology. Cars, boats, television sets, stereophonic sound equipment, transistorized radios, electric leg shavers, and hair curlers, and an endless array of gadgetry (including even the electric toothbrush!) were all produced — and purchased. It was felt, not without good cause, that since technology had accomplished so much in the product and convenience

(30) Buckminster Fuller proposed the Dymaxion house as early as 1927. As a prepackaged home, it would have rotated as the sun moved, thus maximizing light in its small but efficient interior.

There is no question but that packaged housing is feasible (consider the casing for the electric refrigerator and the assembly line for the automobile), but the sums of capital involved are very large.

From 1945 onward, the United States government (specifically the FHA) put its money into guaranteed low-interest home loans. The result was an enormous growth in suburbia, the continued insistence on individuality, and single-family houses.

(31) The Seagram Tower in New York City (1958), by Mies van der Rohe, is recognized by many as the last great building of the International style.

markets, it could also be applied to the housing industry.(30) The suburban dream became an almost-reality, and the middle class expanded to include the plumber, the electrician, and the beauty parlor operator, as well as the traditional professional white-collar worker.

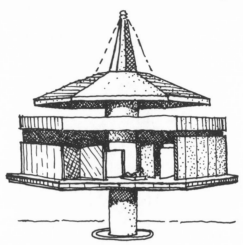

In the larger, business sense, the corporation became the keystone to expanding markets, and capitalism became associated, not with small privately owned enterprise, but rather with multinational companies dealing with new nations. For these companies the International style became both obvious and desirable. A functional, clearly detailed box rising to forty, fifty, sixty, even one hundred stories in height, became a prestigious means of identifying power. And no Gothic cathedral spire could outdo the care lavished by a design master on these pristine and elegant corporate towers.

Accepting the mantle of the leading practitioner of the International style, Mies designed many such buildings, culminating in the Seagram Tower in New York City.(31) Probably more than any other, this building became a symbol of functionalism, the International style, and the perceived predominant aesthetic of the modern movement.

Despite the preeminence of the International style, however, it did not, in fact, express either the inner heady social goals that had originated the modern movement or the new goals that had emerged as a result of the war. For in addition to its physical damage, the Second World War had profoundly disturbed our sense of well-being and our understanding of man's relationship to society. Goebbel's propaganda had demonstrated that the organized social state did not always produce better individuals with richer lives, but in fact often resulted in an inhumane society capable of monstrous acts.

The earlier 1920s belief that society and architecture working together would produce a clean, healthy, and better environment for the people had been proven false. Society and architecture had rarely cooperated, and even when they did, the results were often detrimental rather than beneficial.(32) The goals and aesthetics of the modern movement, at least in the United States, became confused, as American society became increasingly complex. The International style — never more than one style, one direction, within the modern movement — became identified in the public's eye with corporate high-style modern architecture, while functionalism, as championed by the Bauhaus, was designed, not as clean, well-proportioned, and finely detailed architecture, but rather as cheap boxes, built to save money and to maximize profit. Both commercial and public architecture in the United States floundered in this aesthetic conflict. Flat-roofed campus-plan school boxes, highway strip development, and suburban sprawl (bearing little resemblance to the elegance of Mies) proliferated and became the norm during the country's economic boom in the 1950s.(33)

(32) The architect Albert Speer's book Inside The Third Reich *carefully documents the frightening implications when an artist abandons his personal convictions in favor of those of the socialized state.*

Not all architecture produced for societal goals, of course, is necessarily evil — the Blue Ridge Parkway, the Cloisters museum in New York, Rockefeller Center, and the Greenbelt New-town housing developments, are all examples of vital and meaningful projects built in the United States during the 1930s and 1940s for many of the same social goals as those expressed in more dictatorial states.

The problem after 1946 in the United States — although not in Europe — was that socially inspired architecture lost its appeal in the individualistic tide of middle-class affluence.

(33) Louis Sullivan's famous dictum "Form follows function" had lost its meaning. Sullivan's intent was that a bank should look like a bank — i.e., its aesthetics and its form should convey the symbolic meaning of its functional use. This dictum was not easy to achieve in 1890, when banks, civic buildings, commercial towers, etc., were being built to look like Greek and Roman temples.

In addition, those critics who claim functionalism itself always means cheap boxes should consider again the Farnsworth House, built in the 1950s near Plains, Illinois, by Mies van der Rohe — an elegant "functionalist" (and International style) box that is certainly not cheap!

(34) The pragmatic tradition can be seen in the best work of Eero Saarinen — later to be carried on by Skidmore, Owings and Merrill; Edward Larrabee Barnes; I. M. Pei; Roche and Dinkeloo; etc.

The Brutalist movement, centered in England, grew out of an admiration for the new directions (after 1946) begun by Corbusier. In particular, the housing projects by Stirling and Gown are exemplary.

The technologists thrived in California, where Eliot Noyes and Charles and Ray Eames influenced a host of younger architects, including Cesar Pelli, and the Los Angeles greys, a group using technology in combination with an aesthetic espousing the life-styles of the West Coast. In England the archigramists espoused pop-art mechanics, and more recently the minimalists have carried on the technologist's tradition.

The metabolists in Japan built on futurist theory, as well as additive (organic) form, to espouse a striking new architecture.

(35) In 1982, Team 10 still existed, although the dynamism of its earlier days was gone. The best expression of the Team's beliefs can be found in the Team 10 Primer, *first published in 1962, and edited by Alison Smithson and republished in 1968 (Cambridge, Mass: M.I.T. Press). The members in 1968 included Bakema, Van Eyck, Candilis, the Smithsons, Woods, de Carlo, Coderch, Pologni, Soltan, Wewerka, and Erskine.*

Without a clear, commonly agreed-upon aesthetic held by both the public and the building professions, a plethora of submovements and "isms" appeared. From 1945 to 1970, these mini-movements included pragmatism, Brutalism, existentialism, technologism, metabolism, neo-humanism, and neo-rationalism, as well as back-to-earth environmentalism and the always-present anarchism and socialism groups.(34) At least two of these groups, one in Europe and one in the United States, deserve special consideration, however.

Team 10, a humanist-oriented group, grew out of the earlier CIAM movement in Europe, who had based their "Athens Charter" of 1933 on Corbusier's goals of urban design. Feeling that the older group was too rigid in its planning principles, particularly in the field of mass housing, this group of younger architects in 1954 founded their own movement.

From the beginning, Team 10 was a loose association of architects championing two broad areas of mutual concern.(35) The first of these was the continued need by society for new and rationally designed housing. The expression of this concern was led by Jacob Bakema, Alison and Peter Smithson, George Candilis, and Shadrach Woods, who argued that large-scale housing should not merely be large, but that it should also reflect the social needs of the family, with streets for people, balconies, separated traffic walkways, and a humane scale.

A second concern was the perceived need to reexpress individualized spaces where each human could feel comfortable and at home while still a part of the larger whole. The argument for this second, more theoretical, concern was led by Aldo Van Eyck, who (frequently phrasing his beliefs in almost poetical language) stated that continuity, linkages, and the thresholds from one spatial scale to another — such as the door, the window, and the gateway — were means by which man could comprehend his place within the larger urban structure.

His best-known and most often quoted remarks concern his definition for place and occasion:

What ever space and time means place and occasion mean more...

For space in the image of man is place, and time in the image of man is occasion. ...

Is man able to penetrate the material he organizes into hard shape between one man and another between what is here and what is there,
between this and a following moment?

Is he able to find the right place for the right occasion?

Is he able to linger?

No — so start with this: articulate the inbetween. Make a welcome of each door.

a countenance of each window.

Make of each place; a bunch of places each house and each city (a house is a tiny city, a city a huge house). ...

Man still breathes in and out.
When is architecture going to do the same?(36)

This concern for the intermediary space is brilliantly espoused in Van Eyck's design for an orphanage in Amsterdam.(37) Within this building, he creates a series of interior children's streets, each with resting places, small playing areas, and doorways into "intermediary places." Few buildings have better expressed the social dreams of the modern movement, in combination with a personal and humane architecture.

(36) Aldo van Eyck quoted in Progressive Architecture, *September 1962, p. 155.*

(37) These two drawings illustrate Van Eyck's concern for both personal and intermediary places. Sketch (a) shows a reading room (or alcove) within a larger domed room — a place where girls may gather to talk, read, or just be alone. Sketch (b) shows a seating area, half outside and half under a covered walkway — a place of linkage and continuity between "here and there."

(a)

(b)

(38) The Philadelphia School, like Team 10, embraced a wide range of particular interests, only loosely organized in and around Philadelphia and the University of Pennsylvania. Some of the members included Le Ricolais, Komendant, Geddes, Bacon, Tyng, McHarg, Venturi — and Romaldo Giurgola, who continues through his quiet insistence on quality of construction, combined with humane scale, to influence young architects in the Philadelphia area.

(39) Kahn's importance has been acknowledged elsewhere in this book, see: Introduction (Richards Medical Center); chapter 1, note 26 (the Trenton Bathhouse); chapter 4, notes 28, 29 (an extensive existentialist quote); and chapter 5 (text discussion of "what the building wants to be").

(40) From the Louis Kahn Notebook *(Cambridge, Mass.: M.I.T. Press, 1973).*

(41) The plan of the Dacca Assembly Hall shows how the hall is surrounded by

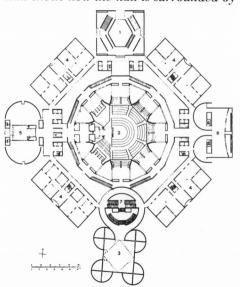

An American group called the Philadelphia School had many of the humanist goals found in Team 10; unlike Team 10, however, this group had a clear spiritual leader — the architect-leader Louis Kahn.(38) Using the graduate design program at the University of Pennsylvania as a base, Kahn preached an almost mystical blend of humanism, craftsmanship, and existentialism.(39)

In search of an elemental or a priori reason for architecture, Kahn argued that before form, there is always a human idea or need, which has an "existence-will."

I have learned that a good question is greater than the most brilliant answer. . . . A man is always greater than his works because he can never fully express his aspirations. . . .

. . . Turn to feeling and away from thought. In feeling is the psyche. Thought is both feeling and presence of order. . . . This Existence-Will is in the psyche. All that we desire to create has its beginning in feeling alone. . . .

Realization of this nature is the merging of feeling and thought when the mind is in closest rapport with the psyche, the source of what a thing wants to be. It is the beginning of form.(40)

Again and again, Kahn was to make the proposition that before form, there exists an idea that wills itself, through order, into being. Thus, he was always to search for elemental, almost abstract, forms, which expressed for him a sereneness and fundamental correctness. Any of his later works, such as the unfinished capitol of Bangladesh at Dacca,(41) express this idea of existence-will in powerful forms. Squares, circles, pyramidal sections, and intersections of basic geometrics — all complexly interact in apparent simplicity.

As a teacher, however, Kahn's greatest contribution probably lies, not in his design work, but rather in his philosophic insistence that form does *not* necessarily follow from function, but rather is ordered from prior human feelings or desires. These teachings became the first clear American alternative away from Bauhaus functionalism, and they influenced not only the Philadelphia School but a generation of younger architects looking for new directions and inspiration.

By 1970 it had become apparent that the modern movement no longer had any clearly believed-in direction for its aesthetics. Internationalism had ended, but no single "ism" had emerged to replace it. Aesthetics had become plural rather than singular. In large part, this was due to social and cultural change. As older societies ravaged during the Second World War reemerged, often with great material advances in technological production, and as entirely new societies, new nations, arose where only primitive livelihood had formerly existed, there arose the corresponding need for regional richness, a return to historical precedent, and the desire for local control and preservation of both the natural and the man-made environment.

Not only had the modern movement's cry for functionalism been misinterpreted, but material increase in and of itself was not enough. A surfeit of sterile and stripped boxes was not better than one box.(42) In addition, the modern movement's early insistence on originality and newness — necessary perhaps for the overthrow of the Beaux Arts tradition — had in the ensuing years also overthrown both continuity in history and the older linkages in architectural form itself. Buildings never photographed within a context or architectural fabric were constructed as jewels to be set on sites conceived in independent separateness.

Two cities — both frequently cited as being of architectural interest — are good examples of this malaise. One of them, Columbus, Indiana, a showcase for prominent American architects, has, under the patronage of an industrial philanthropist, been filled with isolated jewels, which despite their sometimes splendid forms, bear little relation to either the social and cultural life or the architectural fabric of a small Midwestern town.

the ancillary facilities. Simple, elemental geometrics — squares, circles, ellipses, etc. — are used in a complex grouping.

For Kahn, the act of gathering together became the "existence-will" expressed as the central form. The Prayer Hall, as a particulary important Islamic building, is nonetheless given its own unique form (a square inside of four cylinders) and is rotated slightly off the main axis, for further emphasis.

The overall result is a rich mix of special forms, creating striking shades and shadows beneath the strong sun of the Indian subcontinent.

(42) Some historians believe that the box-like sterility of anonymous giant public-housing projects is at least partly due to Marxist political thought: the proletariat political demands resulting in more buildings but not better ones.

Nonetheless, the dream of providing better housing for the masses is fundamental to the modern movement. As Candilis and Woods stated, in our age it is "impossible for each man to construct his house for himself. It is for the architect to make it possible for the man to make his house his home." (Team 10 Primer, 2nd ed., p. 74).

(43) Venturi's book Complexity and Contradiction in Architecture, *published in 1966 (New York: The Museum of Modern Art), has had an immense influence within schools of architecture and on the later postmodernist group. The inherent problem of Venturi's argument is that buildings that are ordinary, commonplace, and full of contradictions are also often banal, and when one champions the banal, he frequently gets it.*

(44) The plan of the Byker Wall housing project shows how the major building forms — a long wall that encloses and protects the interior low-scale units - is used as a buffer from highway noise.

Through color, changing of material, and a constant personal contact with residents during the design of the project, Erskine was able to construct an environment commented on favorably by both its occupants and its architectural critics.

The other city, Las Vegas, has been hailed as the queen of strip development, its gambling casinos representing pop-art palaces for the masses. The architect-writer Robert Venturi has gone so far as to suggest that the ordinary and commonplace should be studied to bring back a richness in architectural aesthetics.(43) But while Las Vegas's multicolored, lighted palaces are indeed dazzling, it is not clear that they represent any real subconscious desire of our society. Las Vegas can also be seen as the ultimate environmental crassness that results when the only architectural criteria is unbridled economic profit.

One final current problem of the modern movement is its title, for after more than eighty years of existence, the modern movement is no longer modern. As a word, *modern* implies a certain revolutionary fervor — stressing originality, newness, and a sweeping away of the old. Whatever is current, i.e., avant-garde and modern, will be correct. While the title was proper when the movement was indeed new, it now seems inappropriate in light of our current need for a contextual architecture rooted within historical continuity.

The 1970s and 1980s reactions to the problems of the modern movement's aesthetic have been as varied as the situation and the place. In Europe, architects are reawakening to the historical importance of the modern movement's early heroes, in particular Frank Lloyd Wright and Le Corbusier. (Being closer to history, Europeans never completely threw it away, despite futurist and Bauhaus enjoinders to do so.) Humane scale and historical context are being reconsidered in conjunction with the goals of a social architecture possible through advanced construction technology. Typical of these concerns is the Byker Wall housing project in England by Ralph Erskine.(44) Utilizing a technology that allows for a giant housing framework, Erskine has relied upon individual family infill to create a rich urban fabric, both socially and architecturally.

In the United States, a loose grouping of architects, referred to as postmodernists, have drawn the most attention. Like so many groups in opposition to the recent past, postmodernists are allied more by what they are against than by what they are for. The modern movement, they say, is now sterile (if not dead) and possesses a false functionalism that has destroyed the richness of architecture, once possible through ornament and historical symbolism. Suggestions toward starting a new aesthetic, however, are as varied (and often as contradictory) as the diverse interests of each subgroup of postmodernists.

One group, exemplified by the work of Robert Stern, suggests that historical allusion, ornament, and a rich contextual symbolism are necessary. This group, openly eclectic, argues art for art's sake and freely borrows classical, Beaux-Arts details to add richness.

Another group, influenced by Venturi, argues for commonplace vernacular (recent-history regionalism) and an architecture filled with ambiguity, irregularity, and popular values.

Yet another group suggests that a new language is needed — one that is more abstract and deals with the logic of pure architectural form. Peter Eisenman builds exercises in intricate geometric forms and numbers his houses 1, 2, 3, 4, etc. Michael Graves does painterly compositions with layers of entry facades, each carefully colored to create symbolic illusions of depth (in addition to the real layers of the building walls).

One of the more interesting of the postmodernists is Richard Meier, who does not formally reject the modern movement, but rather uses elements of Corbusier's purist period in new sculptural explorations of space. His Atheneum in New Harmony, Indiana, has curved walls, ramps, flying projections, and sinuously twisting railings, all to express a circulation system more symbolic than needed for functional reasons.(45)

(45) An axonometric drawing of the Atheneum. This drawing style — a popular technique with postmodernists — shows well Meier's use of architectural elements to express a fragmented sculptural architecture, in which spatial movement (and excitement) becomes the building idea.

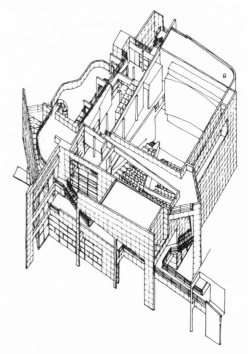

(46) Some critics have been scathing. In his review of the book Post-Modernism: The New Synthesis, *by Charles Jencks, Wolf Von Eckhardt, the architectural critic for the* Washington Post, *says: "Jencks' scholarship manifests itself mainly by the heap of names that covers the floor under his tenuous theoretical constructions. And Post-Modernism is as yet only a side show attracting mainly young architecture students and editors of chic magazines" (*AIA Journal, *September 1981, p. 77).*

(47) Quoted from a lecture given by Huxtable at the American Academy of Arts and Sciences and published in the January 1981 Architectural Record, *p. 79. This lecture, "The Troubled State of Architecture," and its sequel, "Is Modern Architecture Dead?" (*Architectural Record, *October 1981), are an excellent introduction to the theoretical fervor sweeping the American architectural community since the late 1970s.*

(48) "The Troubled State of Architecture" (p. 79). Mrs. Huxtable is often even more biting and pungent. In the same address, she also states:

> *Small ideas are delivered in large words and weighed down with exotic and private references. Intellectual trendiness is rampant. . . .*

> *I have been harboring a chilling thought: some architects really are building the way they are thinking, if that is the right word for what is going on in their heads. (p. 75)*

While Mrs. Huxtable expresses concern that today's students fail to see the heroic, humane goals of the modern movement,

But postmodernism has itself come under serious attack. Many trained professionals still feel deeply that they perform a needed service for society. Unwilling to throw out the baby with the bathwater, these architects argue that it is possible to acknowledge the reemerging need for aesthetical concern with historical context, cultural continuity, and regional richness without abandoning the goals of a dedicated social art.

In addition, postmodernism (like modernism) also suffers from mislabeling, for if modernism is what is new and current, then something that comes later cannot, by definition, exist concurrently! Indeed, the semantic jargon and the pretentious (and often intentional) misuse of language that surrounds postmodernist theory makes much of the movement's questioning appear trivial and irrelevant.(46)

Perhaps the noted architecture critic Ada Louise Huxtable has best stated both the positive and the negative aspects of postmodernism. On the positive side, she suggests that "all of this is part of something deeper: a search for meaning and symbolism, a way to re-establish architecture's ties with human experience, a way to find and express a value system, a concern for architecture in the context of society."(47) Mrs. Huxtable also sounds a negative alarm, however: " . . . two factors disturb me deeply: the danger of architects increasingly addressing each other, with a widening comprehension gap between the professional and the public, and the sharp trend away from sociological to exclusively aesthetic concerns." And again, "It [architecture] is now backing away blindly . . . from a sociological or environmental context and into the realm of pure art again — back into an ivory tower with a vengeance, surrounded by an unsettling aura of ecstasy and unease."(48)

This brings us to the real and pertinent question: Is the modern movement dead?

One purpose of this chapter — as an outlined and shortened history — has been to show that far from being dead, the modern movement remains alive and well and is vitally responding to new challenge. For the underlying social needs present at the movement's beginning remain with us. Improved city environments, better housing, functional buildings, and an architecture more egalitarian — open and accessible to a larger audience — are still desires of our society. And, while today's world is infinitely complex and pluralistic and no longer naively expects architecture to solve social problems, it still sees architecture as symbolically expressing its cultural goals.

Thus it is that a healthy reappraisal of aesthetical values is refreshing — for our comprehension of space has changed, just as our understanding of architecture's role has changed. To realize that architecture as an art does not mold the society, but rather culturally enriches it, does not deny the validity of the underlying social concerns of the modern movement. At this moment, serious architects continue to reexamine their aesthetical directions, learning again from history (the recent history of the modern movement as well as the preceding classical history) and building a shared aesthetic clearly within the tenets of modernism — an aesthetic less strident than that espoused by many postmodernists, an aesthetic socially conscious, yet individually humane. A prime example of this new awareness of the importance of recent history and humanist attitudes is the interest now being shown in the work of Alvar Aalto.

Aalto, who was born in 1898, was a prodigious architect, with more than 300 buildings, town plans, and projects to his credit. Despite its quantity, his work remains difficult to assess — for Aalto followed no dogma or easily discernible aesthetical path — but one personal quality underlies all of his creative output: He was a humanist, who never let his participation in the functionalist direction of the modern movement overshadow his deeper concern for creating a humane architecture. And there is every reason to believe that in our current reappraisals of the modern movement, Aalto will continue to grow in stature as the architect who best united the rationalist and the empiricist, or intuitive, strains of the new architecture.

not even bothering "to wonder what the excitement was all about," it is possible this is an unfounded worry. Already, many students see the revived interest in history as refreshing, but the studied historicism of much of postmoderism — like the archigram movement of the 1960s — may die from its own simple irrelevancy. And, fortunately for architects, architecture, and society, much of what gets published in dogmatic avant-garde magazines as being postmodern and theoretically important never gets built.

(49) A sketch of the Turun Sanomat newspaper plant reveals Aalto's early acceptance of Corbusier's five points of architecture. Less than a year later, he was to move forward from this position to a more unique and personal, yet still modern, style.

(50) The first-floor plan of the Sanatorium at Paimo (a) is reflective of the free-plan compositions advocated by the Bauhaus. While the sanatorium is completely functional and clear, it also shows Aalto's fascination with the sudden curve (or the irregular form) added within the orthagonal grid. The entry desk (b), with its curve at that place the visitor first asks for directions, is indicative of this fascination.

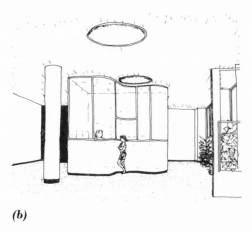

(b)

Aalto, who was schooled in Helsinki, started on his own in 1922, and his early work reflected the National Romantic and Classic Revival styles then popular in Finland. He was soon to embrace the underlying tenets of the modern movement, however, and his 1928 design for the Turun Sanomat newspaper plant at Turku is perhaps the first modern building in Finland.(49) Two other projects, however, catapulted him into the first ranks of European architects: his 1927 competition entry for the municipal library in Viipuri, which was not finished until 1935, and his 1929 design for a tuberculosis sanatorium at Paimo, also a competition winner.

In particular, the sanatorium surprised many critics by its sophistication.(50) In this group of buildings, he oriented each room carefully to receive sunlight, but not glare. The ceilings were painted a soft color, and light fixtures were designed to avoid direct light in the patients' eyes. His famous sun-trap was a daring cantilevered structure, but

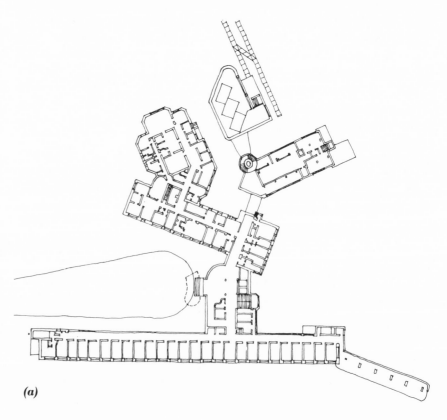

(a)

more importantly, his disposition of the buildings was informal, yet in character with the nature of the site. The critic Kenneth Frampton says of the sanatorium (and the Viipuri library), "Aalto's lifelong concern for the overall *ambience* of a space and for the way it may be modified through the responsive filtration of heat, light, and sound, was first fully formulated in these works."(51)

It was but a short time before Aalto's concern for modifying technology to serve a purpose greater than functionalism, led him to spatial organizations that were more organic and free-flowing than those of other Heroic Age architects. His restrained designs always show a concern for human use, and he detailed railings, stairs, light fixtures, wall surfaces — i.e., anything one could touch, feel, or see at an immediate level — with infinite care.(52)

The building that most clearly established his international stature was (again, a competition winner) his design for the Finnish Pavilion at the 1939 World's Fair in New York.(53) The walls of this pavilion, sloping inward from floor to ceiling, allowed for displays on each higher level, all to be seen from the main floor. Aalto called this arranging products like a country store. In addition, the sloping curves were covered with small, randomly patterned wooden battens, and the entire building was a testament to the advanced industrialized wood technology then to be found in Finland. The pavilion represents Aalto's final development within the tenets of functionalist architecture. Henceforth his buildings were always to express a more personal style of intuitive organic form combined with rational technology — a style sometimes referred to as romantic modernism.

Several motifs, or concerns, can be found in all of Aalto's final work from 1944 until his death in 1976. Among these are:

1. Defining a clear circulation path (ease of human functional movement) despite the often complex forms of the building. One never gets lost in one of his designs; there is always a hierarchal sense of direction.

(51) Kenneth Frampton, Modern Architecture: A Critical History (New York: Oxford, 1980), p. 198.

(52) In 1960, at the Royal Institute of British Architects, he was to state, "To make architecture more human means . . . a functionalism much larger than the merely technical one."

(53) Aalto won first, second, and third places in this competition! The plan (a), with its overlapping curved lines, cannot be understood without also viewing the perspective sketch (b). Every surface is in movement, yet the overall functional organization is easily perceived.

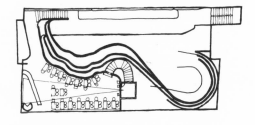

(a)

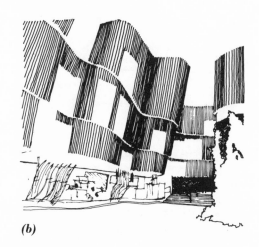

(b)

2. Harmonizing light quality through the use of skylights. Perhaps as a result of the seasonal, uneven light qualities to be found in Finland, Aalto preferred to equalize, soften, and yet maximize incoming light intensities. This concern for even skylighting also led him to deemphasize the window.

(54) In this regard, Aalto clearly was at odds with the mainstream of the modern movement — which, since Wright's Prairie houses, has been fascinated with destroying the traditional wall between outside and inside. This fascination has been abetted by lightweight structural columns and beams that technologically allow the removal of the older, solid walled corner.

3. Creating an outside as outside and an inside as inside. Perhaps again as a result of Finland's climate, characterized by harsh winters, he liked the grand interior room, or atrium (sometimes even expressed as an open courtyard). Despite his love of organic, free-flowing interior space, however, he did not (as Frank Lloyd Wright did) open his walls to dematerialize the line between indoors and outdoors.(54)

(55) The sketch (a) shows the symbolic grass-stepped entry to the upper level of the town hall. The actual paved entry is on the other side of the courtyard, adjacent to a parking area, as shown at the top right in the plan (b). The courtyard is also more symbolic than functional, and is meant to be looked into rather than traversed.

4. Enriching his buildings with texture, color, and decoration, most often from the use of warm wood and soft brick. Many of his later buildings have walls modeled with screens, overhanging trellises, and bright-colored tiles, all of which create a layering of surfaces.

All of these concerns can be seen in the town hall at Saynatsalo, built in 1952.(55) Constructed *around* a small hill-rise, the building combines

(a)

The meeting room has an intricate wooden-truss design reminiscent of traditional Finnish structures. Saynatsalo demonstrates Aalto's mastery of small-scale projects in addition to his later large town-planning proposals.

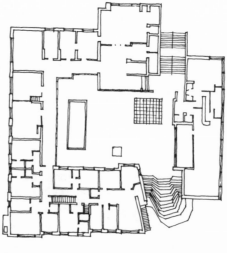

(b)

small-scale commercial enterprises on the lower level with civic functions above, where it opens to a small raised courtyard (or atrium). The sloped roof of the town meeting room marks it as the dominant and most important form within the complex. While the overall size of the project is small, its composition gives it a grandeur in keeping with its function. Finally, its construction of dark brick, with natural-wood roof trusses and windows, gives the entire design a domestic, intimate quality much admired by critics. While Aalto was to design many more buildings,(56) none has been more universally acclaimed than Saynatsalo.

(56) *Typical of these is the Institute of Technology (1964) at Otaniemi. Although vastly larger than Saynatsalo, the project has many similar concerns. Particularly striking is Aalto's use of the lecture hall (a) as the focal point of the composition. A dramatic and powerfully irregular form, the hall is inserted into the regularized grid. Note in the plan (b) that the smallest and last grouping of buildings — in this case the school of architecture — has its own small courtyard, and irregular lecture-hall form, reminiscent not only of the overall Otaniemi concept but also of the town hall at Saynatsalo.*

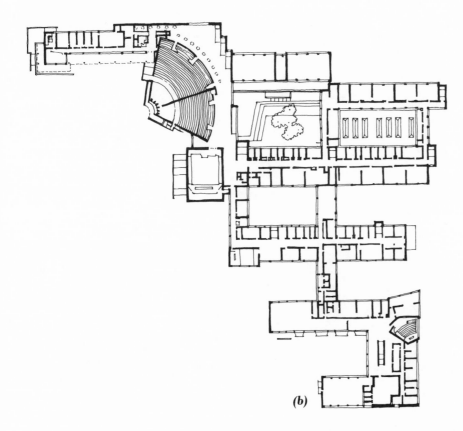

(b)

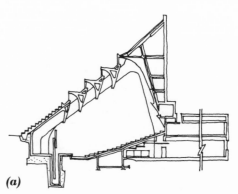

(a)

Taken as a whole, Aalto's career demonstrates how a sensitive architect can build upon the original goals and aspirations of the modern movement in creating his own personal aesthetic.

A final question remains: In what new direction are the architectural aesthetics of the modern movement now headed? Clearly, no one knows. What is certain is that we are living in a period of great social change: At least on a surface level, new fashions, new styles, and new submovements will rapidly appear and as rapidly be discarded.

At a philosophical level, one that deals with deeper societal and personal values, we can only speculate and hope that the humane and worthwhile goals and dreams of the modern movement reemerge in a lasting architectural aesthetic.

XI   EDUCATION AND AN AFTERWORD

This chapter is, first, about education — specifically an education in architecture at the college level; second, it is a final plea, or an afterword, for developing an aesthetic rooted in humanism — an aesthetic guiding us toward an architecture that may be shared.

Architectural education has as its first priority the same goal as all higher education: teaching the student how to think imaginatively. For it is at the university that the typical American student is first commonly asked to convert knowledge — the minutiae of facts, details, and dates — into the ability to organize, to conceptualize, to think creatively.

Alfred North Whitehead stated this goal succinctly when he said, "The ideal of a university is not so much knowledge, as power. Its business is to convert the knowledge of the boy into the power of a man."(1) The university must seek to help each student bring together discontinuous experiences and unorganized thought into more coherent patterns, into structured concepts that help in understanding man, nature, and the world within which we exist.

Learning how to think at this conceptual level is particularly important in our present complex age. For no student, no individual, can master the whole of our society's accumulated knowledge — we each live but a part of it. Our inherited culture(2) is so vast that in order to grasp its significance, we must convert fragmentary glimpses of it into our larger understanding. This ability to use knowledge to think at a deeper level remains the first goal of all university education.

This goal can only be achieved, however, if knowledge is considered imaginatively. Again, Whitehead stated this well: "This atmosphere of excitement, arising from imaginative consideration, transforms knowledge. A fact is no longer a bare fact: it is invested with all its possibilities. It is no longer a burden on the memory: it is energising as the poet of our dreams, and as the architect of our purposes."(3)

(1) Alfred N. Whitehead, The Aims of Education *(New York: The Macmillan Co., 1949), p. 97.*

(2) As noted in the Introduction, note 12, Jacques Barzun, a historian-philosopher at Columbia University, stated that our culture is transmitted to the next generation both by individual trained intelligence and by our inherited intellect.

Barzun's point is even more relevant to recent history when we consider the vast new potentials of stored knowledge — slide collections, microfilm manuscripts, and computer disks.

(3) Whitehead, Aims of Education, *p. 1. Whitehead's thoughts are so cogent on this point that a further quote is warranted:*

> *The proper function of a university is the imaginative acquisition of knowledge. . . . a university is imaginative, or it is nothing . . . imagination cannot be measured by the yard, or weighed by the pound, and then delivered to the students by members of the faculty. It can only be communicated by a faculty whose members themselves wear their learning with imagination. [p. 101]*

And again:

> *Students are alive, and the purpose of education is to stimulate and guide their self-development. It follows as a corollary from this premise that the teachers also should be alive with living thoughts. [p. 1]*

(4) J. S. Bruner, On Knowing (New York: Atheneum, 1967), p. 119. The idea of excellence has been espoused by every architectural school. The problem is always in deciding what constitutes an idea of excellence. Each cultural generation defines this differently. What is surprising is the great number of ideas that seem to transcend their own age — the Parthenon (used by romanticists, classicists, Corbusier, and Nashville, Tennessee, as being aesthetically correct), Jefferson's Lawn, the Brooklyn Bridge, the Pantheon, the Pyramids, etc.

(5) Bruner, On Knowing, p. 120. Bruner continues this argument as follows:

> . . . the structure of knowledge — its connectedness and the deviations that make one idea follow from another — is the proper emphasis in education. For it is structure, the great conceptual inventions that bring order to the congeries of disconnected observations, that gives meaning to what we may learn and makes possible the opening up of new realms of experience. (p. 120.)

This point, of course, also relates to chapter 5 and its discussion of conceptual ideas — those ideas that have great generating potential for further ideas.

A wonderful anecdote relates that Frank Lloyd Wright used to hold up his thumb and say: "See this thumb? I am not interested in 'thumb,' I am interested in 'idea of thumb.'"

To excite, to help the student think imaginatively, Whitehead asks for an exposure to greatness, or, as J. S. Bruner suggests, for "the idea of excellence."(4) If we translate this suggestion into a pragmatic architectural example, we can see that a careful study of Thomas Jefferson's design for the University of Virginia's Lawn helps us begin to understand how an educational idea of excellence can be translated into an equally exciting architectural idea of excellence. Or again, understanding Frank Lloyd Wright's early training and education, with its strong nineteenth-century transcendental roots, makes more exciting his later emergence as an architect of new and stimulating twentieth-century form. In each case, deeper perspectives and understanding can be developed if the conceptual structures of knowledge are presented imaginatively, as fresh and lively.

If a university education has as its first goal learning how to think imaginatively, and if the proper teaching method is exposure to greatness and to ideas of excellence, it follows that the appropriate subject matter should be those great organizing ideas of cultural history that have shaped our understanding of our world. Jacob Burckhardt argued this well in his classic eighteenth-century book *The History of the Civilization of the Italian Renaissance*. Burckhardt's contention was that the interconnectedness of knowledge could only be understood by studying cultural history as being alive, inhabited by flesh-and-blood people with perceptions and dreams of societal change, economic growth, and political power inextricably linked at the level of conceptual thought. Bruner states: "The history of culture is the history of . . . ideas that inevitably stem from deeper values. . . . the power of great organizing concepts is in large part that they permit us to understand and sometimes to predict or change the world in which we live."(5)

One of the strongest, and most poetic, arguments for Jacob Burckhardt's approach can be found in Hermann Hesse's 1943 masterpiece, *The Glass Bead Game*. In this novel, Hesse creates a young man, Joseph Knecht, who is studying in an idealized quasi-monastic educational teaching order called Castalia. The highest achievement in Castalia is to be allowed to participate in a theoretical contest of abstract intellectual ideas called the glass bead game. While Hesse never defines with precision how the glass bead game is actually played, we are led to believe it involves the organizing ideas of cultural history as espoused by Burckhardt, with one important exception — the ideas are treated as dry intellectualizations, devoid of the rich human context found in Burckhardt's treatise.

In Hesse's book, Joseph Knecht meets an older teacher, Father Jacobus (obviously standing in for Jacob Burckhardt!), who argues against the teaching of cultural history as a glass bead game of conceptual abstractions. Father Jacobus says:

> You Glass Bead Game players have distilled a kind of world history to suit your own tastes. It consists of nothing but the history of ideas and of art. Your history is bloodless and lacking in reality. You know all about the decay of Latin syntax in the second or third centuries and don't know a thing about Alexander or Caesar or Jesus Christ. You treat world history [as something] in which nothing but laws and formulas exist, no reality, no good and evil, no time, no yesterday, no tomorrow, nothing but an eternal, shallow present.(6)

At this point Joseph Knecht interrupts to argue that it is nonetheless important to try to bring order into history. Father Jacobus's reply is particularly cogent and appropriate:

> Of course one should bring order into history. . . . We think we have recognized a few laws in history and try to apply them to our investigations of historical truth. Suppose an anatomist is dissecting a body. He does not confront wholly surprising discoveries. Rather, he finds beneath the epidermis a congeries of organs, muscles, tendons and bones which generally conform to a pattern he has brought to his work. But if the anatomist sees nothing but his pattern, and ignores the unique, individual reality of his object, then he is a Castalian, a Glass Bead Game player; he is using mathematics on the least appropriate object. I have no quarrel with the student of history who brings to his work a touchingly childish, innocent faith in the power of our minds and our methods to order reality; but first and foremost he must respect the incomprehensible truth, reality, and uniqueness of events. Studying history, my friend, is no joke and no irresponsible game. . . . To study history means submitting to chaos and nevertheless retaining faith in order and meaning.(7)

(6) Herman Hesse, The Glass Bead Game, *trans. Richard and Clara Winston (New York: Holt, Rinehart and Winston, Bantam Books ed., 1970), p. 150.*

(7) *Ibid.*

In this book, Knecht, after becoming the Magister Ludi, or ruling monastic head of Castalia, comes to realize the truth of Father Jacobus's criticism, and he resigns as the head of the order to become a private tutor to one boy. Knecht says: "Above all we forget that we ourselves are a part of history, that we are the product of growth and are condemned to perish if we lose the capacity for further growth and change. We are ourselves history and share the responsibility for world history and our position in it" (p. 325).

(8)   This is the history vs. historicist argument, alluded to in chapter 10. Where the line is drawn between learning and borrowing is often hotly debated.

However, one aspect of studying history appears irrefutable: A proper acknowledgment of the past teaches us how better to appreciate the present. Thus, while occasional nostalgia may be pleasurable, prolonged academic living in the past is both pointless and boring.

(9)   Whitehead says: "The importance of knowledge lies in its use, *in our active mastery of it — that is to say, it lies in wisdom. It is a convention to speak of mere knowledge, apart from wisdom, as of itself imparting a peculiar dignity to its possessor" (Aims of Education, p. 39). The ideal of the university is thus not mastery over people or learning how to acquire money — it is, rather, mastery over knowledge and learning, both how to acquire wisdom and how to share it.*

(10)   In the field of architecture, this process of sharing demands the highest quality of teaching, for the felt, or intuitive, language of architectural form is more difficult to explain at a personal experiential level than at the more analytical level.

Perhaps this is why there are not many great schools of architecture — or great schools of business, law, medicine, education, etc.; sharing demands the highest standards of teaching, and there are few faculty, or students, capable of the intensity necessary.

In this remarkable passage, Hesse (through the voice of Father Jacobus) is warning us that there is an inherent danger in studying cultural history: It can be taught as something dead, a dry intellectualization, rather than as something vibrant and alive. The study of cultural history is thus the study of ideas full of human toil, sacrifice, and joy. When we learn from history, we apply and adapt cultural precedent in ways that address our present human condition and our present problems. Therefore, to borrow ideas from history in an abstract manner and without an understanding of their human cultural context is, at best, only a form of shallow eclecticism.(8)

Let us summarize what Bruner, Whitehead, Hesse — and Burckhardt before them — have all been expressing:

1. The primary goal for a university should be to help emerging young minds learn how to think, converting the knowledge of the boy into the power of the man.

2. The proper method for university teaching should be to demonstrate how knowledge can be structured into conceptual systems that lead us toward a better understanding and ordering of our own experience — an understanding leading to wisdom.(9)

3. The proper subject matter should be a human cultural history, taught with freshness by a faculty who are alive to students who are also alive, and who want to learn how to think imaginatively.(10)

How may these more general thoughts be applied specifically to an architectural education, both at the undergraduate level and at the more-specialized graduate or professional level?

First, we need to reexamine the traditional organization of university course work. It has long been recognized that to become well educated, the student needs a thorough grounding in a number of subdisciplines or areas of thought, and that among these are: *language,* both written and verbal; *scientific inquiry,* including logic, mathematics, analytical method, and both the physical and the natural sciences; the *social sciences*, including political studies, economics, sociology, anthropology; the *humanities*, including philosophy and history; and the *arts*, including music, literature, painting, sculpture, design, and architecture.(11)

If we consider these subdisciplines, not as ends within themselves, but rather as a general beginning framework for learning how to think through acquiring an understanding of Bruner's great organizing ideas of cultural history, we begin to see the difficulty in correctly placing architecture as a field of study.

For not only is architecture an art, dealing in metaphorical meaning, it is also a science and must rely upon many of the other subdisciplines of knowledge. Within the traditional university curriculum, correctly placing architecture as an area of study might be accomplished by creating a new subdiscipline, entitled the *man-made environment*, which would include architecture, both structural and civil engineering, and much of today's ecological and environmental studies.

The importance of such a subdiscipline is immense, for we now possess for the first time in our history the real potential to so alter the man-made environment as to seriously affect the larger natural environment within which we exist. And while we are beginning to sense the damages of ecological pollution, what of the damages of visual pollution? As the eastern seaboard of the United States becomes a vast megalopolis of often-ugly built form, how do we at least protect, if not improve, our aesthetical well-being?

Considering architecture and the man-made environment as an important subdiscipline remains difficult, however, within any traditional university framework, for the simple reason that within the university community, architecture has never been seriously considered an intellectual discipline.(12) Largely for this reason, many schools of architecture have reorganized their own internal curricula so as to offer a broad liberal-arts program at the undergraduate level. Despite the irony involved(13) in this shift, it is healthy, for it helps the architecture student, through an understanding of cultural history, to learn how to think creatively in his own later design work.

(11) While almost all universities give lip service to the idea of well-roundedness, few actually offer a curriculum that makes this possible. Different schools frequently teach the same courses — e.g., engineering and architecture schools, each teaching structural analysis; or business and liberal arts schools, each teaching speech, or public speaking. In the typical arts and sciences college, this specialized secularization even extends down to the department level. The end result is often a student who has remained within a single department without attending any classes in other departments or meeting students with different majors — e.g., architecture students who have taken "architectural physics" without ever having met a student of physics.

(12) The visual illiteracy so prevalent among both faculty and students at the college level is not surprising if traditional elementary school curricula are considered. As a nation, Americans have no formative childhood training in understanding how architecture is a manifestation of cultural history. And in an environmental sense, we have always treated land as being inexhaustible, maintaining the attitude of a frontier aesthetic.

(13) The irony exists within a larger context in which every college student — indeed, every thinking individual — should be concerned with how society makes its marks upon the land, and why it is doing so.

As part of a needed subdiscipline concerning the man-made environment, architecture courses would also make for better later clients, capable of discernment in architectural aesthetics.

(14) Translated into traditional course work, this means that students would take a wide diversity of subjects — mathematics, English, literature, history, sociology, environmental systems, etc. — with subdiscipline groupings. What are missing in many university programs are those special subdiscipline courses that tie the many loose ends together into organized larger concepts of thought. Some colleges, in an effort to resolve this problem, offer required core courses such as The Cultural History of Western Civilization, which gives an overview of diverse subject matter. These classes, usually taught by preeminent scholars, are, at least, a good beginning.

(15) There are at least three paths for traditional professional training in architecture:

1. the five-year program, which generally contains two years of liberal-arts course work and three years of technical architectural training;
2. the 4-2 program, which contains two years of liberal arts, two years of modified liberal arts / architectural course work (usually within the framework of the man-made environment), and two years of graduate professional training;
3. the three-year graduate program, which assumes the student enters professional studies with no prior architectural background. Some schools of architecture offer all three programs; some one or two. The wide range of these programs attests to the broadness of the field once architecture is no longer considered to be simply and solely the profession of building.

(16) Architecture, by its very nature, demands generalists who must deal with a wide range of persons with varied in-

In a general sense this means that the beginning years in a school of architecture would cover each of these subdisciplines of knowledge discussed above, stressing their interconnectedness at a deeper level of values. Architecture courses at the conceptual level — specifically those in history, theory, and visual communication — would be offered to all interested university students within the subdiscipline framework, as one of the means toward a better understanding of the man-made world.

Sometime during the third and fourth years of his undergraduate education, the student in architecture would decide on a major area of interest, such as history, planning, architecture, or landscape design, and would then begin to direct his energies toward a more specific focus. But it would always remain paramount for the undergraduate student to remember that all knowledge is interrelated, and that assimilating and converting knowledge into wisdom remains a primary goal for education.(14)

At the graduate level,(15) architecture schools should offer as many finely honed programs of instruction as there are perceived areas of professional need — ranging from environmental protection to historical preservation to the traditional roles of architecture. What must be assumed at the professional level is that the student has learned how to think and is now ready to apply this ability to rigorous intellectual exercises. What is equally important is that the student remains devoted to conceptual understanding and does not abandon this commitment for the narrow concerns of an academic technocracy.(16)

This means, for example, that architectural drawing will be taught as one of the basic means of visual communication, not as drafting "technique," which is far better learned in a professional architectural office. Likewise, the principles of architectural detailing will be taught as an important element in design, not as sophisticated dimensioning procedures — which again are better learned in an office. A final example might be the study of roadway and circulation networks, a key field in any advanced urban-planning program. While the common dimensional widths of highways, streets, and sidewalks must, of course, be learned, it is mastery of the concepts of movement systems that is the proper course emphasis at the graduate level.

This does not imply that the college-trained professional will be so generalist oriented that he possesses no specialist abilities. Indeed, each particular profession will have specific and particular concerns; the danger is not in having special directions, but rather in a too-narrow specialization that excludes larger human conceptual issues. For example, in the best-known of all architectural curricula — training to become a design-oriented architect — design courses must cover a wide range of special subject matter. Fire-code requirements, high-rise construction process, basic formal organization, and the symbolic cultural issues of our day, as well as many other issues, must all be integrated into the larger concern of a humane and societally shaped, architecturally formed environment.

Keeping in mind these deeper issues will help schools and faculty overcome the natural desire to be always new, in the forefront, avante-garde, and fashionable.(17) For it behooves both architectural schools and the profession as a whole to look beyond prevailing fashion to find the concepts that express well the human need. The age-old questions remain: Who is this architecture for? How can it be programmed and shaped into meaningful form?

And finally, What does it mean to make this mark upon the land?

terests, but I would argue that all professional schools — such as law, medicine, commerce, and engineering — should first train generalists, who are then capable of being specialists in a particular area of concern.

(17) The emergence of an avante-garde could only occur with the rise of a strong bourgeoisie and their patronage in the late 1800s of the salons, the art galleries, and later the museums. When art, music, and architecture were really financed only by the wealthy patron, an avante-garde polemic was not possible, and the aesthetic intellectual did not exist.

It is unfortunate but true that for a more egalitarian middle-class society, architecture carries with it the constant search for newness and fashion. This so exasperated Mies van der Rohe that he is widely quoted as having said, "I don't want to be interesting; I want to be good!"

(18) *Erwin Panofsky,* Meaning in the Visual Arts *(Garden City, N.Y.: Doubleday and Company, 1955), p. 2.*

(19) *Ibid., p. 3.*

(20) *In the introduction to this book I said that Claude Lévi-Strauss was incorrect when stating: "Humanism has failed . . . it has misunderstood man . . . it has tried to cut him off from all other manifestations of nature" (*Time*, June 30, 1967). In a limited sense, however, Lévi-Strauss is correct, for he is speaking of an academic interpretation — a dry abstraction in which one can study the intellectual ideas of Corbusier, Gropius, Mies, or Wright without their respective frailties, errors, and humaneness. Humaneness acknowledges a larger framework of nature within which man exists.*

One can also add that Lévi-Strauss's theories on structuralism treat man just as abstractly as that dry humanism to which he refers.

Throughout this book there has been an underlying plea for an architectural aesthetic shared by all those who practice architecture with an attitude deeply rooted in humanism. Indeed, I do not believe it is even possible to become educated, in the sense I have just outlined, without practicing humanism. Humanism, however, is not in itself a philosophy or a value system. Rather, it is an attitude, a way of looking at problems that can guide us toward our own philosophy. In *Meaning in the Visual Arts,* Erwin Panofsky defines this attitude well when he says it is "the conviction of the dignity of man, based both on the insistence of human values (rationality and freedom) and the acceptance of human limitations (fallibility and frailty); from these two postulates result — responsibility and tolerance."(18)

In other words, man has the freedom to think as he pleases. This freedom, however, brings with it responsibility; the responsibility to think well and not abuse the privilege of freedom. In addition, man is not perfect; we are instead frail and prone to error. Knowing this, we must have humility and must practice tolerance. The humanist will construct his own philosophy, his own aesthetic, for he must freely exercise his own mind responsibly. But his aesthetic will be humane, for it will also be cognizant of man's frailty.

The humanist, Panofsky says, "rejects authority. But he respects tradition."(19) The humanist, then, is a cultural historian in the best sense intended by Jacob Burckhardt and Herman Hesse. He studies the records of the past so that he may learn guidelines for the future, but he always remembers that cultural history is full of error and fallibility, just as it is full of wisdom and truth; that it is human; and that not only must it be cherished and protected, it must also be interpreted tolerantly, humanely.(20)

Rigorously applied, this questioning humanist attitude can lead us toward a shared aesthetic, and an architecture that addresses those still-valid social goals and human needs of the modern movement. In the preceding chapter I suggested that although these basic social goals are still with us, a problem has occurred in an often narrow interpretation of functional need. The humanist attitude can help us redress this imbalance. Through a more proper interpretation of cultural history, we can relearn that functionally correct buildings should also be correct culturally. In the process, we can rediscover both pleasure and dignity in our architecture.(21)

A humanist attitude can also help us understand that our way of perceiving architectural form is still changing. We now know that to the traditional three dimensions of spatial form, we have added a fourth — time. And we are beginning to understand that the meaning of architecture lies in what we choose to remember. And what we remember spatially is conditioned by our culture and by our own perception as we pass through and experience sequential places.(22)

When Aldo van Eyck says that architecture is the marriage of "place and occasion," he is implying that when human activity occurs in an identifiable place, the opportunity for architecture exists. While shaped space may connote architecture in its physical sense, it is only place that connotes human involvement, perception, and an understanding of architecture in its cultural role. All good architecture thus possesses significant *remembered place*.(23)

(21) The loss of dignity is a common dilemma in the twentieth century. Only when there is a basic dignity inherent in our buildings can we rediscover the dignity inherent in our architecture, and inherent in our cities. When a city repossesses its dignity, it commands respect, and we can say again that it is a pleasant place in which to live.

(22) The noted critic S. E. Rasmussen has stated: "Understanding architecture, therefore, is not the same as being able to determine the style of a building by certain external features. It is not enough to see architecture; you must experience it" (Experiencing Architecture *(Cambridge, Mass.: M.I.T. Press, 1954), p. 33*

(23) Aldo van Eyck, Team 10 Primer *(Cambridge, Mass.: M.I.T. Press, 1968) p. 101. Since 1950, critics have made much of different kinds or types of space. Christian Norberg-Schultz lists no less than five types:*

1. pragmatic
2. cognitive
3. Euclidean
4. perceptual
5. schematic (or existential) space.

For Norberg-Schultz, existential space is composed of the intellectual ideas or archetypes that we share with our society. Existence, Space, and Architecture, *(New York: Praeger, 1971), pp. 9-11.*

Not surprisingly, Aristotle said much earlier that space was the sum of all places. As an attempt to synthesize spatial meaning, Artistotle's work is strikingly similar to Kevin Lynch's more recent thoughts on spatial linkages from node to node as found in Image of the City *(Cambridge, Mass.: Harvard University Press, 1960).*

(24) These many linkages, of course, can only be remembered as forms experienced through time and movement. In chapter 10, mention was made of the importance of Einstein's theories of relativity. Equally important in this recognition of time and movement are the writings of the great French philosopher Henri Bergson (1859-1941), who stressed the open flow of time, or time that is lived or remembered as opposed to scientific time of the exact moment.

Bergson was a firm believer in the importance of intuitive reasoning, and his most famous work, Creative Evolution *(1907), argued that a duration of time, or a continual process, is necessary for an understanding of evolution. This duration of time, or perpetual flux, is inexpressible and can only be understood through intuition.*

(25) In this sketch of a proposed design for a new elementary school, an attempt has been made to express the linkage system as a sequential place in itself — a "learning street" composed of mini-nodal points, resting places, study areas, an aquarium, a greenhouse, and threshold foyers into classrooms.

An emergent aesthetical issue (which we have only recently begun to understand) is that our perception of remembered place is highly conditioned by the quality of the linkages that tie specific places together. In other words, the passageways, corridors, hallways, foyers, thresholds that link and hold together the total architectural form have in themselves the potential for significant architectural meaning.(24)

A humanist attitude will help us discover this meaning — elevating the ceremony of social movement and progression, celebrating this human passage as a cultural event unique to our time and place.(25) This is the greatest contribution a correct humanism will make in an emerging shared aesthetic — a constant humane reappraisal of our built form, keeping it fresh and symbolic of our own culture.

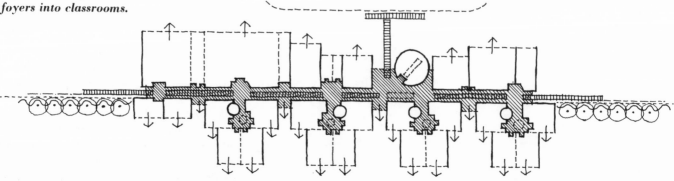

The questioning and searching professional will grow more humble as he grows in architectural stature. He will develop an even stronger sense of ethics, and an understanding that helping resolve human spatial need brings a special pleasure to the responsible architect.(26)

Indeed, the practice of architecture is always joyful, for the dedicated architect knows that his next creative act may help to elevate the human spirit. He labors because he cares, and in caring he shares. He is not afraid to dream, knowing that the goal is to dream well.(27) He searches for the dream that is worth sharing, and for those who will understand in their own way why this search is important and who are capable, in their own right, of joyfully sharing architecture.

(26) These thoughts refer back to the first chapter and its definition of architecture. For it is a humanist position to believe that architecture grows out of a profound statement in physical form about man and his relationship within nature, and that the significance of architecture is that it may help us better understand the human predicament.

(27) In her book Memoirs of Hadrian *(New York: Farrar Straus and Giroux, 1963, p. 126), Margaret Youncenar has the Roman Emperor Hadrian say:*

To build is to collaborate with earth, to put a human mark upon a landscape, modifying it forever thereby. . . .

To reconstruct is to collaborate with a time gone by, penetrating or modifying its spirit, and carrying it toward a longer future. . . .

The Villa was the tomb of my travels, the last encampment of the nomad. . . .

Each building-stone was the strange concretion of a will, a memory, and sometimes of challenge. Each structure was the chart of a dream.

ACKNOWLEDGMENTS

First, I must thank my father, Robert L. Vickery, and my brother, Walter Ray Vickery, not only for their continual support and encouragement but also for their kindness in lending me the support of their newspaper staff at the *Salem* (Missouri) *News*, who did all of the work needed to prepare the book's camera-ready layout. Without this assistance, the book simply could not have been printed at a price affordable to students of architecture. In particular, I should like to thank Mrs. Patricia Medlock, who typeset the entire manuscript on the data computer.

Next, I must thank all of our past and present staff at The Vickery Partnership, Architects, in Charlottesville. My partners, Lawson Drinkard, Bob Moje, and David Oakland, have always been more than patient as I have filled our office with books, notes, and scraps of sketches, often to the detriment of more profitable business. Again, special thanks must go to Mrs. Wendy Valley and Mrs. Linda Giles, who each typed portions of the original manuscript several times over.

With the exception of a few of my own sketches, the line drawings have all been prepared especially for this book and have been done by former students and friends: William Deal, Martin Brandwein, and Frank Lucas (chapters 1, 2, 3, and 5); Bruce Donnally (chapters 6 and 7); Jeff Bushman (chapters 8 and 9); and Peter MacKeith (chapters 4 and 10). My gratitude goes to all of them.

Colleagues at the School of Architecture of the University of Virginia have also been encouraging, as have many former students of my Concepts in Architecture course, who for twelve years now have been prodding me to finish the book rather than promising to do so.

My thanks also to my family — Kevin and Clare and my wife, Mary, who more than anyone knows how painful this enterprise has been.

Finally, a special thanks to two special teachers: my aunt, Dr. Verna Vickery, who first brought Susanne Langer and Jerome Bruner to my attention — thus awakening in me the awareness that teaching deserves scholarship — and Professor Roland Bockhorst, who by his own example demonstrated the joy of faculty and students together sharing architecture.